Strategic Shortfall

Strategic Shortfall

THE SOMALIA SYNDROME AND THE MARCH TO 9/11

Robert G. Patman

Foreword by Martin N. Stanton

Praeger Security International

PRAEGER

AN IMPRINT OF ABC-CLIO, LLC
Santa Barbara, California • Denver, Colorado • Oxford, England

Library of Congress Cataloging-in-Publication Data

Patman, Robert G.
    Strategic shortfall : the Somalia Syndrome and the march to 9/11 / Robert G. Patman ; foreword by Martin N. Stanton.
        p. cm.
    Includes bibliographical references and index.
    ISBN 978-0-275-99362-7 (hardcover : alk. paper) — ISBN 978-1-57356-726-8 (ebook)
    1. Operation Restore Hope, 1992–1993—Influence. 2. Somalia Affair, 1992–1997—Influence. 3. Security, International. 4. National security—United States. 5. United States—Military policy. 6. United States—Foreign relations—1989– I. Title.
    DT407.42.P38 2010
    355'.03307309049—dc22   2009053922

14 13 12 11 10   1 2 3 4 5

This book is also available on the World Wide Web as an eBook.
Visit www.abc-clio.com for details.

Praeger
An Imprint of ABC-CLIO, LLC

ABC-CLIO, LLC
130 Cremona Drive, P.O. Box 1911
Santa Barbara, California 93116-1911

This book is printed on acid-free paper ∞
Manufactured in the United States of America

Contents

Foreword

About a decade ago I was stationed in Qatar as the commander of the U.S. Army pre-positioned equipment site there. In my spare time I wrote a book about my experiences in Somalia as an infantry battalion operations officer during Operation Restore Hope in 1992-93, pecking away at the prodigious rate of about 2-3 pages a week. To my surprise the book was published in early 2001 and received generally favorable reviews (although some reader reviews on Amazon said it was boring compared to Blackhawk Down). That project done, I went on with other things and then 9/11 happened and I went to war . . . again and again.

I completed my last trip to Afghanistan in September of 2009 and retired from the Army on the last day of that month. I was in my new civilian job for less than a week when I unexpectedly received an e-mail from New Zealand asking if I'd write the foreword for a book by Professor Robert Patman on the international impact of the "Somalia Syndrome." Feeling humbled and honored, I agreed.

Robert Patman's book brings back a lot of memories, not all of them pleasant. He has certainly done his research. As a participant in not only Operation Restore Hope, but also operations Desert Thunder I and II and Desert Fox, I can say that his retelling of events is accurate. He has a particularly good eye for the policy decisions that naturally, as a lowly major and lieutenant colonel, at the time I was not involved in. In that sense I can assure the reader that he will find this book wonderfully informative. I certainly learned things I didn't know, even though I was there.

Robert Patman and I share a belief that 9/11 did not just happen. Rather, 9/11 was the cumulative result of bungled policies, cultural misunderstandings, wishful thinking, and intellectual sloth, both in America and in the rest of the Western world. Partisans in U.S. politics are quick to point fingers at each other, but there's more than enough blame to go around among previous administrations. Mainly our present difficulties come from an inability over the past three decades (and probably before that) to see the world as it really is and not how we would wish it.

There's a commercial for FRAM oil filters on U.S. television. In it a mechanic in oil stained coveralls stands in front of car with a disassembled engine. He talks to the camera and says that if the owner of this car had bought a $12 oil filter six months ago he wouldn't be paying $600 for an engine repair bill now. The mechanic looks over his shoulder at the torn down car, shrugs, looks back at the camera, and says, "So you see it's really a simple choice, you can pay me now"—holding up the oil filter—"or"—motioning to the car—"you can pay me later." The commercial is a perfect metaphor for the reaction of America and the Western world to the chaos of failed states in the 1990s and the nascent al Qaeda threat. We knew the threat was there but it was too hard, too inconvenient, and too incongruent with the nice clean decent Western way we looked at the world. And so nothing was done. We didn't buy the oil filter, and now we're fixing the car.

The great American humorist P. J. O'Rourke once wrote: "We are fools when we fail to defend civilization." I believe this to be true. I believe civilization is worth defending. I believe that Somalia could have been different if the United States and the international community had been intellectually honest with themselves as to what they were undertaking and its true cost. Failure was not inevitable; the opposition in Somalia was nowhere near as formidable as the Sunni or Shia militias in Iraq or the Taliban in Afghanistan. Had we succeeded in Somalia it's a reasonable possibility that the slaughter in Rwanda could have been prevented or at least curtailed. The Western world could have stood against chaos and genocide. But it was too hard, it didn't matter enough, there were other things domestically that were more important, and Africa was so far away. And so we quit. Somalia was, at the same time, small stakes and too rich for our blood. And the barbarians of the world watched and drew their own conclusions.

These conclusions were reinforced in 1998 when our embassies were attacked in Africa. Kill a dozen or so Americans (and hundreds of Kenyans and Tanzanians) and we'll send a few cruise missiles your way. That's it, an attack met by a neat no-muss, no-fuss response. That our tepid counterstrokes missed and were not followed up mattered less to our leadership at the time than the appearance that we had done "something." Again al Qaeda drew its own conclusions.

Somehow, somewhere along the line we had gotten it into our heads that war was easy and a technically soluble problem . . . that the fanatics who attacked us would slink away from their Afghan hovels in horror at our cruise missiles and say in a Snidely Whiplash stage whisper, "Curses!

Foiled again by American technology!" . . . that fanatics who would tear at our civilization did not merit a serious response. We know better now.

But do we really? As I write this, Somali pirates prey on the world's commerce, and civilization reacts in a feckless and legalistic manner. For all its myriad frustrations, the war in Afghanistan is nothing short of a war between two visions of what man can be. Yet we (the West) vacillate—as if the consequences of a "Somalia–like" withdrawal from Afghanistan would not have repercussions around the world for decades to come.

Robert Patman takes you back to a period when much more was possible in the world than we imagined at the time; back to a fork in the road where, sadly, Western civilization led by America made the wrong choice and picked the path of least resistance. And he chronicles the consequences. It's a tragic story in the classic sense of the word and one that Professor Patman has told well. Maybe one day we'll learn. I hope so.

Martin N. Stanton
Colonel, Infantry, US Army (Retired)
Author of *Somalia on $5 a Day* and *Road to Baghdad*

Preface

For many observers, 9/11 was a transformative event. President George W. Bush claimed that this event ushered in a new strategic era. According to this view, the global security environment of September 12 was fundamentally different to that of September 10. Such a reaction assumed that the events of September 11 came out of a clear blue sky. It was a position that struck a chord with many citizens, who were struggling to comprehend why America was attacked in this way. Interestingly, in 2008, this perspective was still widely held in the United States. Commenting on Wall Street's financial crisis, Democratic presidential contender Senator Barack Obama insisted that "[it] isn't 9/11. We know how we got into this mess."[1]

However, the view that 9/11 suddenly transformed the international security environment is profoundly mistaken. The environment had been radically changing since the end of the Cold War. This book locates the origins of 9/11 in an increasingly globalized security context of the early post–Cold War period. In particular, the book seeks to illuminate the connection between the disastrous U.S.–UN humanitarian intervention in Somalia in 1992–1994 and the emergence of a permissive security environment that ultimately made the events of September 11 possible. In many ways, the Somalia crisis was a defining moment for the United States in the early post–Cold War era. According to former Secretary of State, Warren Christopher, "we learned a lot from that painful experience."[2]

Among other things, the Clinton administration believed that it had learned two key lessons from Somalia: failed or failing states were not geostrategically significant to the American national interest, and multilateral institutions such as the UN could not be allowed to exercise any constraining effect on issues relating to American security. The upshot of the United States' experience in Somalia was a risk-averse approach in Washington to intervention in civil conflicts, especially if such involvement ran the risk of U.S. casualties. This approach was known as the Somalia Syndrome and had far-reaching international repercussions. Because the United States had enormous structural power in military and economic terms in the post–Cold War international system, the Somalia Syndrome had a very significant impact on the evolution of a transnational terrorist organization, al Qaeda. In fact, we now know, the connection was even more direct. Through its involvement in the episode known as Black Hawk Down in October 1993, the al Qaeda leadership believed it had actually helped create the Somalia Syndrome in American foreign policy. Thus, the Somalia crisis was an important catalyst in emboldening the bin Laden network to gradually escalate its terrorist campaign against U.S. interests during the period after 1993. While the Clinton administration somewhat belatedly recognized the al Qaeda danger after 1996, the second Bush administration stubbornly refused to take the threat seriously until it was too late. In short, policy choices made by the administrations of Bill Clinton and George W. Bush played a significant role in creating a strategic shortfall that enabled al Qaeda to grow to the point at which it was capable of mounting the devastating terrorist attacks of 9/11.

The structure of the book reflects the central objective of explaining America's strategic shortfall. Chapter 1 discusses the emergence of the post–Cold War global context and how this development was linked to the collapse of the Somali state. Chapter 2 examines the decision of the first Bush administration to launch an armed humanitarian intervention in Somalia. Chapter 3 considers how and why the U.S.–UN intervention in Somalia did not live up to international expectation. Chapter 4 examines the Australian experience in the Somalia operation, an experience that suggested there was nothing inevitable about the failure of the U.S.-led intervention. Chapter 5 examines the link between the advent of the Somalia Syndrome and the emboldening of al Qaeda. Chapter 6 chronicles how the long shadow of Somalia continued to temper the increasing efforts of the Clinton administration to address the dangers presented by the bin Laden network. Chapter 7 focuses on the conceptual reluctance of the second Bush administration to respond to repeated high-level warnings about the al Qaeda threat. Finally, Chapter 8 seeks to explain why the Clinton and the second Bush administration failed to address America's strategic shortfall in the pre-9/11 period.

Acknowledgments

In the course of preparing this book, I have received considerable assistance from a number of people and institutions whom I wish to acknowledge—though, of course, the responsibility for the views expressed in the book belongs only to me.

My first thanks go to six academic colleagues who encouraged me to pursue this project, and who also provided wise counsel and intellectual inspiration after I began the research for it. Four of them, Emeritus Professor Jim Flynn, Professor Philip Nel, Professor Marian Simms, and Dr. Chris Rudd, have worked alongside me in the Department of Politics at the University of Otago in New Zealand for a number of years. I owe a huge debt of gratitude to these individuals. At the same time, Professor David A. Welch, CIGI Chair of Global Security at the Balsillie School of International Affairs and Professor of Political Science at the University of Waterloo, and Dr. Dirk Nabers, Senior Research Fellow at the German Institute of Global and Area Studies at the University of Hamburg, deserve special thanks. David and Dirk generously provided insightful comments and observations on the manuscript.

Second, I would like to thank three people who provided excellent research assistance at various stages of the project. Two former Ph.D. students in the Department of Politics at the University of Otago, Dr. Marjolein Righarts and Dr. Andreas Reitzig, and another former postgraduate student from the same department, Mr. Jeremy Hall, all did a splendid job in helping the author locate the relevant material for researching this book. I should add that Andreas provided further technical assistance in the preparation of the final manuscript, and that Jeremy also offered useful feedback on various draft chapters. To each of these individuals I am deeply grateful.

Third, I was fortunate to have the very able assistance of the staff of Praeger Security International. Ms. Hilary Claggett, then Senior Editor in Politics, Current Events, and International Affairs, firmly supported the idea of the book and played an important role in helping to get the project off the ground. Mr. Robert Hutchinson, Hilary's successor at Praeger, brought helpfulness, commitment, and patience to the project. Such support was critical to bringing the manuscript to fruition. It was a pleasure to work with Robert.

Fourth, I would like to thank a large of number of people who kindly agreed to be interviewed for the research effort that underpinned this book. Such generous assistance has been much appreciated.

Fifth, there is an institutional debt to acknowledge. In 2007, I was the recipient of a University of Otago Research Grant that helped fund research assistance for this book project, and also helped me defray the costs of conducting research in the United States.

Finally, and most importantly, I should especially like to thank my family. I have been blessed to have the loving support of my wife, Dr. Martha Bell, and our three beautiful daughters, Jennifer, Stephanie, and Carolyn. Martha is a talented researcher in her own right and has made considerable sacrifices to support our family and the completion of this book. Martha and our three young girls devised various incentives to try and nudge me across the finishing line. These included a chocolate cigar and a visit to the Chinese Gardens venue in Dunedin. I should add that my mother and father have also been supportive in every way; and so has my sister, Elaine, who has always taken a keen interest in this book project.

Abbreviations

ABC	American Broadcasting Corporation
ABCA	America–Britain–Canada–Australia
ABM	Anti-Ballistic Missile
AID	Agency for International Development
ANZUS	Australia, New Zealand, United States Security Treaty
APC	armored personnel carrier
BBC	British Broadcasting Corporation
CIA	Central Intelligence Agency
CMOT	civil military operations team
CNN	Cable News Network
CSG	Counterterrorism Security Group
CTBT	Comprehensive Nuclear Test Ban Treaty
DDO	Deputy Director for Operations
DPG	Defense Planning Guidance (document)
EIJ	Egyptian Islamic Jihad
EPLF	Eritrean People's Liberation Front
EPRDF	Ethiopian People's Revolutionary Democratic Front
EU	European Union
FAA	Federal Aviation Administration
FBI	Federal Bureau of Investigation
HMMWV	Highly Mobile Multi-Wheeled Vehicle (Humvee)
HRS	Humanitarian Relief Sector
ICC	International Criminal Court
IG	*Gama'at al-Islamiyah*
IO	State Bureau for International Organization
JCS	Joint Chiefs of Staff
JSOC	Joint Special Operations Command

MiG	Mikoyan-i-Gurevich
MRC	major regional conflict
NAFTA	North American Free Trade Agreement
NATO	North Atlantic Treaty Organization
NBC	National Broadcasting Corporation
NEC	National Economic Council
NGO	nongovernmental organization
NIF	National Islamic Front
NSC	National Security Council
NSPD	National Security Presidential Directive
OAU	Organization of African Unity
ODF	Operational Deployment Force
OFDA	Office of Foreign Disaster Assistance
OPR	Operation Provide Relief
PCCA	Policy Coordinating Committee for Africa
PDD	Presidential Decision Directive
PLO	Palestine Liberation Organization
PNAC	Project for the New American Century
QRF	Quick Reaction Force
RAF	Royal Air Force
RMA	Revolution in Military Affairs
ROE	Rules of Engagement
RPG	rocket-propelled grenade
SALT	Strategic Arms Limitation Talks
SDM	Somali Democratic Movement
SGSE	Secretary General's Special Envoy
SLA	Somali Liberation Army
SNA	Somali National Alliance
SNM	Somali National Movement
SPLF	Somali Peoples' Liberation Front
SRRC	Somali Reconciliation and Restoration Council
SRSG	Special Representative of the Secretary-General
SSA	Somali Salvation Alliance
TNC	Transitional National Council
TNG	Transitional National Government
TOW	tube-launched, optically tracked, wire guided (missile)
UF	United Front for the Liberation of Western Somalia
UN	United Nations
UNHCR	United Nations High Commissioner for Refugees
UNICEF	United Nations Children's Fund
UNITAF	Unified Task Force
UNOSOM	United Nations Operation in Somalia
UNSC	UN Security Council

UNSCR	UN Security Council Resolution
USC	United Somali Congress
WHO	World Health Organization
WSLF	Western Somali Liberation Front
WTC	World Trade Center

Chapter 1

The New Global Context and the Disintegration of the Somali State

Radical changes in the international system in the late 1980s challenged the traditional, realist conception of security known as national security. This state-centered perspective dominated international relations from 1945 to the end of the Cold War and was characterized by the core belief that international security is essentially defined by the military interactions of sovereign states. But realist thinking failed to anticipate the demise of the Cold War system and the subsequent break-up of the Soviet Union in 1991. Those events left the United States the world's only superpower and even prompted some observers to describe the post–Cold War era as "the American unipolar age."[1]

At the same time, the end of the Cold War was both a symptom and a cause of deepening globalization. This term has been generally associated with the growth of international linkages, an erosion of the autonomy of the state, and the emergence of a new security environment in which the pattern of conflict has moved beyond the protection of the state. Because the Cold War magnified a sense of external threat—be it international communism or capitalist encirclement—it tended to promote internal cohesion in most states by constraining preexisting ethnic and subnational aspirations.[2] However, the removal of this structural constraint in the late 1980s undermined the system of superpower patronage and unleashed centrifugal forces in states that no longer had the resources to keep various demand-bearing groups at bay or shield them from the powerful forces of economic and political liberalization.

In many ways, Somalia epitomized the international transition that was occurring. The country was transformed in the space of a few years from an important Cold War player to the status of a geostrategic discard. In 1989, the U.S. Congress, citing human rights violations by Somalia's regime under Siad Barre, forced the Bush (Senior) administration to suspend its military and economic aid program to Mogadishu. By January 1991, Barre was overthrown in an armed rebellion led by the United Somali Congress (USC). But instead of heralding stability, the overthrow of Barre's regime intensified a civil war that had started in 1988 and led to the complete collapse of central governance in the country.

U.S. NATIONAL SECURITY AND THE HORN OF AFRICA DURING THE COLD WAR

For much of the post-1945 era, the nature and scope of international security was defined by the parameters of the Cold War. This term was used to describe a climate of hostility and rivalry that developed between the Western (capitalist) and Eastern (communist) blocs shortly after World War II. A pervasive sense of threat meant that the respective hegemonic bloc leaders, the United States and the Union of Soviet Socialist Republics (USSR), engaged in a political competition, not only with each other, but also for the allegiance of the world at large.[3]

The Cold War had a profound, but very different impact on the political life of the two superpower rivals. For the United States, the Cold War brought about a fundamental change in its security thinking. The same could not be said for the Soviet Union. From 1947, the United States had to become organized for perpetual international confrontation with the Soviet Union and the prospect of war in order to protect its core national interests—security, promotion of democratic values, and economic prosperity. The new state of permanent preparedness required an unprecedented coordination of attitudes, policies, and institutions and involved the creation of what Daniel Yergin and other scholars have called America's "national security state."[4]

Unlike the concept of national defense, centered on the physical protection of the continental United States, the doctrine of national security was a much broader notion and postulated the linkage of many different political, economic, and military factors so that developments around the globe could be seen to have a direct impact on America's core interests. By 1948, for example, President Truman could state that the "loss of independence by any nation adds directly to the insecurity of the United States and all free nations."[5] The policies adopted by the United States during the Cold War included containment, confrontation, and intervention.

No continent was spared from the effects of Cold War competition between the superpowers. In Africa, the United States pursued a policy of "selective engagement." Washington essentially treated African countries as pawns in a global strategic contest with the Soviet Union. Republican and Democratic administrations alike supported American allies on the

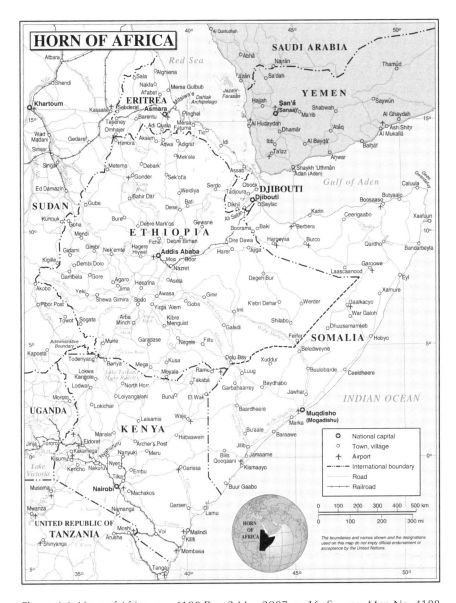

Figure 1.1: Horn of Africa, no. 4188 Rev. 2 May 2007, p. 16. Source: Map No. 4188 Rev. 2 United Nations, May 2007, Department of Peacekeeping, Cartographic Section, Available online: http://www.un.org/Depts/Cartographic/map/profile/horne.pdf. Courtesy of the UN Cartographic Section.

African continent and sought to weaken African regimes that were friendly toward Moscow. This tendency was certainly evident in the United States' policy toward the Horn of Africa, a region that was targeted for its geostrategic location. As Figure 1.1 shows, the Horn flanks the oil states of Arabia, controls the Bab el Mandeb Straits (which are a busy international shipping lane), dominates part of the Gulf of Aden through which oil tankers pass, and overlooks the passages where the Red Sea, the Gulf of Aden, and the Indian Ocean converge.[6]

For the first three decades of the Cold War, U.S. policy in the Horn was centered on Ethiopia. In 1953, the United States obtained a twenty-five-year lease on the Kagnew communications facility in Asmara as part of a quid pro quo for American diplomatic support in the United Nations (UN) for Ethiopian trusteeship over Eritrea. During the next two decades, the Kagnew station served as an important link in the worldwide network of U.S. military communications, which stretched from the Philippines through Ethiopia and Morocco to Arlington, Virginia. Thus, Ethiopia was regarded in Washington as the principal buffer against communism in black Africa. Between 1953 and 1970, Emperor Haile Selassie's government in Ethiopia received 20 percent of all U.S. economic aid ($350 million)—and 50 percent of all U.S. military aid ($278.6 million)—that went to sub-Saharan Africa.[7]

Unlike Washington, the USSR did not establish a foothold in the Horn until much later. In November 1963, Moscow outbid three Western countries—the United States, Italy, and West Germany—by offering Somalia a military aid package worth US$35 million. It was during the 1960s, when Mogadishu was ruled by a Western-style parliamentary regime, that Somali Islamist groups began to emerge. Two Muslim Brotherhood-inspired groups, the *Waxda al-Shabaah al-Islaami* and the *Jama'at-Islaami*, strove to be key players in shaping the agenda of the young Somali state. But the degeneration of Somalia's democracy, exemplified by a left-wing military coup that brought Major General Mohammed Siad Barre to power in October 1969, dealt a substantial blow to the Islamist cause.

Barre, a general in the Soviet-trained army, pledged to introduce in Somalia what Moscow liked to call "scientific socialism".[8] Groups like Jama'at al-Islaami were forced to disband or, as in the case of the Waxda al-Shabaab al-Islaami, were driven underground. By 1974, Somalia had acquired one of the best equipped armies in black Africa, with a large numbers of Mikoyan-i-Gurevich (MiG) fighter planes, T-54 tanks, and a vast assortment of heavy arms. In return, the Soviet Union obtained a major naval facility at Berbera in northwestern Somalia and access to several Somali airfields. In July 1974, Moscow codified its alliance with Somalia through a "Treaty of Friendship and Co-operation." Nevertheless, while Barre's military regime curbed the activities of Islamist organizations, it was careful to stress that socialism and Islam were fully compatible. On

February 15, 1974, Somalia joined the Arab League, a move sponsored by conservative Saudi Arabia. As far as Moscow was concerned, "the religious problem" remained a major obstacle in Soviet–Somali relations.[9]

While U.S. engagement in the Horn was largely shaped by global Cold War competition, developments on the ground did sometimes shape Washington's containment strategy toward Moscow. Having been displaced in Ethiopia by the Soviet Union in April 1977, the Carter administration found itself on the back foot as Moscow launched a massive military intervention to determine the outcome of the Ethiopian–Somali War of 1977–1978.[10] That experience helped to end the era of superpower détente. "SALT [the Strategic Arms Limitation Talks]," President Carter's national security adviser, Zbigniew Brzezinski, noted, "lies buried in the sands of the Ogaden."[11] The very success of the Soviet–Cuban intervention prompted the Carter administration to establish a "rapid intervention" capability in the Horn of Africa, the Red Sea, and the Indian Ocean region and propelled the United States toward a "Second Cold War" under the leadership of the Reagan administration in the early 1980s.

The Ethiopian–Somali War also precipitated a remarkable superpower realignment. In August 1980, the United States and Somalia signed an agreement whereby access to air and naval facilities at the port of Berbera were granted to U.S. Rapid Deployment Forces in exchange for American support. Over the next decade, President Barre's government received more than $700 million in economic and military aid from the Reagan and Bush administrations.

However, with the demise of the East–West divide in the late 1980s, the repressive regimes in Somalia and Ethiopia began to lose their superpower life-support systems. In 1988, the United States and the Soviet Union pressed their respective allies in the Horn to sign a peace accord to put the bloody Ethiopian–Somali dispute over the Ogaden territory on hold.[12] While the Cold War did not cause this regional conflict, both parties to the dispute had exploited superpower rivalry to advance their own local interests. But if the 1988 peace accord was a cynical attempt to buy time for two increasingly embattled dictatorships, it failed to deliver. In northern Somalia, for example, the 1988 peace accord prompted an invasion by Somali National Movement (SNM) rebels after their bases in Ethiopia were closed down. Fierce fighting, centered on the provincial capital of Hargeisa, ensued. It marked the beginnings of a civil war that would eventually destroy the Barre dictatorship in January 1991.

THE END OF THE COLD WAR AND AMERICA'S NEW FOREIGN POLICY

The end of the Cold War in the late 1980s offered an extraordinary opportunity for a reappraisal of U.S. foreign policy. The interpretation

given to this stunning change would help frame any subsequent understanding of the new global context. According to President George H. W.
Bush, the collapse of Soviet communism meant that America had "won
the Cold War."[13] That view was widely shared in the United States, and
the outcome was considered, in no small way, to be a triumph for the
American model of national security that had evolved since 1947.[14]

Rather less attention was given in the United States to alternative
explanations for the end of the Cold War: the view that Mikhail Gorbachev's policies and personality were the single biggest factor behind the
dramatic improvement in superpower relations;[15] the view that the end
of the Cold War was a result of the internal degeneration of the
Marxist–Leninist political system that forced the Soviet Union to opt out
of Cold War competition with the United States;[16] and the argument that
the advent of globalization in the early 1980s facilitated the intersection of
external pressures from the Reagan administration on Moscow and long-
term domestic pressures within the USSR to create a new impetus for
change.[17]

While interpretations of the Cold War's demise varied, several distinctive features of the new landscape became immediately apparent to all
concerned. Most obviously, there were no longer military confrontations
of a system-threatening character. During the Cold War, a conflict
between the United States and the Soviet Union could have threatened
the entire world with nuclear devastation. But after 1989, it was difficult
to conceive of likely conflicts of the same magnitude.

The United States emerged from the Cold War as the world's only
superpower, with no real geopolitical or ideological competitors in sight.
The collapse of the USSR produced a new Russian state, shrunken east-
ward and northward by nearly a third of its former territory.[18] Europe was
preoccupied with German reunification and the reconstruction of a post-
Communist Eastern Europe. Japan experienced a severe downturn in its
economic performance in the 1990s, and China, the world's fastest-growing
economy, found itself involved in a tremendous transformation that limited its global aspirations. Thus, for the first time in the modern era, the
United States could theoretically operate on the global stage largely without the encumbrance of other great powers. In terms of interstate relations, the relative power of the United States had sharply increased.

The post–Cold War world was subject to deepening globalization. The
latter could be broadly defined as the intensification of technologically
driven links between societies, institutions, cultures, and individuals on a
worldwide basis. Globalization implies "a shift in geography" whereby
borders have become increasingly porous.[19] Among other things, the
process of globalization involves a compression of time and space, shrink-
ing distances through a dramatic reduction in the time taken, either physically or representationally, to cross them. As a consequence, the world is

perceived as a smaller place as issues of the environment, economics, politics, and security intersect more deeply at more points than was previously the case.[20]

Beyond that, however, there was little agreement concerning the likely impact of globalization on role of the sovereign state in the making of foreign and security policy. Three rival schools of thought could be identified. For the hyperglobalists, the growing interconnectedness of national economies through globalization would gradually negate the significance of territorial boundaries and pave the way for the demise of the sovereign nation-state.[21] The hyperglobalists contended that one of the crucial effects of globalization is to reduce and ultimately eliminate the space for states to manage national security policy. In contrast, the skeptics basically believed that little had changed in the international arena. Rejecting the hyperglobalist position as politically naive, the skeptics argued that the impact of globalization on the sovereign state has been much exaggerated. In this view, the state was not the victim of this process, but instead its main architect.[22] It was argued that the sovereign state was still the sole institution tasked with the responsibility for establishing the preconditions for governance: political stability, the rule of law, education and training, and security are among the elements that play a part here.[23] Finally, the transformationalists rejected the tendency to juxtapose state sovereignty and globalization. According to this perspective, the state was not automatically diminished by globalization, nor unaffected by it. Rather, the role of the sovereign state in the international system was being transformed by states themselves in the face of perceived costs and benefits imposed by the globalization process. For transformationalists, transnational pressures on the sovereign state from without and within were promoting a broader and more cooperative approach to security.

Interpretations of how globalization affects the state are important in assessing how globalization has interacted with the changing structure of the international system since the end of the Cold War. This is important not only for understanding the actions of the United States in the post–Cold War era, but also for any conception of the ramifications of these changes in regard to weak and failing states. As the case of Somalia will show, globalization can have unexpected effects on weak states. This was particularly the case during the late 1980s and early 1990s, when the changing international security environment was having profound effects on how the United States and the USSR interacted with the developing world.

At the risk of oversimplification and some foreshortening, the U.S. foreign policy orientation at the beginning of the 1990s seemed to place it somewhere between the views of the skeptics and transformationalists. The George H.W. Bush administration, as well as the following administration of Bill Clinton, appeared confident about constructing a "New

World Order," with a number of key elements observable in the new vision. The main goal articulated by Bush for the New World Order was the maintenance of international peace. It was implied that the new order should preserve security, defend freedom, promote democracy, and enforce the rule of law.

Bush's speeches indicated that the key diplomatic and political institution for operating and managing the new global order was the UN. In the late 1980s, dramatic changes in the international system expanded the contexts in which the UN could act. The United States and major powers, no longer limited by the Cold War constraints that had incapacitated the UN for its first forty years, turned to the organization to respond to a host of new challenges, including the management of internal conflict and humanitarian emergencies. It was the UN that was the central forum for mobilizing international opinion against Iraq's invasion of Kuwait in August 1990. Moreover, in the aftermath of the Persian Gulf War, the United Nations Security Council (UNSC), confronted with large numbers of displaced Kurds in northern Iraq, Turkey, and Iran, as well as vulnerable Shiites in southern Iraq, assumed new powers. It declared in Resolution 688 of April 5, 1991, that a member government's repression of its people constituted a threat to international peace. Such a declaration was unprecedented.

Bush's references to a New World Order clearly anticipated a strong and active leadership role for the United States, albeit one either through partnership with the UN or in coalitions that enjoyed a wide measure of international support. In the eyes of many Americans, the United States had not only prevailed over Soviet totalitarianism, but was now spearheading the process of globalization. The scene seemed set, according to Francis Fukuyama, for a new world system based on Western values of liberal democracy, market capitalism and international cooperation.[24] In a memorable phrase, Fukuyama argued that the end of the Cold War marked the "the end of history."[25] Indeed, the crushing military victory of the U.S.-led coalition over Saddam Hussein's Iraq in the Persian Gulf War of 1990–1991 did seem to affirm a New World Order based on U.S. global leadership through a reinvigorated UN.

Yet, it was not apparent to policymakers in Washington that the vision of a New World Order was anathema to, at least, one former partner in the Cold War battleground of Afghanistan. During the 1980s, the Red Army was ensnared in Afghanistan in a costly Vietnam-style quagmire that united the Muslim and Western worlds against Moscow. It was during this time, at the height of Cold War tensions, that the United States extended substantial financial and military support to the Afghan *mujahideen* and the International Muslim Brigade—a fundamentalist Islamic group headed by a Saudi national, Osama bin Laden, and a Palestinian, Abdullah Azzam—that were fighting the Soviet invasion.[26] With the winding down of the Afghan war in 1989, bin Laden formed a multinational insurgent organization, known as *al Qaeda* or "the base," to pursue *jihad* against the next major enemy of Islam, America. For bin Laden and his followers, the victory against the Soviets and Afghan Communists was first and foremost a victory for Islam and had demonstrated the "myth of superpower."[27] Long angered by America's support for Israel, a state that had occupied Palestinian territories since the 1967 war, and embittered by the willingness of the Saudi government to station American troops on holy Muslim territory after Iraq's invasion of Kuwait in 1991, bin Laden and his supporters were eager to confront the remaining superpower—the United States—and its allies.[28]

Meanwhile, during the period 1989–1992, the impact of Washington's vision of a New World Order in the Horn of Africa was quite uneven. A one-party regime in Ethiopia, previously sustained by Soviet superpower patronage, found itself swept away by a tide of internal demands for greater participation and democratization. Barely six months after Gorbachev cut off military aid to the regime under Mengistu Haile Mariam in 1990, spectacular military gains by the Eritrean People's Liberation Front (EPLF) and the Ethiopian People's Revolutionary Democratic Front (EPRDF), a broad coalition of resistance groups, forced Mengistu to flee the Ethiopian capital of Addis Ababa. After Mengistu's exit, the United States played a crucial role in establishing transitional arrangements in Ethiopia by backing an EPRDF takeover of the country and endorsing the EPLF proposal for a UN-supervised referendum to decide the issue of Eritrean independence.[29] At the same time, low levels of economic development, colonially imposed borders, and the virtual absence of civic institutions retarded the democratization process in neighboring Somalia. In fact, the embryonic liberalization process in Somalia enhanced its tribal divisions and helped plunge the country into chaos.

THE NEW WORLD ORDER AND THE DISINTEGRATION OF THE SOMALI STATE

Somalia was a spectacular example of state disintegration following the end of the Cold War. In fact, the collapse of Somalia, and the international community's response to it (or lack thereof) were a depressing forerunner to events that would plague the 1990s. By the beginning of 1992, Somalia had dissolved into a Hobbesian "state of nature." A many-sided civil war had destroyed any vestiges of central authority in the country, in the process turning a severe drought into a catastrophic famine. Moreover, around 70 percent of the country's livestock was lost, and much of Somalia's farmland belt in the south was devastated.[30]

The reasons for the failure of the Somali state are complex and widely misunderstood. On the one hand, a number of commentators have attributed the demise of the Somali state to the overwhelming impact of a "natural" disaster, the Somali famine of 1991–1992. On the other hand, some analysts who saw politics rather than nature at the heart of the Somali crisis focused either on the divisive legacy of the Siad Barre dictatorship or on the destructive effects of abundant weapons provided by both superpowers during the Cold War. In reality, the roots of this political cataclysm were local and international in character.

Historically, the notion of Somali statehood was problematic. Prior to independence in July 1960, the Somalis did not have a cohesive state. As a nation of mainly pastoral nomads, the Somalis traditionally had a decentralized political community based on an extensive clan structure. Here political identity and loyalty was largely determined by clan affiliation or descent. By eking out an existence in the arid planes of the Horn of Africa, the Somali lifestyle was marked by independence, assertive self-reliance, and a general distrust of central government.

From the time of Somalia's independence, the persistence of clan politics frustrated the efforts of central government in Mogadishu to build an enduring sense of Somali nationalism based on allegiance to the state. The task was complicated by the fact that the boundaries of independent Somalia did not fully correspond to the aspirations of Somali nationalism. As Figure 1.2 illustrates, over a million Somalis living in French Somaliland (later to become Djibouti), the Northern Frontier District of Kenya, and the Ogaden region of Ethiopia were left outside the borders of the new state. Thus, from the very beginning of its existence, Somalia sought to expand its boundaries so that they coincided with those of the "nation."[31] This goal quickly brought Mogadishu into conflict with all its neighbors. But if Pan-Somalism encouraged solidarity against external threats, it failed to erase antagonism among Somalia's clans.

By using Somalia's strategic location as a lever in the Cold War, Barre had exploited superpower rivalry to maximize aid for his dictatorship. Alliances were formed first with the former Soviet Union and then with the United States. Altogether, after twenty-two years in power, the Barre regime had received more than $1 billion worth of military aid and around $300 million in economic assistance.[32] In this way, Barre established the basis for a centralized state apparatus. The centrifugal tendencies of clan politics were curbed through a combination of foreign aid–funded patronage and military coercion.

Barre's political dominance, however, diminished with the end of the Cold War. It is true that the Bush administration responded in 1988 to an armed rebellion by the SNM by shipping automatic rifles and ammunition worth $1.4 million to Barre's dictatorship. But this military and economic aid program in Somalia was suspended in 1989.[33] Other clan-based

Ethnic Groups

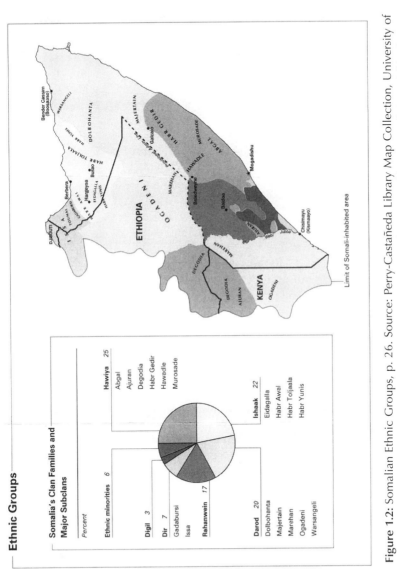

Figure 1.2: Somalian Ethnic Groups, p. 26. Source: Perry-Castañeda Library Map Collection, University of Texas, Ethnic Groups from Somalia Summary Map, CIA, 2002, http://www.lib.utexas.edu/maps/africa/somalia_ethnic_grps_2002.jpg. Courtesy of the University Libraries, The University of Texas at Austin.

opposition groups took up arms in southern and central Somalia. By 1990, the Barre regime, bereft of virtually all foreign aid, exercised only limited control over the regions surrounding Mogadishu. Because of the civil war, the Somali state had, in political and institutional terms, already collapsed before the final ousting of Barre in January 1991 by the United Somali Congress.[34]

Instead of heralding stability, the overthrow of Barre accelerated the process of disintegration. The leaders of the USC, which drew its support from the Hawiye clans, became absorbed in a bloody power struggle almost as soon as they had driven Barre from Mogadishu. The USC military commander, General Mohamed Farah Aideed, who played a key role in defeating Barre,[35] refused to accept Ali Mahdi Mohamed as interim president of a new USC government. The struggle also had a tribal dimension. Mahdi's support base was in the Hawiye subclan, Abgal, while Aideed's backing derived from another Hawiye subclan, Habar Gidir.

Fighting was not limited to Mogadishu but spread chaos and starvation throughout southern Somalia. As well as the confrontation between the heavily armed factions of Aideed and Mahdi, there was fierce fighting involving these groups and forces loyal to the Barre regime, led by Barre's son-in-law General Siad Hersi Morgan. The intensity of the fighting was fueled both by the vast arms stockpile accumulated during the Cold War and a thriving local arms trade, partly stimulated by the disbanding of the huge army of the former Ethiopian dictator, Mengistu Haile Mariam, in 1991.[36]

Somalia's continuing descent into chaos also facilitated the growth of a variety of Islamist organizations. *Al Itihaad Al Islamiya* (Islamic Union) emerged as the most militant Islamist group in Somalia. Other Islamic fundamentalist organizations surfaced in Somalia, such as *al Islah* and *al Wahda*, but these groups tended to focus on social and educational aims.[37] In contrast, al Itihaad transformed itself toward the end of the Barre dictatorship from a nonpolitical group into a jihadist organization dedicated to promoting its vision of a pan-Somali Islamic state through military means. The details of this transformation remain murky, but it is highly likely that returning Somali mujahideen veterans, who had resisted the Soviet occupation of Afghanistan as holy Islamic warriors, played a decisive part in this.[38] But despite having its own militia, al Itihaad was loosely structured and soon found itself squeezed out of Mogadishu by clan-based factions led by warlords such as Mahdi and General Aideed.[39] Nevertheless, remnants of al Itihaad retreated to more rural centers, especially to southwest Somalia, and, as will be explored later, managed to attract quite significant external support that helped it remain a military player in the country.

Alongside these relatively organized factional wars, looting, random killing and banditry was carried out by gangs of *khat*-chewing, armed teenagers known as *Mooryaan*.[40] At the same time, drought, a cyclical problem in Somalia, magnified the impact of the manmade damage to the country. By 1992, the UN estimated a death toll of 300,000 from starvation, while 400,000 Somalis sought refuge in Kenya and another 300,000 did the same in Ethiopia.[41]

Meanwhile, in northwest Somalia, the victorious Somali National Movement insurgents, confronted with virtual anarchy in the south, declared unilateral independence from Somalia in May 1991. While the "Republic of Somaliland" failed to achieve any international recognition, it did attain a measure of stability and embarked upon a process of political reconciliation.[42]

INTERNATIONAL DYNAMICS OF THE SOMALI COLLAPSE

Despite the prolonged dissolution of the Somali state between 1988 and 1991, the international response to the suffering it occasioned was largely slow and ineffective. With the heroic exception of the Red Cross and a number of nongovernmental relief organizations, Somalia was abandoned in 1991 by much of the international community. In part, this was a reflection of the attitude of the permanent members of the Security Council, especially the United States. When the fighting escalated in the Somali capital in January 1991, the U.S. embassy helped organize the evacuation of virtually the entire foreign diplomatic community. It was almost as if America and the UN regarded the situation in Somalia as hopeless.

Furthermore, the first Bush administration initially ignored sporadic pleas from representatives of NGOs and pleas from Senators Paul Simon (D-IL) and Nancy Kassebaum (R-KS) in April 1991 "to actively explore possible United States initiatives to reconcile the conflicting factions and should encourage efforts by outside mediators."[43] Indeed, senior officials in the administration resisted recommendations to put Somalia on the UN Security Council agenda until January 1992. According to a State Department official, Washington initially viewed Somalia as just another humanitarian crisis in Africa.[44] Besides, the Bush administration was preoccupied with the Persian Gulf conflict, the disintegration of the USSR, and the unraveling of Yugoslavia. In the words of T. Frank Crigler, former ambassador to Somalia, America "turned out the lights, closed the door and forgot about the place."[45]

In addition, the UN found it difficult to operate in an environment where there had been a total collapse of the structure of central government. The UN Secretariat in New York was alerted to the gravity of the Somali situation some months before the fall of the Barre regime.[46] Nevertheless, the UN and its specialized agencies the United Nations

Children's Fund (UNICEF), the United Nations High Commissioner for Refugees (UNHCR), and the World Health Organization (WHO) withdrew all their staff from Mogadishu for security reasons. This absence was, in the words of one UN insider, the organization's "greatest failure"[47] after the Cold War. As an upshot, the UN provided no assistance in 1991 and showed little sign of understanding the depth of the catastrophe until late 1991, when Mogadishu became a killing field. Meanwhile, with the Arab League and the Organization of African Unity (OAU) largely ignoring the Somali political crisis, it was left to a handful of nongovernmental organizations (NGOs) such as the International Red Cross, the Save the Children Fund, and Médecins Sans Frontières to give humanitarian aid in appalling conditions. These organizations found it necessary to employ Somali guards to protect their houses, offices, stores, and hospitals.

According to Mohamed Sahnoun, the United Nations Secretary-General's Special Envoy (SGSE) to Somalia between April and October 1992, the UN missed three opportunities to prevent the catastrophic collapse of the Somali state before 1992.[48] The first chance came in 1988, when the UN failed to put pressure on the Barre government to halt the savage repression against the Isaaq population in northern Somalia. Sahnoun argued the UN should have mediated between Barre's regime and the SNM movement. A second opportunity came in May 1990 with the publication of a manifesto in Mogadishu signed by a coalition of over 100 Somali politicians, intellectuals, and businessmen, calling for a national reconciliation conference and democratic elections. While the United States confirmed that bilateral aid would not be resumed until Barre's regime respected human rights, the UN failed to support the Manifesto Group. Consequently, many members of the Manifesto Group were arrested by Barre. The third opening came shortly after Barre fled the presidential palace. Instead of evacuating its staff, Sahnoun maintained, the UN should have worked on the ground to promote a dialogue between the contending factions. In July 1991, the UN refused an invitation from the government of Djibouti to participate in a political reconciliation conference between representatives of the main Somali clans. Then, in October 1991, Mahdi's USC faction requested a special session of the General Assembly be dedicated to Somalia. The UN Under Secretary for Political Affairs, James Jonah, sent a message urging the UN Nairobi office in Kenya "to endeavor to discourage at the local level any idea for holding a special session on Somalia."[49]

Still, if the United States and the UN had problems dealing with the lawless and stateless Somalia, several regional actors had fewer qualms about operating in such an environment. From the second half of 1991, and well before any U.S.–UN engagement in Somalia, al Qaeda started to provide armed assistance and military training to al Itihaad Islamist elements in Hargeisa in northern Somalia and Gedo in southwest Somalia, as well as similar assistance to al Itihaad forces in the Somali-populated Ogaden region in neighboring Ethiopia.[50] In addition, a number of senior al Qaeda officials were sent to Somalia by Osama bin Laden to conduct reconnaissance, oversee the delivery of the aforementioned assistance, and hold discussions with al Itihaad officials. These officials included Jamal al-Fadl, L'Houssaine Kherchtou, Saif al Adel, and Mohammed Odeh.[51] In early 1992, al Itihaad also began to receive financial and military assistance from Iran and Sudan.[52]

Meanwhile, one year after the Barre government fell, the UN Security Council finally addressed the issue of the Somali conflict. In January 1992, United Nations Security Council Resolution (UNSCR) 733 called on new UN Secretary General Boutros Boutros-Ghali to mediate in the civil war and impose an arms embargo on Somalia. The latter was largely meaningless given the vast leftover stocks of superpower weaponry inside the country and the ethnically porous frontiers with Kenya and Ethiopia that facilitated a thriving local arms trade.[53] But on the mediation front, Jonah was dispatched to Mogadishu during January to try and persuade the major factions to negotiate an immediate ceasefire.

At this point, a problem arose that was to haunt UN diplomacy in Somalia thereafter. The UN Secretariat, presumably unaware of the political nuances of the Mahdi-Aideed conflict, "accepted by default Mahdi's status as interim-President."[54] While such recognition provided a formal link between the UN and a country without a government, it compromised the UN's impartiality in Aideed's eyes. He sensed that the UN was siding with the self-appointed President of Somalia, Mahdi. As a result, Aideed rejected Jonah's mission. It was not until early March that the UN managed to broker a shaky ceasefire, but only after the UN gave Aideed fresh reassurances of its impartiality.[55]

The reduction in hostilities in Somalia highlighted the growing problem of the looting of humanitarian aid. Factions in control of ports, such as Aideed's in Mogadishu, levied taxes on cargoes, took cuts of 10 to 20 percent of the incoming food shipments (some of which were sold outside Somalia), and also provided "technicals"—trucks with mounted guns—to "protect" food deliveries. Furthermore, food convoys were frequently robbed by those hired to defend them. Thus, while food aid was subject to such racketeering, it was actually contributing to the very conflict that had caused the famine in the first place.[56]

In a bid to overcome this problem, the UN Security Council passed Resolution 751 on April 24, 1992, which authorized a United Nations Operation in Somalia (UNOSOM I) under the overall direction of Mohamed Sahnoun. The Resolution approved the deployment of fifty UN Observers to monitor the ceasefire and the deployment of 500 Pakistani UN troops in consultation with "the parties in Mogadishu" to provide security in and around the focal point of the relief effort, Mogadishu.[57]

Appointed in April, Sahnoun quickly made a favorable impression by seeking to implement Resolution 751 through pursuing a "bottom-up" strategy in Somalia. While working hard to establish good relations with major warlords like Aideed and Mahdi, Sahnoun also bypassed them by cultivating the support of clan elders, a traditional source of authority in Somali society, for a sustained grassroots reconciliation effort along the lines initiated in northern Somalia.[58] In this way, Sahnoun hoped to gradually neutralize the power of the warlords by winning the backing of their own tribal elders for UN mediation and the international protection of emergency relief aid. The strategy was analogous to plucking the feathers of a bird until the bird could no longer fly.[59]

But Sahnoun's approach needed time to work and overlooked the fact that the horizons of many of the elders were defined by the narrow interests of their clan or subclan. More importantly, the warlords, and particularly Aideed, were in no mood to passively accept the plucking of their feathers. It took two months just to persuade Mahdi and Aideed to accept the deployment of the fifty UN observers. Mahdi agreed immediately, but General Aideed initially insisted that observers be in civilian attire rather than uniform.[60] At the same time, the UN itself complicated these negotiations. In mid-June 1992, a Russian Antonov plane with UN markings delivered military hardware and newly printed Somali currency to Mahdi's airfield in north Mogadishu. The UN had no ready explanation for this highly disruptive blunder, which prompted an already suspicious Aideed to accuse the UN of favoring his archrival Ali Mahdi.[61]

Tortuous negotiations also preceded the deployment of the UN security force. Again, Mahdi accepted with alacrity as Aideed appeared to drag his feet. Aideed extended the talks with Sahnoun, demanding that the UN train a 500-strong Somali police force to replace the UN force when it departed. The talks then got bogged down over wage demands for the Somali force. Eventually, on August 12, four months after Resolution 751, Aideed and his Somali National Alliance (SNA) allies signed an agreement with Sahnoun for the deployment of the 500 peacekeepers. As part of the agreement, Sahnoun stated that any increase in the number of UN troops would require the consent of Aideed's SNA leadership.[62] The protracted discussions reflected Aideed's concern that the introduction of peacekeeping troops would not only erode his competitive position with Mahdi in Mogadishu—his faction exercised control over the lucrative Mogadishu harbor and airport facilities—but also affect his political base elsewhere in Somalia.

Nonetheless, despite the desperate humanitarian situation in Somalia, it took yet another month before the first group of Pakistani peacekeepers arrived in mid-September. Complications in UN decision-making due to the unprecedented use of peacekeepers in a humanitarian role,[63] and the apparent reluctance of the White House to raise the profile in an election year contributed to this. Whatever the reasons, the delay meant that no UN troops had arrived when the Security Council, on August 28, under the terms of Resolution 775, authorized a further deployment of 3,500 troops across four operation zones in Somalia. That UN decision was made without consulting the UNOSOM delegation in Mogadishu, the governments of neighboring countries, or the militia leaders and tribal elders, as had previously been the case. Yet the additional deployment was once again contingent on the consent of the local warlords.[64] The response from Aideed was wholly negative. Convinced that the UN announcement contravened his August agreement with Sahnoun, Aideed threatened to send UN troops home in body bags. The security environment in Somalia rapidly deteriorated.

While all of the Pakistani blue-helmets had arrived by late September 1992, the force's terms of reference, based on traditional notions of what constituted peacekeeping, proved to be totally inadequate to the Somali challenge. There was no durable ceasefire to preserve, and cooperation with the warring parties was either non-existent or unreliable and inconsistent. Far from fulfilling their mission to secure the airport, the seaport, and the lines of communication in and around Mogadishu, the lightly armed Pakistani struggled to protect themselves from repeated militia attacks and were pinned down in their barracks, near Mogadishu airport, for the first two months after arriving. Restrained by very limited rules of engagement, the lightly armed Pakistanis were powerless to stop the looting or secure the peace.

This debacle intensified pressure on the UN and the United States "to do something" about famine-stricken Somalia. Since the beginning of 1992, many NGOs publicly criticized UN ineffectiveness in a country where over a million people faced the very real prospect of starvation. Then, in July 1992, the international media took up the story, beaming horrific TV pictures of starving Somalis to the United States and other countries. These extremely powerful, but misleading, media images reinforced Boutros-Ghali's own desire for quicker results. During a UN debate on Bosnia in July 1992, the Secretary General rebuked the Western countries for paying more attention to the "rich man's war" in the former Yugoslavia than to the Somalian tragedy.[65]

Meanwhile, stung by domestic criticism, President George H. W. Bush launched a spectacular airlift of food aid to Somalia in August 1992. However, this initiative was soon overshadowed by the basic problem of looting. Some relief agencies even claimed that something like 50 percent of all humanitarian aid delivered was being stolen by gunmen linked to the warlords.[66] In September, food ships were shelled and turned away at the Mogadishu port, and UN officials were assaulted at the southern Somalian port city of Kismayo. A frustrated Sahnoun criticized the UN for its bureaucratic inertia and pleaded for more time from New York to secure

Aideed's consent for the deployment of 3,500 peacekeepers. But the UN leadership was getting "very impatient" with Sahnoun's meager results.[67] From New York's standpoint, there were few signs that he was on the verge of a diplomatic breakthrough. Indeed, a suspicion existed within the UN Secretariat that Sahnoun was misreading the Somali situation. With thousands of Somalis dying from hunger each week and warlords like Aideed effectively exercising a veto on UN action, the organization perceived it faced a crisis of credibility. On October 27, Sahnoun was forced to resign. He was replaced by Ismat Kittani, an Iraqi diplomat who soon reached the conclusion that Aideed would never agree to a substantial UN peacekeeping presence.

The contrast between the New World Order rhetoric of the Bush administration and the UN and the grim realities of life in Somalia could not have been greater. By mid-1992, the collapse of central government authority in Somalia was total. But the country's traditional clan structures, backed by a surfeit of modern weapons, had reasserted themselves with a vengeance, dividing the capital, fragmenting the country, and condemning thousands of Somalis to death by starvation.

THE NEW GLOBAL CONTEXT AND SOMALIA

Globalization, the end of the Cold War, and the disintegration of Somalia were related through both direct and indirect channels. How the end of the Cold War affected the Somali state seems fairly clear: without superpower support, what was a highly incoherent, corrupt and fragmented state could no longer withstand the centrifugal pressures that were being brought to bear upon it, particularly due to clan rivalries, a lack of respect or trust in the state, and ongoing border tensions. While the Barre regime could contain these forces with the help of first the USSR and then the United States, there was little opportunity to do so once not only the superpowers but also the international community in general lost interest in what had apparently become a strategically unimportant area of conflict.

Not only did globalization affect the forces that brought about the end of the Cold War, but it has also had profound effects on Somalia before, during, and after its disintegration into chaos. Globalization, with its opposing forces of integration and fragmentation, shaped the new international security environment that so profoundly affected Somalia during and after the Cold War. Western, and in particular the United States', interpretation of why the Cold War ended meant that countries such as Somalia were seen as lacking strategic significance with the demise of the Cold War. By underestimating the powerful impact that globalization was having in the world, the international community missed an important piece of the puzzle that has defined the security environment of the post–Cold War world.

While Barre's dictatorship effectively kept Somalia isolated from many foreign influences, [68] once Barre was overthrown and Somalia fell into a governmental vacuum, globalization acted to both reinforce and reconfigure the situation inside the country. The global strategic status that Somalia and Ethiopia had attained during the Cold War resulted in massive amounts of arms being traded both across borders and more locally. The availability of these weapons was important in maintaining a situation of statelessness. The rapid spread of international influences within Somalia after the advent of civil war in 1988 helped transform Somalia into a highly globalized territory.[69] Furthermore, lack of governmental regulation in Somalia allowed the movement of people and products, which would not otherwise have been the case. While Somalia remained a state without government, racked by warlord politics and fighting, the same time the people of Somalia were simultaneously opened up to a contradictory world of technology and opportunity. Seen in this way, the effects of globalization before the end of the Cold War played out in Somalia in the aftermath of the fall of Barre regime to exacerbate civil conflict—but at the same time, globalization thrived in this stateless environment to open up a new world to Somali people and increase their interaction with that world.

CONCLUSION: SOMALIA AND THE EMERGENCE OF THE NEW SECURITY PARADIGM

The post–Cold War environment of the early 1990s was one in which two important forces collided. First, the rise of the United States as the sole "superpower" in the international system, combined with a U.S.-centric interpretation of why the Cold War ended, led to a U.S. foreign policy that tended to underplay the geostrategic importance of weak or failing states. Second, globalization, which, it is argued here, actually had an important role to play in ending the Cold War itself, was an important force in buttressing Bush's New World Order, particularly through financial and technological developments. However, at the same time that globalization acted to integrate the world, it also had powerful fragmentation effects. The changing structure of the international system, interacting with globalization, had profound effects on the situation in Somalia. But Somalia, as we shall see, was by no means unique in the post–Cold War era.

In many ways, the Somali crisis was a paradigm of the emerging security order. It highlighted several key features of the post–Cold War environment. Weak or failed states were now the main source of threat and instability in the world, and these new civil conflicts were often characterized by the absence or inadequacy of legitimate governance.

Furthermore, many of the "new wars" were driven by issues of identity and involved the mobilization of movements along ethnic, tribal, racial, and religious lines. Civil conflicts such as Somalia served to stimulate calls for higher standards of governance, including the spread of democracy. The Somali crisis also highlighted the way that globalized mass media now had the ability to help internationalize internal conflicts— often described as the "CNN Effect."

The potential for economic and military overspill from intrastate conflicts also challenged the old sovereign distinction between domestic and external policy in the field of security, and finally, the capacity of the international community to respond to major security challenges was largely determined by the stance of the United States, the sole superpower.

It is no exaggeration, then, to say that the Somali crisis was very literally at the point of transition between a bipolar world marked by superpower competition and the new era of intensifying globalization, rising complexity, and a single dominant power rising above it all: the United States. To understand the eventual international response to Somalia's plight in 1992, it is necessary to examine the decision-making process in the US that underpinned it.

Chapter 2

About Face: President Bush's Decision to Intervene in Somalia

The offer by President George Bush on November 25, 1992, to commit U.S. forces to lead a humanitarian military mission in Somalia, under UN auspices, was an abrupt departure from previous American policy. Convinced that the UN's attempts to reverse starvation and disorder in Somalia were "no longer tenable," the Bush administration determined there was little alternative but to adopt more forceful measures to ensure that starving Somalis got fed. This view had also been floated by the UN Secretary General's former Special Envoy to Somalia, Mohamed Sahnoun, and publicly advocated by a number of aid agencies operating in Somalia.[1] After a week of intensive U.S.–UN negotiations, Boutros-Ghali accepted the U.S. proposal; it was unanimously endorsed on December 3, 1992, by the Security Council. Resolution 794 recognized that the Somali situation constituted "a threat to international peace" and authorized the U.S.-led Unified Task Force (UNITAF) to use "all necessary means to establish as soon as possible a secure environment for humanitarian relief operations."[2] The force was to be large—37,000 troops, the bulk of which were to be Americans.

This intervention was a landmark decision for both the UN and the United States. It was the first time the Security Council had sanctioned a major enforcement action under Chapter VII of the UN Charter in a theoretically sovereign state. It was also the first time in recent memory that the United States explicitly justified sending its troops to a foreign country not to safeguard U.S. strategic interests, but to perform a humanitarian mission. In Bush's words, U.S. troops would "do God's work"[3] in Somalia by acting to help those in desperate need of food.

At the same time, Bush's decision to intervene in Somalia marked a major change in U.S. policy toward UN peacekeeping. The administration

indicated before Operation Restore Hope even began that a portion of
U.S. forces deployed in Somalia would stay on to serve as full members
of the UN peacekeeping force that would replace the U.S.-led coalition.
Thus, in a clear break from the past, the United States was prepared for
the first time, in principle, to allow its forces to operate under UN military
command.[4]

Bush's initiative startled many Americans, including those within the
ranks of his own administration.[5] It also took much of the international
community, particularly the aid organizations involved in Somalia, by
surprise.[6] For almost fifteen months after Somalia's descent into chaos following the collapse of Barre's dictatorship, Somalia seemed to be off the
U.S. foreign policy agenda. Indeed, in early 1992, before the suffering in
Somalia became front-page news, officials in the Bush administration dismissed the idea of armed humanitarian intervention in that country as
"ridiculous."[7] There was little public indication of this undertaking before
President Bush announced his intention to launch it.

So what were the reasons for this change of heart by a lame-duck
President? How did the Bush administration come to make a decision that
had truly momentous consequences for U.S. foreign policy and the
post–Cold War world? Was Bush's decision simply an impulsive response
to heart-rending TV images of starving Somalis and mounting domestic
and international pressures that "America must act?" Or was this decision
a product of careful debate within the Bush administration that forged a
consensus among senior civilian and military officials on the purposes
and limits of what one official called a "classic humanitarian intervention?"[8]

This chapter seeks to grapple with these issues by examining the U.S.
decision making process that led to America's largest ever military
involvement in Africa. Rather than focusing exclusively on the ultimate
presidential decision, the decision to intervene in Somalia is examined
here in the wider context of three consecutive phases in the decision making process from 1991 to 1992. The first phase of policy, that of minimal
U.S. engagement in Somalia, covers the period from the collapse of the
Barre dictatorship in January 1991 to June 1992. A second phase, the
period of partial U.S. engagement, extended from July to September 1992
and encompassed a U.S.-led airlift of international aid known as Operation Provide Relief. The third phase, beginning in October 1992, was one
of active U.S. engagement in Somalia and culminated in President Bush's
offer on November 25, 1992, to lead a UN-authorized armed humanitarian
intervention in Somalia.

The argument that emerges here is that the U.S. decision to commit
U.S. forces to Somalia was more a product of intergovernmental policy
dynamics and domestic politics than broader foreign policy concerns such
as the strengthening of the UN's peace enforcement capabilities in a collapsed state like Somalia. The decision to intervene was more ambiguous

and less clear-cut than it appeared. Above all, the final decision to intervene was the product of a delicate interagency consensus forged by presidential leadership and a sudden convergence in the views of the State Department and the Department of Defense in mid-November 1992.

PHASE ONE: MINIMAL U.S. ENGAGEMENT IN SOMALIA (JANUARY 1991–JUNE 1992)

Despite a Cold War alliance with the dictatorship of Siad Barre, the United States began to distance itself from its ally in the late 1980s when civil war engulfed the northern part of Somalia and spread southward. By January 6, 1991, the United States had ceased to have a diplomatic presence in Somalia. Citing security concerns, the United States evacuated its embassy staff and that of the entire foreign diplomatic community from Mogadishu as rebel forces of the United Somali Congress closed in on the Somali capital. On January 27, President Barre was overthrown and fled toward his clan homeland in southwestern Somalia. Thereafter, Somalia was assigned only a modest priority in the making of U.S. foreign policy.[9]

Nevertheless, the continued disintegration of Somali political and economic structures led to an ominous disaster situation. Within days of Barre's departure, the leaders of the victorious USC became absorbed in a violent power struggle. Mogadishu turned into a bloodbath as two heavily armed factions, led by Ali Mahdi and General Mohammed Aideed, slugged it out for control of the Somali capital. The fighting was not confined to Mogadishu. Barre's retreating troops adopted a "scorched earth" policy as they retreated from Mogadishu. At the same time, the severe drought further magnified the impact of civil strife.

In Washington, the initial response to the Somali crisis was one approaching indifference. As outlined in Chapter 1, the end of the Cold War had seen a rapid evaporation of Somalia's strategic value. For nearly eighteen months, the U.S. government was reluctant to lead on the Somali crisis. This reticence manifested itself in a number of ways. In July 1991, the United States endorsed the reconciliation conference at Djibouti, showing its hope for an African solution to the crisis.[10] The U.S. Assistant Secretary of State for Africa, Herman Cohen, was sent as an observer. But the Djibouti process made little headway. The Bush administration also sought to lay the issue at the feet of Siad Barre himself, as well as the former colonial powers, Britain and Italy.[11]

For much of this period, the Bush administration was preoccupied with other international and regional issues. In the words of Cohen, there was "a lot going on:"[12] the Persian Gulf conflict, the disintegration of the USSR, the escalation of the Bosnian crisis in former Yugoslavia, and U.S. mediation in Angola, Sudan, and Ethiopia loomed large in Washington.[13]

Thus, the United States blocked diplomatic efforts to put Somalia on the UN Security Council agenda until January 1992.[14] In this context, the absence of a UN presence in Somalia in 1991 certainly did not help matters. Moreover, Boutros-Ghali's attempts in early 1992 to adopt a more proactive UN policy toward Somalia encountered U.S. resistance.[15]

After the UN brokered a shaky ceasefire in Somalia in March 1992, the U.S. representative in the Security Council watered down a draft UN resolution, which called for the dispatch of 550 peacekeepers to guarantee the stability of the ceasefire in Somalia.[16] At this stage, the United States was determined to limit UN involvement to humanitarian relief. The main reason was financial. A dozen UN peacekeeping operations had been authorized in the previous twenty-four months. The Cambodian operation alone was budgeted for $2 billion. According to Cohen, the U.S. picked up 30 percent of the cost.[17] Considering that the United States was previously paying approximately $70 million toward peacekeeping per year, it is not difficult to see that the U.S. government was alarmed at spiraling peacekeeping costs. In particular, the administration was concerned not to incur the displeasure of Congress by spending even more in the area of peacekeeping.

The initial reluctance of the Bush administration to take a strong lead in the worsening Somali crisis had several important consequences. One was that the U.S. role remained largely humanitarian until July 1992. During this period, the State Department and the Agency for International Development (AID) undertook a substantial list of emergency response measures in an attempt to contain the Somali crisis. Money and food was given to the Save the Children Fund, Médecins Sans Frontières, Cooperative for Assistance and Relief Everywhere (CARE), UNICEF, the World Food Program, the International Medical Corps, the UN High Commission for Refugees, and the International Red Cross. Despite its reservations on expanding the UN involvement in Somalia, the United States quickly became the world's largest donor of humanitarian assistance to Somalia.[18]

In addition, Somalia began to feature in interagency discussions within the U.S. government. The intensity of these discussions grew as 1992 drew on. Representatives from the State Department, including the Assistant Secretary of State for Africa, State Bureau for International Organization, Department of Defense, Joint Chiefs of Staff (JCS), and Agency for International Development, as well as National Security Council (NSC) representatives and (sometimes) officials from NGOs, all participated in these discussions.

The Assistant Secretary of State for Africa, Herman Cohen, said that those like himself calling for an activist policy toward Somalia through the UN Security Council were initially "lonely voices" within the U.S. government.[19] Cohen's Africa Bureau said that Somalia's humanitarian crisis was essentially a security problem generated by the effects of the country's multisided civil war in a country that for all intents and purposes had imploded. But the problem was that for much of 1992 the State Bureau for International Organization (IO)—the agency concerned with the UN—did not accept this analysis. Assistant Secretary for IO John Bolton and his deputy John Wolf strongly argued that Somalia was simply suffering from a food shortage problem. This view was shaped by budgetary concerns, as well as the conviction that the United States had no national interest in supporting substantive UN efforts to improve the security situation in Somalia. As an upshot, IO officials blocked efforts by the Africa Bureau to table the Somalia issue at the UN Security Council. The IO view was backed by the Department of Defense and the JCS.

For well over a year, General Colin Powell and the Joint Chiefs of Staff had steadfastly opposed the idea of UN-backed armed humanitarian intervention in conflicts like Somalia, Liberia, Bosnia, and elsewhere.[20] Such opposition was based on the assumption that as the world's only superpower, the United States, would have to lead any such operation and that to do so could, in turn, embroil the United States in historically entrenched conflicts that were not relevant to U.S. vital interests. From General Powell's perspective, the crisis in Somalia was a humanitarian tragedy, but not a direct threat to the national interests of the United States. The basic position of the Joint Chiefs and the senior White House staff was that U.S. forces would not be able to safeguard themselves or effectively facilitate the distribution of humanitarian aid in a civil war situation in which it was very difficult to distinguish friend from foe. Thus, in the words of General Powell, "I was not eager to get us involved in a Somalian civil war . . ."[21]

The stance of General Powell and the Joint Chiefs was shaped by several factors. First, in historical terms, there was little precedent in American public life for undertaking such a venture. It is difficult to imagine, for example, that the Founding Fathers would have envisaged or approved the dispatch of American armed forces to another country far from home in order to conduct a major police action where no defensive American interest appeared to be at stake.[22] Second, and not unrelated to this point, the so-called Powell Doctrine, formulated in the wake of U.S. reverses in civil wars in Vietnam (1965–1975) and Lebanon (1983), was regarded by the Pentagon and senior White House staff as "a practical guide" for committing American troops to combat. According to General Powell, former Defense Secretary Casper Weinberger identified six tests in 1984 for use in determining when to commit American forces: "Commit only if our or allies' vital interests are at stake"; "If we commit, do so with all the resources necessary to win"; "Go in only with clear political and military objectives"; "Be ready to change the commitment if the objectives change, since wars rarely stand still"; "Only take on commitments that gain the support of the American people and the Congress"; and "Commit US forces only as a last resort."[23] In other words, the key question for deploying U.S. troops in Somalia or any other country is whether "the [U.S.] national interest is at stake?" According to Powell, "if the answer is yes, go in and go in to win. Otherwise, stay out."[24]

Both President Bush and Secretary of Defense Dick Cheney had a lot of confidence in General Powell's judgment, particularly after the Persian Gulf War in 1990–1991. Powell saw himself as a disciple of the great Prussian strategic thinker, Carl von Clausewitz, and claimed that Clausewitz himself "would have applauded" the logic of the Powell Doctrine.[25] Relatively few policymakers in Washington in the early 1990s were in a position to seriously question the appropriateness of the Powell Doctrine in the post–Cold War era. Nevertheless, new conflicts like Somalia certainly challenged the notion, attributed to Clausewitz, that wars are waged by sovereign states against sovereign states to enhance the power and well-being of sovereign states. Although some wars in the post-Cold War era would continue to fit this interpretation, "postmodern wars" like Somalia did not.

Cohen responded to the interagency impasse on Somalia by engaging in what he called "bureaucratic politics."[26] As Assistant Secretary of State for Africa, Cohen had the right to convene what was called the Policy Co-ordinating Committee for Africa (PCCA). He chaired the meetings of this committee, which initially occurred every three weeks or so. These meetings included factual briefings on Somalia from Central Intelligence Agency (CIA) and Defense Intelligence officials. One regular participant was Walter Kansteiner, a Republican political appointee serving as Director for African Affairs on the National Security Council Staff. He took detailed notes, and it was through his reports to General Brent Scowcroft, the National Security Adviser, that news about Somalia reached President Bush.[27]

While Cohen's chairing of the PCCA constrained him from championing Somalia too openly, such sessions, which included important contributions from Andrew Natsios, Director of the Office of Foreign Disaster Assistance (OFDA), and Jim Bishop, Deputy Assistant Secretary for Human Rights and Human Affairs (and former U.S. ambassador to Somalia), helped to gradually tighten the institutional focus on Somalia.[28] Both Natsios and Bishop advocated a proactive approach to Somalia, vigorously arguing that the United States should be doing much more. Furthermore, in early 1992, Natsios launched weekly press releases, chronicling the horrors of the Somali situation in systematic and statistical terms. Natsios's efforts helped to gradually stir U.S. public opinion, whether through the *New York Times*, CNN, or Congress.[29]

In January 1992, Senator Paul Simon (D-IL), chairman of the African Subcommittee of the Senate Foreign Relations Committee, along with his committee colleague Senator Nancy Kassebaum (R-KS), called for urgent international action to save the Somali people from starvation.[30] They were to devote much of their energies in the next few months to urging U.S. support for UN peacekeeping efforts, eventually calling for U.S. "volunteers" to undertake humanitarian intervention. In Africa Subcommittee hearings in March 1992, the two senators argued that the UN Security Council's reluctance to send peacekeeping forces to Somalia would only condemn thousands of Somalis to a premature death.

The first six months of 1992 also witnessed growing pressure from humanitarian NGOs. In late March, two groups, Africa Watch and Physician for Human Rights, harshly criticized the role of both the United States and the UN in Somalia. In a joint report, the groups accused the United States of making no serious effort to head off the disaster in Mogadishu and of failing to press the UN to act earlier in Somalia.

The PCCA meetings had certainly increased the governmental spotlight on Somalia but until late June 1992 the Bureau of IO, tacitly supported by JCS, effectively "roadblocked" attempts to expand U.S. involvement in the Somali crisis through the UN as well as outside it. Thus, despite an intensifying debate about Somalia, the so-called realists still held the upper hand at the interagency level at a time when a large number of issues competed for foreign policy attention in Washington.

PHASE TWO: PARTIAL U.S. ENGAGEMENT IN SOMALIA (JULY–SEPTEMBER 1992)

The month of July was a turning point for U.S. policy toward Somalia. It was the month in which President Bush resolved, in the words of Lawrence Eagleburger, the Acting Secretary of State, to be "forward learning"[31] on Somalia. That is to say, the President was now inclining toward a more active policy toward Somalia. Why did this happen in July?

For one thing, the international mass media began to give constant, almost saturation coverage of the civil war-fueled famine in Somalia. Haunting images of starving Somalis on the BBC and CNN shocked public opinion in the United States and much of the Western world. Newspapers such as the *New York Times* and *The Guardian* began to produce a series of stories detailing Somalia's humanitarian crisis. While the White House was not impervious to the public impact of this new media attention on Somalia, it should not be forgotten that frustrated elements within the Bush administration, such as Cohen and Natsios, had worked hard to alert the media to the horrors of the Somali situation since early 1992. Clearly, these members of the Bush administration were hoping to mobilize U.S. public opinion in order to put pressure on those of their colleagues within the government who were resisting a more engaged policy approach toward Somalia.[32]

In addition, the U.S. Ambassador to Kenya, Smith Hempstone, sent a cable on July 10 to the White House regarding the Somali famine; it became known as "The Hell Called Somalia."[33] The cable was sent after Hempstone and two of his staff had undertaken reconnaissance visits to Somalia and gained good firsthand knowledge of the Somali situation. It certainly had a powerful effect on the President, who, according to Kansteiner, scribbled in the margin of the cable "something must be done about this."[34] The cable had called for a large-scale infusion of American food aid in Somalia. Hempstone's deputy chief of mission, Michael Southwick, happened to be in Washington at the time and confirmed that interest in the Somali situation "was beginning to perk up."[35]

Boutros-Ghali's unusually blunt and widely publicized criticism of Western countries paying more attention to Yugoslavia than to the Somalian tragedy added to the pressure to act. Amongst other things, Boutros-Ghali implied that the most powerful Western country, the United States, cared more about the loss of life in Europe than in Africa. The timing of Boutros-Ghali's intervention came shortly after the publication of his report "An Agenda for Peace." This envisaged a more active role for the post–Cold War UN in new areas such as peacemaking and peace-building in countries "torn by civil war and strife."[36] According to Scowcroft and Kansteiner, the public criticism by Boutros-Ghali certainly registered with President Bush. Moreover, it followed an earlier, private expression of concern by the UN Secretary General in the Oval Office in May 1992 that many developing countries felt that the UN Security Council was somewhat indifferent to humanitarian concerns in the Third World.[37] Apparently, Boutros-Ghali had also reminded the Bush administration that it had received full support from the UN for ejecting Saddam Hussein's forces from Kuwait and anticipated that the United States would be equally responsive when another Muslim state, Somalia, found itself in desperate need of humanitarian assistance.[38] Such sentiments were not lost on an American president who had publicly articulated a vision of U.S.–UN partnership in a New World Order after the Cold War.

At the same time, there were signs that the "interventionist" side of the interagency debate was beginning to make some headway. In spring 1992, Bishop arranged a meeting with Kassebaum, the Republican Senator for Kansas. In the course of the meeting, Bishop explained that the situation in Somalia was far worse than was generally realized and that the strictly humanitarian approach of the United States and the UN in Somalia was not working[39]—it had taken all of three months just to obtain the agreement of the warring factions in the country to allow fifty UN ceasefire observers to complete their deployment to Mogadishu as authorized by UNSCR 751.

Senator Kassebaum responded sympathetically but was not optimistic about there being much political support in America for U.S. military involvement in any humanitarian operation. Nevertheless, two months later, Senator Kassebaum visited Somalia and returned to testify before the House Committee on Hunger on July 22 with the following message: "I believe the U.S. has a moral obligation to Somalia. Throughout the years of the Cold War, Somalia and the rest of the Horn of Africa were of strategic importance. We must demonstrate that our concern for human beings is as great as was our past fear of the Soviet empire."[40] Such statements from a highly respected Republican like Senator Kassebaum could not, in the view of Kansteiner, be safely ignored, particularly in a presidential election year.[41]

Taken together, the above factors placed President Bush in an awkward political position. On the one hand, the Democrats were attacking him as a president who cared only about foreign policy. Candidate Clinton was already developing the theme by mid-1992 that greater attention had to be given to the U.S. economy. On the other hand, a failure to act decisively and effectively on Somalia's endless crisis exposed Bush to charges that his leadership was weak and that his call for a New World Order was just rhetoric. Again, Candidate Clinton led the charge on this. He said that troops should be sent to Somalia to alleviate the appalling starvation that was seen on U.S. television from mid-July 1992 on, and also questioned the Bush administration's policy toward Bosnia and Haiti as well as China.[42] Interestingly, after the Cold War, liberal humanitarian groups in the United States, traditionally suspicious of the projection of American military power since the Vietnam War, began to advocate the use of military force to protect human rights in places like Somalia.[43]

At this point, there was a rise in the tempo in of the interagency debate[44] within the U.S. government on how best to deal with the Somali crisis. In July 1992, Cohen proposed that the United States use its logistical and military capabilities to airlift food to Somalia, but the JCS reacted negatively to the suggestion. The JCS maintained that a humanitarian operation of this nature should be funded from the AID budget and that it would be more appropriate and cheaper to do this using commercial airlines.[45] This response could be seen as another way of saying that the JCS did not favor a U.S. government airlift. Cohen countered by saying perhaps President Bush wanted to do something about the Somali tragedy. There was no consensus within the administration over what to do, but the momentum toward a more active U.S. role was gathering steam.

On July 27, the UNSC unanimously adopted Resolution 767, urging the Secretary General to mount an airlift of food supplies. On the same day, the Department of State made a public statement in favor of dispatching armed UN security elements to Somalia; as Cohen later noted, this was "the first US 'pro-security' statement"[46] since the crisis began.

Then, in early August, the U.S. Senate entered the picture. Frustrated by the apparent reluctance of General Aideed to allow the deployment of 500 peacekeepers into Somalia to protect the distribution of famine relief operations in Mogadishu (something to which he eventually agreed, on August 12), the Senate passed a resolution on August 3 calling for the dispatch of 500 UN troops to Somalia "with or without the consent of the Somalia factions."[47]

Still, Cohen was "totally surprised"[48] by an August 14 White House announcement that the United States would mount an emergency food airlift into the interior of Somalia, using U.S. military transport aircraft, and would offer an air-transport capability to 500 Pakistani troops who would serve as UN peacekeepers in Mogadishu. More than 130 U.S. troops, along with three or four C-141 Starlifter transport aircraft and ten C-130 Hercules cargo planes, were sent to Mombasa in order to distribute food to Somali refugees in Kenya and southern Somalia. However, the mission of the U.S. airlift was to deliver food rather than provide security for the distribution of food.

This airlift, known as Operation Provide Relief, was authorized just before the Republican Convention for the Nomination of the Presidential Candidate in late August. Significantly, the President also appointed Andrew Natsios as Special Coordinator for Somali Relief.[49] He had already demonstrated at the PCCA meetings that he was a "well-organized, tough and articulate guy" who could get things done.[50] On August 28, the United States began Operation Provide Relief with a military airlift of emergency food supplies into Somalia from Mombassa.

Unfortunately, Operation Provide Relief failed to ensure that starving Somalis who most needed food actually received it. Much of the airlifted food was captured by the warring militias. This was frankly acknowledged by the Chair of the JCS, General Powell, in his memoirs: "We rarely knew what happened to the relief supplies. Local warlords stole the food from warehouses. They hijacked relief agency trucks. The UN effort was practically at a standstill, while images of the fleshless limbs and bloated bellies of dying children continued to haunt us."[51] Moreover, the airlift intensified competition and conflict between the factions and therefore made the security situation even worse for humanitarian NGOs working on the ground. This was particularly the case in the cities of Baidoa and Bardhere in southern Somalia, where militias fought for the control of the valuable supplies.

The lack of security at the ports and along the roads either made the moving of food impossible or created opportunities for bandits or factions to seize food shipments in transit. Clearly, more needed to be done. But what—and by whom? President Bush's August decision to mount an airlift had changed the terms of the debate within the administration but had not yet created an interagency consensus. In late summer 1992, the JCS rejected an idea by Bishop. He had advocated a "zone of tranquility" concept that built on the ideas of Fred Cuny.[52] This plan envisaged the use of 12,000–15,000 U.S. marines, plus helicopter gunships to neutralize Somali "technicals." The idea was to set up feeding areas outside Mogadishu—where the two major militias were concentrated—to get food to the Somalis who desperately needed it. According to Bishop, the JCS not only turned down the idea, but also rejected the idea of contingency planning for such an eventuality. Yet, such contingency work, according to Bishop, was already underway in Florida.[53]

PHASE THREE: ACTIVE U.S. ENGAGEMENT IN SOMALIA (OCTOBER–DECEMBER 1992)

Throughout the fall of 1992, interagency efforts to devise a more effective strategy toward Somalia intensified further. The scale of the disaster was extraordinary. It was reported that 25 percent of all Somali children under five years had perished from malnutrition between 1991 and 1992.[54] Out of a total population of fewer than 6 million, hundreds of thousands of Somalis faced starvation. Several things became increasingly apparent: the expanded humanitarian effort was failing. Shooting and looting incidents at airfields and ports receiving emergency food supplies in early October illustrated a stark reality about the U.S.-led emergency airlift: the airlift in itself would never bring the problem of starvation under control.

Meanwhile, diplomatic efforts to strengthen the UN peacekeeping presence in Somalia stalled. On August 28, 1992, UN Security Council Resolution 775 authorized a further deployment of 3,000 troops across four zones in Somalia. According to Sahnoun, that decision in New York was made without informing the UNOSOM delegation in Mogadishu, without informing the governments of neighboring countries, and without consulting tribal elders. Yet, as in the case of the Pakistani peacekeepers, the deployment of the 3,000 UN troops was contingent—once again—on the approval of the local warlords.

The failure of the U.S.-led airlift, Operation Provide Relief, and the besieged Pakistani peacekeepers to protect food distribution operations into Somalia led to increasing calls from humanitarian organizations to provide greater security for relief operations there. In early November, a large number of international relief groups and representatives from the office of the UNHCR again urged the international community to step up its efforts to ameliorate the famine. InterAction, a coalition of 160 U.S.-based nongovernmental relief organizations, issued public and private appeals to the Bush administration, including a letter to President Bush himself in mid-November,[55] detailing the extensive problems that relief groups were facing in Somalia owing to the lack of security against armed militias and bandits. InterAction requested that the United States step up its support for the UN to provide greater security for the distribution of humanitarian aid.[56] Furthermore, Boutros-Ghali restated his criticism that the Bush administration was devoting a lot of attention to the Bosnian war in Europe while largely ignoring the terrible plight of millions of black Africans in Somalia.

Certainly, by September 1992, there was growing pressure on the Bush administration to intervene in the Bosnian conflict. After the chilling disclosure in August 1992 that there were Serb-controlled concentration-style camps in Bosnia, members of Congress and significant elements of the American media openly began to challenge the administration's view that the conflict was a spontaneous and multisided ethnic conflict. Alarmed by the public furor, General Powell decided to step up his efforts to keep U.S. troops out of the conflict. As well as lobbying within the U.S. administration against a U.S. commitment, he took the opportunity to assail the proponents of limited military intervention in the *New York Times*: "You bet I get a little nervous when so-called experts suggest that all we need is a little surgical bombing or a limited attack. When the desired result isn't obtained, a new set of experts comes forward with talk of a little escalation. History has not been kind to this approach."[57]

But Powell's allusions to Vietnam and Beirut failed to quell the demand for action in Bosnia. A day later, the *New York Times* strongly criticized Powell and his reluctance to intervene in Bosnia: "The war in Bosnia is not a fair fight and it is not war. It is slaughter . . . President Bush could tell General Powell what President Lincoln once told General McClellan: 'If you don't want to use the Army, I should like to borrow it for a while.'"[58] By his own admission, Powell was frustrated that his arguments concerning the historical, ethnic, and religious complexities of the Bosnian situation had not made more impact in what was an election year. Such were the pressures on Powell and his colleagues in early November when Bill Clinton, who had campaigned on an activist policy in Bosnia, won the 1992 presidential election. And Powell's concern that America might launch an ambiguous, feel-good military intervention in Bosnia was deepened during his first meeting with President-elect Clinton on November 19, when the possible use of air power in Bosnia was raised by the new president.[59]

It was within this new political context that American policy toward Somalia rapidly developed. On November 12, 1992, Robert L. Gallucci, the Assistant Secretary for Political-Military Affairs, presented Lawrence Eagleburger with proposals for intervention in both Somalia and Bosnia. Alerted by John Praizza, the Director of Regional Security Affairs, to the problem of low morale among those government staff engaged in humanitarian work in Somalia—the problem, according to Gallucci, was caused by the continuing American reluctance to recognize the security dimension of the Somali crisis—Gallucci consulted with Eagleburger and decided to act.

These proposals were presented on paper without letterhead, unsigned, to Eagleburger.[60] In the case of the Somali proposal, Gallucci argued that the United States should lead an international coalition to save Somalia from starvation under a UN Security Council authorization to use "all necessary means"—including armed force. The Somali proposal was described as "low risk" and "low cost," whereas the Bosnian proposal was characterized as "high risk" and "high cost."[61] Within a relatively short period of time, Eagleburger informed Gallucci that President Bush had accepted in principle the proposal for intervening in Somalia, although the question of how to operationalize it remained to be worked out. However, President Bush had rejected in principle the second proposal concerning U.S. intervention in Bosnia.

The Gallucci proposal coincided with several other significant developments. In an address to the UN General Assembly in late September, President Bush announced that the United States would become involved in complex emergency situations that were a feature of the post–Cold War era—and, therefore, that the U.S. military would have a new and more active role in peacekeeping in the 1990s. The speech, according to James Mayall, "rang bells"[62] in the Department of Defense; the Pentagon's opposition to humanitarian intervention began to soften. Deputy Assistant Secretary of State for African Affairs Robert Houdek agreed. Bush's UN speech certainly "turned heads" in the JCS and signaled to the Pentagon that having "lost its primary mission" at the end of the Cold War, it should be prepared to take on new roles in the post–Cold War era.[63]

Then, in mid-November, there was the circulation inside Washington of an important cable from the diplomatic mission to the UN. Among other things, the U.S. mission emphasized the need to increase the credibility of UN peacekeeping in the post–Cold War era.[64] Because President Bush's "New World Order" perspective envisaged partnership with the UN, it was important that it had a credible partner to sustain the new post–Cold War order. The fact that President-elect Clinton had embraced the idea of a strong UN role—he even endorsed the idea of a standing UN army during the course of the 1992 campaign for the White House[65]— indicated that this was, at the time, a bipartisan diplomatic concern.

At the same time, President Bush's electoral defeat helped to free up the decision making process in relation to the Somali crisis. For at least six months prior to the 1992 presidential election, electoral considerations weighed heavily on interagency discussions in relation to the Somali crisis. However, after Clinton's victory, the interregnum provided a fresh chance for President Bush to focus on Somalia and made officials in the lame-duck administration sensitive to signals from the incoming government on what was acceptable.[66] And, generally speaking, the signals received on Somalia tended to be proactive. This could not but affect the direction of interagency discussion on the Somali problem. In mid-November, a Senate delegation headed by Senator Simon, as well as a House of Representatives delegation under Representative John Lewis (D-GA), were calling for more security after visits to Somalia. According to Colonel Kevin Kennedy, Chief of Staff at the Operation Provide Relief base in Mombasa, these high-level delegations signaled, at the very least, that the Democrats were not adverse to a more forceful approach toward Somalia.[67] These signals complemented Clinton's campaign message that America should exert more leadership in complex emergencies such as that in Somalia. Indeed, an official who worked on the Africa Desk of the CIA recalled attending a forum in which a member of the Clinton camp, Morton Abramovich, effectively told the outgoing Bush administration to get on with the job of addressing the humanitarian disaster in Somalia.[68]

Shortly after his election defeat, Bush had soon refocused on Somalia. He asked NSC staff for an assessment of Operation Provide Relief. Had this airlift worked? If not, what could be done? Gallucci's proposals for intervention in both Somalia and Bosnia on November 12 should be seen in that context. Having agreed to explore the idea of intervening in Somalia, President Bush asked his staff to prepare some policy options. Four meetings of the NSC Deputies Committee, a prominent interagency panel of officials just below the Cabinet level, were scheduled between November 20 and 24 to consider options. Three options were tabled at the first meeting on November 20: increased U.S. support for UN peacekeeping efforts; a U.S.-organized coalition effort that provided logistical support but no ground troops; and a U.S.-led multinational force in which U.S. ground troops would take the leading role, as had been the case in the 1990–1991 Operation Desert Storm. Although there was little consensus at the November 20 meeting, the third option was not even raised for discussion. Apparently, it was not seen as a serious option.[69]

However, at the second session of the Deputies Committee on November 21, Admiral David Jeremiah, the Vice-Chairman of the JCS and Powell's representative, stunned the meeting by declaring "if you think U.S. forces are needed, we can do the job."[70] That statement was in sharp contrast to the resistance the Pentagon had previously shown about getting involved in Somalia. Jeremiah outlined an initial concept to deploy two divisions, parts of which might consist of units from coalition countries. The Pentagon's abrupt policy reversal on Somalia was described by diplomat Frank Wisner as "amazing";[71] Cohen characterized Jeremiah's statement as a "major mystery";[72] Houdek called Jeremiah's comment "astounding";[73] and Scowcroft noted: "I was struck, and I still am, with the alacrity with which Colin Powell changed gears."[74] But Admiral Jeremiah denied there had been any major shift in the thinking of the JCS.

While he acknowledged there had been "some gap" between the Department of Defense and the State Department over what to do in Somalia, he believed these differences had been "worked through" in the Deputies Committee meetings and that his statement of November 21 reflected the fact that the two sides had moved closer to each other.[75] In any event, the State Department, which had never sought a U.S.-led armed intervention in Somalia, now jumped on the JCS offer and sought to lock it in. When Jeremiah and the IO continued to express concerns about the circumstances under which U.S. forces could withdraw in any such operation, Ambassador Brandon Grove, the new Head of the Somali Task Force in Washington, spelled out in a memo on November 23 for the National Security Council specific exit criteria and strategies "should we become militarily engaged" in Somalia.[76] This was done mainly to reassure the JCS and the IO.

Two more meetings of the Deputies Committee were held at the White House to refine options for Bush. When these discussions were completed, Bush met his senior advisers in the National Security Council on the morning of November 25. He made it clear at the outset that "we want to do something about Somalia."[77] He had three options before him: option "A" was greater U.S. support for a traditional UN peacekeeping operation consisting of a 3,500 UNOSOM force, backed by heavy arms and the authorization to use force if necessary. Option "B" was a UN-led international force of 15,000 troops. This would not include U.S. ground troops; Washington would provide logistical support and a rapid reaction force in the event of an emergency. Finally, under option "C," or what was known as the "sledgehammer" option, a substantial U.S. force would lead to an international coalition, as it had in the liberation of Kuwait, to ensure the effective distribution of humanitarian aid in Somalia.[78]

The critical November 25 meeting lasted less than an hour. Despite fairly strong interagency support for option "B," President Bush and his top advisers opted for option "C"—a large-scale, U.S.-led armed intervention. Some members of the Bush administration were surprised that the President had opted for the strongest option available. Support for an option "B" type approach had been firming up in the State Department for some time. But Scowcroft said that he strongly supported the "sledgehammer" option, and that he believed it to be the "safest" choice for achieving the objective of a humanitarian intervention in Somalia without leaving a messy situation for the incoming Clinton administration.[79] On the evening of November 25, the United States informed Boutros-Ghali that it was prepared to lead a Desert Storm–style humanitarian intervention in Somalia. During "tough negotiations" between the United States and the UN over the next week, it became plain there were operational differences between the two sides, but, ultimately, the U.S. conception of the intervention prevailed. The United States "had the troops," explained

Wisner.[80] On December 3, the Security Council unanimously endorsed the U.S. initiative through Resolution 794.

Interestingly, there were some early signs of dissent within the Bush administration over the decision that led to Operation Restore Hope. Ambassador Hempstone expressed his opposition to the intervention in a government cable that was mysteriously leaked to the *US News and World Report* on December 12: "If you liked Beirut"—a reference to the loss of 243 U.S. marines in 1983—"you'll love Mogadishu."[81] In the cable, Hempstone said U.S. intervention will only "keep tens of thousands of Somali kids from starving to death in 1993 who, in all probability, will starve to death in 1994." Hempstone's view was publicly "trashed" by Cheney and, to a lesser extent, Eagleburger.[82] But the fact that someone other than Hempstone had leaked his cable suggested there were others within the Bush administration that shared his misgivings about Operation Restore Hope.[83]

EXPLAINING THE U.S. DECISION TO INTERVENE

Like so many decision-making processes, the U.S. decision to intervene in Somalia was far from clear-cut. The decision did not emerge as a classical rational choice within the Bush administration. The decision making process, in the words of Admiral Jeremiah, was "not that pretty."[84] President John F. Kennedy once remarked that the essence of decision is often mysterious, even to the participants themselves.[85] Each step in the process can seem trivial, but cumulatively, such steps can result in momentous decisions. That was certainly the case with the Bush administration when it came to Somalia.

Organizations in the U.S. government such as the Bureau for African Affairs in the State Department and the Agency for International Development had pushed hard from early 1992 just to get Somalia on to the U.S. foreign policy agenda. Yet President Bush's ultimate choice, the so-called sledgehammer option, went far beyond what these agencies had ever envisaged for Somalia. This outcome was linked to the fact that the JCS, which had spent the best part of twelve months strongly resisting any military involvement in Somalia, suddenly experienced a "complete turnaround"[86] and offered to undertake a large-scale armed humanitarian intervention there.

It is clear that Jeremiah's statement at the Deputies Committee meeting on November 21 "unlocked the door" to U.S. intervention in Somalia.[87] The offer by the JCS was instrumental in forging what had hitherto been elusive—a broad, interagency consensus within the administration over what to do about Somalia. In particular, it opened the way for an apparent convergence in the positions of the State Department and Department of Defense. So why did the JCS reassess its stance toward the Somali crisis? It is important to note that although the JCS denied it had performed a U-turn on Somalia, it did acknowledge that its thinking had evolved.[88] In fact, there were indications in the early 1990s of an intense internal debate within the Pentagon over the future role of the U.S. military. This debate was principally between traditional "warfighters" and international "humanitarian interveners."[89] According to Ambassador Grove, the internationalist wing of the Pentagon had gained the upper hand by mid-1992.[90] Certainly, the Pentagon's "bottom-up review" of 1992–1993 under General Powell found that U.S. forces still needed to be equipped to fight two major regional conflicts simultaneously. Powell's "two war strategy" required a level of funding that was comparable to the Cold War era, but such demands on the American taxpayer could be more difficult to justify if the JCS remained unwilling to adapt the Powell Doctrine to new intrastate conflicts such as that in Somalia.

However, it should be emphasized that it took some time and increasing presidential engagement with Somalia to bring about this evolution in the thinking of the JCS. Three developments stand out in the decision making stream that culminated in U.S. intervention. First, and most obviously, President Bush's belated recognition in July 1992 that "something must be done" about Somalia. According to Scowcroft and Kansteiner, President Bush was a compassionate man who was deeply moved by Ambassador Hempstone's harrowing cable of that month that detailed the terrible impact of war and famine in Somalia. Perhaps because President Bush had a hands-on foreign policy approach, his first serious encounter with the Somali issue quickly began to affect—indeed, to shape—the interagency discussions on this subject. It was no coincidence that the Department of State made its first statement in favor of sending armed UN security detachments to Somalia since the crisis began in late July 1992. At the same time, Bush's high standing with the Pentagon, especially after the 1990–1991 Persian Gulf triumph, meant that his initial engagement with the Somali problem would have surely registered with the JCS.

Second, Bush's first concrete commitment, the August 1992 authorization of a U.S. airlift of emergency food aid, Operation Provide Relief (OPR), was almost certainly a catalyst in the emergence of the decision to intervene. On the one hand, the operation provided graphic evidence that Somalia was a security—rather than purely a food—problem. That inescapable realization had a considerable effect on the balance of forces inside the U.S. government. It gave new leverage to those who like Cohen had been arguing since the beginning of 1992 for the need for strong military intervention in order to address the problem of war-fueled starvation. On the other hand, the U.S. military, which had long opposed participating in a humanitarian operation, now found itself running OPR at the President's request. In a sense, the Pentagon had now crossed a vital threshold—or, as Kansteiner put it, "the camel's nose was now in the tent."[91] In a bureaucratic politics context, this was an important point. Governmental organizations tend to treat the views and position of other institutions with some suspicion. Just because the State Department was advocating a more active approach toward Somalia, the JCS could not be expected to automatically agree with that assessment. Admiral Jeremiah confirmed that the JCS had not been particularly impressed by many of the proposals put forward by the State Department officials for dealing with Somalia.[92] However, OPR provided the Pentagon with firsthand information regarding both the dangers and the possibilities of involvement in Somalia.

One episode was particularly significant. Admiral Jeremiah paid a flying twenty-four-hour visit to a feeding station at Hoddur in southern Somalia in September 1992. He admitted in an interview that he was profoundly affected by the experience: "I have seen some tough situations before in Asia, but this was absolutely beyond the pale."[93] Admiral Jeremiah then flew straight from Hoddur to Washington via Mombasa and immediately reported on his Somali visit to General Powell.[94] He also presented a photographic record of his visit to Hoddur to his boss. Such episodes helped to challenge JCS's perception of the Somali situation in several ways. For one thing, OPR may have reduced the concerns that the U.S. military had about working alongside NGOs. By most accounts, OPR occasioned some fruitful cooperation in the field. Also, there were indications that the Pentagon enjoyed the praise that was heaped on its management of OPR.

Third, the political interregnum after President Bush's electoral defeat had an important bearing on the ultimate decision to intervene in Somalia. Freed of domestic electoral considerations, Bush was free to concentrate on his strength (foreign policy), and, in particular, on an issue with which he had been fully engaged since September (namely, the Somali crisis). Several factors inclined the President toward decisive action. According to several former members of his administration, the timing of the decision on November 25—one day before Thanksgiving—was revealing. The moral tension between expectations of bountiful family reunions during a traditional national celebration in the United States and haunting TV images of starving Somalis apparently weighed heavily on President Bush.[95] A humanitarian concern to do the right thing also intersected with several political considerations. Consultations with President-elect Clinton's transition team indicated that the new administration was comfortable with a more active approach toward Somalia. Gallucci, who briefed the Clinton transition team on President Bush's decision to lead a humanitarian intervention, found it significant that Clinton's first question at the briefing session was: "Will this stop the kids in Somalia dying?"[96]

At the same time, Bush, while conscious of the need to avoid saddling the incoming Clinton administration with a new international commitment, was attuned to the views and concerns of the JCS under the leadership of General Powell. President Bush had never hidden his admiration for General Powell, and he was fully aware that after his election defeat Powell feared that the new president might escalate U.S. military involvement in Bosnia. And while Powell had no great desire to intervene in Somalia, the JCS under his leadership always saw Bosnia as far more dangerous a place—in Powell's judgment, one that could become a quagmire for American troops.[97] So, by offering the possibility of sending a substantial number of troops to Somalia in a limited operation, the JCS could be seen as doing something humanitarian but—equally important—dampening any demand to send troops to Bosnia, which was seen as the biggest threat to the Powell Doctrine. The option of a limited but large-scale U.S.-led humanitarian intervention in Somalia corresponded to Bush's desire to make an immediate difference in Somalia without tying the hands of his successor. Indeed, President Bush had apparently convinced himself that the Somali operation could be completed before President Clinton was sworn in on January 20, 1993.[98] While Powell and the Defense Secretary always believed that such a timetable was unrealistic, they nevertheless agreed with the President's sentiment that U.S. troops should not stay a day longer than necessary.

RELATIONSHIP BETWEEN THE PROCESS AND THE SUBSTANCE OF THE DECISION

The process of forging a broad consensus within the Bush administration behind a commitment to intervene in Somalia left its mark in both the shape and the substance of the final decision. Bush's choice of the "sledge-hammer option," which formed the basis of Security Council Resolution 794, reflected, above all, the need to accommodate the Powell Doctrine. The support of Powell and the JCS was essential if Bush were to realize his goal of doing something in Somalia before he left office. After the "great military triumph" in the Persian Gulf War of 1991, General Powell was in a position in Washington to strongly shape the operational features of the next U.S. military deployment in Somalia.[99] And Powell insisted that any humanitarian intervention in Somalia be structured in a Desert Storm fashion, in order to meet his earlier reservations concerning "nation-building," "mission-creep," a clear mission, and an exit strategy.

Resolution 794 authorized the U.S.-led UNITAF to use "all necessary means to establish as soon as possible a secure environment for humanitarian relief operations."[100] As far as the Bush administration was concerned, UNITAF was a limited enforcement operation to simply "open the supply routes, to get the food moving and to prepare the way for a UN peacekeeping force to keep it moving."[101] The imprint of Powell's influence was immediately evident in the following ways: first, UNITAF was very large—37,000 troops in all, of whom 27,000 were Americans—and thus had the capability to apply overwhelming force; second, Powell's emphasis on overwhelming force effectively centralized Operation Restore Hope in south Mogadishu, the only location in the country that had the type of air and seaport facilities that could support such a large military build-up;[102] third, the Bush administration stressed the limited and humanitarian nature of the mission, stating that "we do not plan to dictate political outcomes";[103] fourth, because Operation Restore Hope was not considered a strategic intervention, the United States decided to work with the warlords—Powell requested that Robert Oakley, a former ambassador to Somalia with a distrust of nation-building dating back to Vietnam, take on the position of U.S. Special Envoy to Somalia[104]—and ruled out systematically disarming any warring factions; and fifth, the scope and definition of U.S. humanitarian intervention was constrained by the perceived need to exit from Somalia at the earliest possible time.

In short, the substance of the U.S. decision to intervene in Somalia was shaped less by the requirements of correcting a situation in which political disintegration and civil war had generated mass starvation and more by the decision making process and the interests of the key players in Washington that authorized such a decision.

Chapter 3

A Shattered Hope: The U.S.–UN Intervention in Somalia

The armed humanitarian intervention by the United States and the United Nations in Somalia was important because it was the first substantial effort of the New World Order to grapple with the problem of intrastate conflict in the post–Cold War era, and also because it involved experiments in new forms of multilateral peace operations. Unable to ameliorate conditions of civil war and drought in Somalia through emergency humanitarian assistance and traditional UN peacekeeping, the United States and the UN opted for drastic action. This consisted of two phases: UNITAF, a U.S.-led humanitarian intervention with limited enforcement powers; and UNOSOM II, a UN-led humanitarian operation with extensive enforcement functions to uphold law and order, including specific instructions to disarm clan militias.

But the U.S.–UN operation in Somalia proved to be a profound disappointment. Disarmament, which is understood here as a process involving the reduction, removal, or elimination of the means of violence, was not explicitly written into UNITAF's mandate. The effects of this omission became clear in Mogadishu when UNOSOM II's belated program of disarmament encountered the armed resistance of General Aideed's faction in June 1993. This trend eventually culminated in a savage battle between U.S. Task Force Ranger forces and Aideed's militiamen on October 3 that killed eighteen servicemen and more than 1,000 Somalis. Confronted with televised images of chanting Somalis dragging a U.S. soldier's body through the streets of Mogadishu, President Clinton responded to strong expressions of domestic outrage by quickly announcing that all U.S. troops would be withdrawn from Somalia within six months. That announcement effectively ended the UN's experiment in peace enforcement and had extraordinary ramifications for both U.S. foreign policy and global security in the post-Cold War era.

The task of this chapter is to analyze the gulf between the promise and the performance of the U.S.–UN humanitarian intervention in Somalia. The basic argument that emerges is that although the U.S.–led intervention was not wrong in principle, it was flawed in both design and execution and proved highly vulnerable to the ambitions of the power-hungry and myopic leadership of the feuding factions in southern Somalia.

INTERNATIONAL INTERVENTION: A CONTESTED MANDATE

From the outset, UNITAF, or Operation Restore Hope, was plagued by controversy over the definition of its mission. The operation was unchartered territory for the UN. The organization's charter made no provision for how to deal with "failed states."[1] Within a week of launching Operation Restore Hope, there was a public clash between the Bush administration and the UN over whether the mandate for the operation included the disarming of Somali militias. Presidential spokesman Marlin Fitzwater said, "[D]isarmament was not a stated part of our mission and that has not changed."[2] According to Oakley, Security Council Resolution 794 was "a clearly defined mission, which is to establish security conditions in Somalia to provide for the uninterrupted flow of relief supplies. It does not include disarmament."[3] He was supported by U.S. commander of UNITAF Lieutenant General Robert Johnston, who said, "people will need to change the terms of my mission before I get into a wholesale disarmament."[4] As a result, Washington maintained that U.S. troops would only be used to disarm armed groups in Somalia that posed a direct threat to the security of famine relief operations.

The UN, however, took a much broader interpretation of the mandate. In the view of the UN Secretary General and other senior officials, "a secure environment" was inconceivable without disarmament.[5] Indeed, Boutros-Ghali believed he had a private understanding on this matter with the Bush administration. In a letter to President Bush after the Security Council resolution of December 3, Boutros-Ghali set out what he saw as the aims of the U.S.-led operation. These included removing mines, disarming the militias, and seeking to pacify the country, as well as the purely humanitarian tasks.[6] But the Bush administration denied this. Undeterred, Boutros-Ghali said that UNITAF troops should fan out from its designated sectors in Somalia to neutralize heavy weapons belonging to the warlords.[7]

The dispute between the United States and the UN over disarmament centered on different interpretations of what constituted a secure environment in Somalia. The UN wanted UNITAF to use its overwhelming military advantage to create an environment that would be conducive to both humanitarian operations and the process of national reconciliation before it handed over the operation to the UN. Without substantial disarmament, the UN leadership believed it would be acutely vulnerable to the armed menace of the bandits and organized factions in the follow-up peacekeeping operation.[8] Boutros-Ghali feared that if the gangs and factions were not disarmed, the operation would be nothing more than a Band-Aid exercise, with much of the humanitarian work going to waste.

THE U.S. STRATEGY OF LIMITED PEACE ENFORCEMENT

Notwithstanding the public rift with the UN over disarmament, the Bush administration clung to a narrow definition of its mission in Somalia. Political considerations, relating to the Powell Doctrine, shaped a firm distinction between humanitarian and strategic intervention. Because Somalia was deemed to belong to the former category, the Bush administration was anxious to adhere to the norm of non-interference in domestic affairs. In this vein, the Bush administration pledged respect for Somalia's "sovereignty and independence."[9] Underlying this was a tacit recognition that ultimately, civil wars are about the distribution of power, and that disarming would, by definition, affect the position of key competitors for political power. Should disarmament be pursued, the United States would have to get involved in putting a governing structure in place in Somalia, something which entailed a long-term commitment.

The U.S. aversion to such a long-term commitment was closely entwined with the possibility of suffering significant casualties. As one senior U.S. officer put it: "If we go out and try to physically disarm people who don't want to be disarmed, we're talking about going to war against all the factions in Somalia."[10] Johnston was determined to avoid this: "We want to minimise absolutely the risk to our own forces."[11] The Americans were wary of the sheer complexity of the security environment in stateless Somalia. A large part of the population was armed. Guns were an ever-present feature of Somali life, and carrying them in public was commonplace. In these circumstances, according to Eagleburger, it was "impossible to imagine" that U.S.-led forces could ever totally disarm Somalia.[12] How could UNITAF troops distinguish between Somali gunholders who were militia members, outlaws, or those who simply had weapons for self-defense? Such circumstances presented an "enormous challenge," in the words of Johnston.[13] Along with a potentially high cost in blood, proactive disarmament could also prove to be expensive. Washington was already paying an estimated $30 million a day to keep its troops in Somalia—there was little financial stomach to see this cost escalate further.[14] If disarmament was pursued in a purposeful fashion, that figure would have risen sharply, at least in the short term. From the vantage point of the White House, the political consensus supporting Operation Restore Hope was viewed as being likely to collapse if the United States moved toward the UN position on active disarmament.[15]

Boutros-Ghali would have preferred a humanitarian enforcement operation in Somalia under UN command and control. But he recognized that the UN lacked the financial and logistical capacity to carry out a rapid military intervention. Thus, UNITAF represented a convergence rather than an identity of interests between the United States and the UN. UNITAF and UNOSOM I coexisted but were independent of each other.

Exactly two years after the last American forces had departed from their base at Berbera in northern Somalia, they made a large-scale return to the country. The first units of UNITAF, led by the United States, landed on the beaches of Mogadishu on December 9, 1992. Despite some minor glitches, the initial deployment proceeded smoothly, with some 1,800 troops deployed in the first day, and the U.S. flag raised once more over the embassy compound for the first time in two years.[16] Approximately 40 percent of Somalia, mainly the central and southern regions, fell under the mandate of UNITAF, which at its peak comprised 37,000 troops from twenty-five countries, including 26,000 from the United States.[17]

However, when the Bush administration announced in late November that the United States was prepared to lead a UN-backed humanitarian intervention in Somalia, the news was not met with enthusiasm everywhere. General Aideed, the most prominent of Somalia's warlords, feared that UNITAF's presence could weaken his power base within his Habir Gedir subclan and jeopardize his plans to become leader of a new Somalia. During the civil war fighting after Barre's departure in January 1991, the Habir Gedir were able to take over much of the south side of Mogadishu, including the seaport and airport. In particular, they occupied homes and properties of the Abgal subclan—who formed the support base for Aideed's great rival for power, Ali Mahdi—and gained control of the enormous revenues generated by the port and airport. With the intervention of UNITAF, the Habir Gedir lost control of the seaport and airport facilities, and faced the possibility of a political agreement that would force them to return the properties they had seized during the civil war.[18] As leader of the Habir Gedir subclan, Aideed was sensitive to such concerns.[19] But, confronted with the military muscle of the United States in Mogadishu, Aideed decided that cooperation, at least in the short term, was the most prudent option, and he agreed to a ceasefire with Mahdi's faction. By projecting himself as a responsible leader, a wary Aideed hoped (as did Mahdi) to secure U.S. support for his own political ambitions in Somalia.[20]

A more forceful and immediate expression of opposition to the U.S.–UN intervention in Somalia, however, came from Osama bin Laden. Unbeknown to Washington, bin Laden's al Qaeda organization had established a presence in the country almost a year before Operation Restore

Hope was launched.[21] In fact, Nairobi had been used as a support station for al Qaeda people and their allies traveling to and from Somalia.[22] As previously noted, the United States became bin Laden's top enemy after the USSR's demise; thus U.S. troops in Somalia, an Islamic country, presented a tempting target. Bin Laden and his senior colleagues in al Qaeda were convinced that the UN was simply a tool of Washington and believed that the United States would use Somalia as a staging ground to attack or invade neighboring Sudan, where bin Laden was then based. As an upshot, bin Laden issued a *fatwa*, a declaration of war, to the members of al Qaeda calling for the killing of all "infidels" in Somalia, and urging all members to do what they could to drive these infidels out of Somalia.[23]

As a first step, al Qaeda quickly hatched a plan to interdict and attack Somalia-bound U.S. troops. As UN forces assembled for Somalia, some U.S. military personnel transited Aden, Yemen, and stayed at hotels there for several days. Al Qaeda targeted two hotels there, the Gold Mohur and the Mövenpick, which it believed were used by U.S. troops. On December 29, 1992, bin Laden's organization detonated a bomb in the Gold Mohur but got no closer than the carpark of the Mövenpick before the intended bomb exploded. The attacks cost the lives of two tourists and wounded seven other people, including one of bin Laden's bombers.[24] Although there were no U.S. soldiers in these two hotels when the terrorist attacks occurred—some American troops were staying at a nearby establishment—within days of the attacks, all U.S. soldiers left Yemen, a point not lost on al Qaeda. According to bin Laden, the Aden attacks were "the first al Qaeda victory scored against the Crusaders."[25] The irony of such claims was that Washington would remain unaware of the growing threat from al Qaeda for some time to come.

In the meantime, the immediate humanitarian impact of UNITAF was considerable. The overwhelming foreign military presence encountered little resistance and quickly broke the stronghold that rival militias had over supply routes. Most of the needy areas—such as Bardera, in the southwest—started to receive food. The looting of relief supplies and the protection rackets operated by some merchants practically stopped. As a result, an estimated 250,000 lives were saved.[26] Improved security also facilitated some significant improvements to Somalia's shattered infrastructure. UNITAF repaired more than 1,800 kilometers of roads, restored two airfields, and revamped fourteen water wells.[27] In the short term, UNITAF helped to establish a more secure environment for humanitarian supplies in the areas under its jurisdiction.

But there was an operational ambiguity about UNITAF's humanitarian focus. UNITAF broke its own nonpolitical guidelines by quickly establishing a working relationship with the main warlords. Although the UN-led intervention initially put the warlords on the back foot, Oakley publicly embraced Mahdi and General Aideed after they signed a U.S.-brokered ceasefire on December 11, 1992.[28] With this gesture, the warlords gained a spurious legitimacy as political leaders. Many Somalis were dismayed; they had expected the warlords to be arrested by U.S.-led forces.[29] The warlords were widely seen as war criminals who had plunged Somalia into chaos and famine. Moreover, Oakley's embrace deemphasized the "bottom-up" strategy pursued by Sahnoun (and pursued, in a token fashion, by his successor, the aloof Kittani) and thereby reduced the freedom of action of UNOSOM I in searching for a political solution.

In early January 1993, the UN Secretary General opened a peace conference of the Somali faction in Addis Ababa. These talks culminated in a peace accord signed by fifteen of Somalia's factions at a UN conference on national reconciliation in March 1993. But it was clear that the warlords were shaping the political process. Under pressure to put together a Somali government as soon as possible, the UN provided a guaranteed seat to each warlord in a Transitional National Council (TNC) that was to guide the country, over two years, toward elections. The agreement was not signed by the self-proclaimed "Somaliland Republic," which was offended by the UN's characterization of the TNC as "a repository of Somali sovereignty."[30]

On the security front, the impact of UNITAF in Mogadishu was largely cosmetic. The initial display of overwhelming force by the U.S.-led force did intimidate and even frighten the armed factions in Somalia, but the warlords soon realized that such a display did not automatically translate into a willingness to use force.[31] While it was agreed in January 1993 that a UNITAF/UNOSOM I ceasefire monitoring group comprising representatives from the Somali factions would take possession of heavy weapons under the control of these movements and oversee the encampment of militias, there was very little progress in implementing these measures. Although heavy weapons and military trucks ("technicals") disappeared from the streets, many were simply hidden; others were moved into the interior beyond UNITAF's reach. No doubt encouraged by U.S.–UN differences over disarmament, it quickly became plain that the militias had no intention of surrendering their weapons.

The Bush administration maintained that troops would only be used to disable or disarm weaponry threatening food and medical supplies to famine zones, while Boutros-Ghali argued that UNITAF should ensure, before it withdrew, that the heavy weapons of the organized factions were "neutralised and brought under international control."[32] At least one State Department official subsequently admitted it was probably a mistake on the part of UNITAF to leave the heavy weaponry of the warlords untouched in the north and south of the country.[33] Evidently, this was a tactical move to avoid direct conflict with the powerful Somali factions in the early stages of the intervention. Certainly, UNITAF's consensual approach to security generated confusion and meager results.

U.S. forces in Mogadishu also considered various voluntary disarmament schemes such as "food for guns" and "cash for guns" concepts. By late January 1993, the United States abandoned these ideas as being either inadequate or too expensive. As for the warlords, the Addis Ababa peace agreement of March 27, 1993, committed the parties to "complete" disarmament within ninety days. But no timetable was agreed for implementing this. Meanwhile, once it became clear to the armed gunmen that they could keep their weapons if they did not directly threaten UNITAF's activities, interfactional fighting and criminal extortion took off.[34] Relief aid workers became favorite targets as gunmen resumed control of large areas of Mogadishu.

The deteriorating security situation in Mogadishu eventually jolted the UNITAF forces into periodic weapons seizures and a belated concern with law and order. On January 11, 1993, for instance, 900 U.S. marines occupied Mogadishu's main arms market at Bakara and confiscated five truckloads of arms and ammunition.[35] Then, on February 6, a Somali police force became operational in the capital for the first time in two years.[36] Until mid-January, Oakley had insisted that the creation of local police forces was not on UNITAF's agenda. However, increasing attacks against U.S. marines in Mogadishu galvanized UNITAF into supporting efforts to form a police constabulary in Mogadishu. These measures, though, were improvised and did not form part of a comprehensive disarmament or civil affairs plan. Nor were they considered by the United States to be a central feature of UNITAF's mandate.

The preference for quick-fix solutions to Somalia's security reflected UNITAF's determination to withdraw from Somalia and hand over responsibility to the United Nations. In early January, U.S. Marines Colonel Mike Hagee announced that the U.S. troop contribution would be cut by 4,000 while warning the warring factions in Mogadishu in the next breath against further use of heavy weaponry in the city![37] In February 1993, after General Aideed accused the United States of supporting Barre's son-in-law General Morgan's seizure of Kismayo from an ally of Aideed's, Mogadishu was gripped by four days of anti-UNITAF demonstrations and gun battles. The United States strongly denied complicity, but relations between Washington and Aideed were clearly declining. Nevertheless, the U.S. military announced that it was pressing forward with plans to withdraw another 3,000 troops from Somalia, because, in the words of General Johnston, UNITAF had accomplished its mission.[38]

The drawdown of American troops in Somalia was certainly monitored by al Qaeda. In early 1993, bin Laden's global terrorist campaign against the United States had gathered momentum. On February 26, 1993, an Islamist group led by Ramzi Yousef, the nephew of a key bin Laden lieutenant, Khalid Sheik Muhammad, detonated a bomb in the underground garage of the World Trade Center (WTC) in New York City. Six people were killed, and 1,000 were injured, in what was the first major terrorist attack on American soil.[39] Elated by the news of the WTC bombing—bin Laden publicly praised the role of the bomb maker, Ramzi Yousef[40]—the al Qaeda leadership stepped up its efforts to attack American or UN forces within Somalia. Two of bin Laden's top military leaders, Abu Ubaydah and Abu Hafs al-Masri, were given the responsibility for directing al Qaeda's anti-U.S. operations in Somalia.[41] In early 1993, bin Laden dispatched Abu Hafs to Somalia for several brief visits. The first visit was essentially a scouting trip. Among other things, Abu Hafs observed U.S. military operations, assessed the ability of local Muslim militia groups to absorb military assistance—he met with members of local Islamist groups like al Itihaad al Islamiya—and evaluated the prospects of success for "Arab Afghans" that were being deployed to Somalia.[42]

Upon his return to the Sudanese capital of Khartoum, Abu Hafs apparently reported positively to bin Laden in Khartoum but did not believe al Qaeda could "take America head on."[43] In a second visit to Somalia, Abu Hafs held discussions with General Aideed and his advisers and agreed to support Aideed's efforts to resist the U.S. and UN presence in Somalia.[44] It should be stressed that Aideed himself was not sympathetic to Islamism ideologically; but, pragmatically, it was useful for him and his Habre Gedir subclan to have strong external friends at a time when he felt the political need to confront the United States. Support to General Aideed's faction took several forms: teams of bomb makers and insurgency warfare specialists were sent to Mogadishu to train Aideed's fighters. Future Nairobi embassy bombers Mohammed Sadiq Odeh, Mohammed Sadia Howaida, and Fazul Abdullah Mohammed were among those sent to Somalia for that purpose.[45] Altogether, bin Laden said that al Qaeda had sent 250 fighters to help Aideed and Somali leaders fighting U.S.-led forces.[46] In addition, al Qaeda provided some financial and communications assistance for Aideed's faction. The effects of the Aideed-al Qaeda connection would soon become evident in Somalia.

Taken together, UNITAF's lack of a clear political agenda, the failure to eliminate the heavy weaponry of the warring Somali factions, and al Qaeda's covert military assistance to General Aideed's armed faction greatly reduced the likelihood that UNOSOM II, the successor to the U.S.-led force, could avoid a challenge to its position from at least one of the Somali warlords.

THE U.S.–UN STRATEGY OF EXTENDED PEACE ENFORCEMENT

On May 4, 1993, UNITAF was formally replaced by UNOSOM II, a transition authorized by Security Council Resolution 814 on March 26. In effect, it widened the scope of peace enforcement powers from the establishment of a secure environment solely for the protection of human-itarian relief activities to the "consolidation, expansion and maintenance of a secure environment throughout Somalia."[47] Under the new mandate, UNOSOM II had three key functions: maintain a ceasefire, ensure the delivery of humanitarian aid, and create conditions conducive to a politi-cal settlement through an interalia program of disarmament. Thus, the new UNOSOM II force, which consisted, in theory, of 20,000 troops and 8,000 logistical support personnel from thirty-three different countries, was supposed to do what a bigger and better-equipped UNITAF had been unable to do: disarm the warlord militias and take charge of the remain-ing 60 percent of Somalia's territory.[48]

While this unprecedented UN peacekeeping mission reflected the ideas of Boutros-Ghali, the operation also had a very significant U.S. dimension. U.S. diplomats had played a key role in drafting Resolution 814,[49] and although the United States, for the first time, nominally placed around 4,000 of its troops under direct UN command, it was a command structure dominated by U.S. or U.S.-nominated personnel. The new head of the UNOSOM II operation, for example, was Admiral Jonathan Howe, formerly Deputy National Security Adviser in the previous Bush admin-istration. Howe's appointment was strongly backed by both the Clinton administration and the UN General Secretary to ensure close coordination between the United States and the UN after the departure of UNITAF. Nearly thirty other American officers were in key positions, including UNOSOM II's deputy force commander, Army Major General Thomas Montgomery, who was also direct tactical commander of the Quick Reac-tion Force (QRF) supporting the body of UN troops. The only U.S. forces in Somalia that were under direct UN control were the logistics compo-nent, consisting of 2,700 men and women.[50]

Almost immediately, the hastily assembled UNOSOM II force was overstretched. The initial complement of 16,000 UN troops struggled to fill the vacuum left by the 37,000-strong UNITAF force. Key items of mil-itary equipment were missing or in short supply. Some contingents, for example, lacked armored personnel carriers (APCs) to protect their troops from small arms fire.[51] Moreover, the new multinational force was required to impose law and order at a time of growing tension between the UN and Aideed, the most powerful warlord. Despite a pledge to dis-arm, Aideed was busy moving new weaponry into Mogadishu through-out the spring of 1993. At the same time, Aideed publicly challenged the expanded mandate of UNOSOM II through a series of hostile radio broadcasts and attempted to manipulate the new UNOSOM authorities into backing an Aideed-sponsored peace conference in May. Within the U.S. government, it was understood that a major incident was all but inevitable.[52] Sure enough, on June 5, 1993, twenty-six lightly armed Pakistani peacekeepers were brutally killed and another fifty-six wounded during prearranged weapons verification inspection visits to some of Aideed's ammunition stores in south Mogadishu. The Addis Ababa agreement of March 27, 1993, had stipulated that arms would be kept in stock, under the care of the factions, in places listed by UNOSOM until they could be handed over to the future Somali army or be destroyed.

The ambush of the Pakistani peacekeepers occurred near Aideed's radio station, which some of his militia claimed the UN was about to seize. According to a report presented to the UN Secretary General by a committee investigating the events of June 5, Aideed believed the UN was involved in a concerted campaign to marginalize him politically.[53] That cannot be ruled out, but there were other motivations connected to the leadership aspirations of Aideed and his Habar Gidir subclan constituency that prompted this premeditated ambush. In many ways, the attack on the Pakistani peacekeepers was a "shoot-out waiting to happen."[54] Because UNITAF left the Somali gunmen with weapons to use, it was always likely that a well-armed, increasingly hostile, faction like Aideed's would take on a visibly weakened UN presence. As the most formidable warlord in Somalia, General Aideed was acutely aware that UNOSOM II's program of disarmament and political reconstruction was a direct political threat to a power base built on the arms of his followers. Aideed saw himself as the real architect of Barre's demise and, consequently, the rightful leader of a new Somalia.[55]

The June 5 incident starkly illustrated the limitations of Oakley's view that warlords such as Aideed could be somehow transformed into responsible statesmen. From the U.S. perspective, an important principle was at issue—that UN peacekeepers simply could not be killed with impunity. As President Clinton put it: "We cannot have a situation where one of these warlords, while everyone else is cooperating, decides that he can go out and slaughter 20 peacekeepers."[56] The concern was that if UNOSOM II did not respond firmly to such an outrage, peacekeeping nations, like Pakistan, would be tempted to withdraw their troops from Somalia. A related concern was that in the absence of a firm response from the UN, Aideed's Somali opponents would interpret this as tacit support for Aideed and would, therefore, use violence themselves to counter him, and the entire mission would be jeopardized.[57] According to Admiral Howe, if the Somalis thought they could get away with killing the Pakistanis, it would be all over for the international relief effort.[58] On June 6, the UN Security Council passed Resolution 837, authorizing the Secretary General to take "all necessary precautions against all those responsible for the armed attacks" in Mogadishu.

For the next four months, UNOSOM II's mission was dominated by the quest to capture Aideed. It marked a rising tide of escalating violence between UNOSOM II and General Aideed's SNA faction. Admiral Howe, with backing from the Clinton administration, put up a reward of $25,000 for information that led to the arrest of Aideed. The warlord responded by putting a $1 million price on Howe's head.[59] The search for Aideed was spearheaded by the U.S.-commanded Quick Reaction Force, and American heavy weaponry and helicopter gunships were used in a series of devastating military strikes on buildings controlled by Aideed's supporters in south Mogadishu. These strikes caused high civilian casualties and alienated many Somalis, including those that had previously expressed contempt for the fugitive warlord.[60] Aideed and his supporters, quick to exploit these tensions, responded with attacks on UN peacekeepers in a tit-for-tat fashion. Each attack seemed to trigger another in kind.

Then, on July 12, under President Clinton's specific authority, sixteen tube-launched, optically-tracked, wire-guided (TOW) missiles and more than 2,000 rounds of 20-mm cannon fire were directed at a compound described as a "major SNA/Aideed militia command and control center."[61] No warning was given. More than fifty people were killed in this attack, but the victims were not militiamen, but a meeting of unsuspecting clan leaders and religious elders who had gathered to explore the prospect of making peace between Aideed's Habr Gedir sub-clan and the UN. Aideed did not approve of the meeting, because his role as clan leader was being questioned. When a group of international journalists arrived at the scene, four of them, including an American, Dan Eldon, were murdered by a furious Somali crowd. In early August, a remote-controlled land mine was detonated under a U.S. Army HMMWV (Highly Mobile Multi-Wheeled Vehicle; commonly known as the Humvee), and four American military policemen were killed. Then, on August 22, in a similar incident, another land mine was detonated near a U.S. Army Humvee. Six American troops were wounded, and their vehicle was destroyed.[62] Evidently, Aideed's militia was already making use of al Qaeda's training assistance in its war against UNOSOM II. The Clinton administration responded swiftly. In late August, Secretary of Defense Les Aspin and General Powell approved a request for a battalion of U.S. Army Rangers and a Delta Force unit—combined as "Task Force Ranger"—to be sent to Mogadishu to boost the effort to hunt down Aideed. Both Aspin and Powell had reservations about this "fateful decision," but felt they had little option but to comply. Aspin told a colleague: "We're sending the Rangers to Somalia. We're not going to be able to control them, you know. They're like overtrained pit bulls. No one controls them. They're going to push right ahead."[63] Task Force Ranger arrived in Somalia on August 27.

To all intents and purposes, it began to look as if the United States, not the UN, was at the forefront of the campaign to arrest or neutralize Aideed and armed supporters. Ironically, U.S.–UN reprisals melted internal opposition to Aideed within his Habar Gidir clan, and his chairmanship of the USC was extended for six months while he evaded arrest.[64] From Aideed's standpoint, his violent gamble was working. UNOSOM II had been goaded into a confrontation that was casting Aideed as a defiant and heroic nationalist figure. The period of confrontation coincided with Aideed's faction putting a new rhetorical emphasis on its devotion to Islam. Rallies held in Aideed's south Mogadishu stronghold accused U.S. soldiers of desecrating and looting mosques during attacks on Aideed's militiamen and condemned American women soldiers for wearing bikinis on a Mogadishu beach.[65] As well as trying to whip up Islamic fervor to swell national support against UN forces, the Aideed factions were also seeking to use language that would consolidate and perhaps increase support from external backers such as al Qaeda.

The wisdom of pursuing Aideed was openly questioned in the United States and elsewhere. As early as July 1993, Senator Robert Byrd (D-WV), chairman of the powerful Appropriations Committee, said: "The Senate has not bought into a policy action against Somali warlords."[66] Furthermore, after the deaths of American soldiers in early August, there were immediate calls in Congress for a U.S. withdrawal. Senator Byrd led the charge, saying that these deaths showed that "[the UN] operation was crumbling . . . [and] that it was not worth the American lives lost and injuries sustained."[67] Italy, one of the former colonial powers in Somalia, condemned the anti-Aideed stance. For its part, the UN leadership asked Rome to remove the commander of the Italian peacekeeping contingent in Somalia, General Bruno Loi, for refusing to obey orders from the UN military commander.[68] There was also tension between Nigeria and Italy after an incident in which seven Nigerian blue-helmets were killed in South Mogadishu because the Italians had refused to open fire to assist them. Meanwhile, twenty-six international aid agencies, in a joint message to the UN Secretary General, complained that the UN's military tactics were actually hindering the distribution of humanitarian aid.[69]

By September 1993, the spiraling violence in Mogadishu was making Congress distinctly edgy. Task Force Ranger had made at least five raids in September to arrest Aideed or his top advisers. All failed to apprehend Aideed. Then, for the first time since American intervention in Somalia had begun in December 1992, a patrolling Black Hawk helicopter was shot down on September 25 by a rocket-propelled grenade (RPG). That development came as something as a surprise to UNOSOM II and to the American military in Mogadishu.[70] In retrospect, it was probably the first sign that Aideed's militia and gunmen were absorbing the training provided by al Qaeda's "Afghan Arabs." In the meantime, Senator John McCain (R-AZ) was among those on Capitol Hill who echoed Senator Byrd's reservations on the U.S. role in Somalia: "We went to Somalia to keep people from starving to death. Now we are killing women and children because they are combatants. This has to stop. It has to stop, and it has to stop soon."[71]

As an upshot, the U.S. Senate demanded that President Clinton explain his policy in Somalia to Congress by October 15. Under mounting pressure in Washington, Aspin rejected a request from Major General Montgomery on September 23 for the deployment of tanks and other armored vehicles to Mogadishu. Aspin believed that a green light to such a request would have been politically unacceptable to Congress.[72] At the same time, there were signs of a limited rethink within the Clinton administration on its Somalia policy. While the administration supported the UN Security Council resolution on September 23 authorizing the continuation of UNOSOM II's approach in Somalia, U.S. Secretary of State Warren Christopher handed Boutros-Ghali a memo saying that there had to be a new emphasis on a political settlement in Mogadishu.[73]

Nevertheless, the Clinton White House failed to signal that it favored an immediate reversal of policy in Somalia. On October 3, the manhunt for Aideed produced a major crisis that began when a company of U.S. Rangers and Delta Forces launched a heliborne attempt to capture Aideed and some of his key advisers near the Olympia Hotel in the warlord's stronghold of south Mogadishu. However, the operation was conducted independently of the UN mission in Somalia.[74] Rather than going through UN channels to get authorization for the use of military force against Aideed, Admiral Howe went through the U.S. government and the headquarters of the Joint Special Operations Command (JSOC) in Florida to get the decision approved. Indeed, UNOSOM II's force commander, General Cevik Bir, was only informed of the operation minutes before it was launched.[75] This approach would prove costly in an operation that went horribly wrong. While the U.S. forces captured some key Aideed advisers, they were quickly pinned down in a savage firefight that lasted seventeen hours. Two Black Hawk helicopters were shot down. Eighteen American soldiers were killed—the largest number of U.S. battlefield casualties in a single engagement since Vietnam—and perhaps more than 1,000 Somalis were killed.[76] In the end, General Bir's troops helped rescue the surviving Americans, a rescue that cost the lives of two UN soldiers from Malaysia and Morocco, respectively. Moreover, the body of a dead American soldier was dragged through the streets of Mogadishu in front of jeering local crowds shouting *Allah-o-Akbar* (God is great).[77] This appalling humiliation, videotaped by Aideed's supporters, was shown repeatedly on American television. Pictures of Mike Durant, a distressed helicopter pilot held hostage by Aideed's faction, only added to domestic disquiet in the United States over Somalia.

In Washington, officials at the White House, Pentagon and Congress were stunned by the size, scope, and ferocity of Aideed's counterattack on October 3. There is now strong evidence that the stiff resistance of Aideed's militia was linked, in part, to the military training assistance provided by al Qaeda, and also to the actual participation of some of bin

Laden's fighters in the battle of October 3. Although it is true that no one within or outside the Clinton administration "thought that Osama bin Laden had anything to do with Black Hawk down . . . or even knew al Qaeda was a growing concern in October 1993,"[78] such perceptions did not fully reflect the realities on the ground. For one thing, Aideed's gunmen received some expert guidance on the use of rocket-propelled grenades from al Qaeda associates like Mohammed Ibrahim Makawi.[79] In Somalia, Makawi and other al Qaeda trainers demonstrated an innovation that had been developed in the Afghan war to shoot down Soviet helicopters. They instructed Aideed's gunmen how to rig their RPGs with a timing device so that they would not need a direct hit, emphasized that the tail rotor was the helicopter's most vulnerable spot, and said that it was necessary to wait until helicopters passed over and then shoot up at it at from behind a forty-five degree angle from a hole dug into the ground to safely absorb the fiery back blast.[80]

Other bin Laden associates, including Abu Obeida al-Bansheeri, instructed Aideed's militia in effective use of mortars while other al Qaeda operatives, such as Odeh, provided instruction on the use of explosives in an insurgency.[81] According to two al Qaeda fighters now jailed in the United States, bin Laden's operatives were directly involved in two attacks using land mines that killed and injured U.S. military personnel in August 1993 and were responsible for downing one of the two helicopters that fell from the sky on October 3.[82] It is difficult to verify such claims, but it is known that the two U.S. Black Hawk helicopters lost in Mogadishu were hit in the tail rotor area by RPGs. Moreover, U.S. Army Captain James Francis Yacone testified that U.S. military intelligence in Mogadishu intercepted radio signals in Arabic during mortar attacks on American targets, including the U.S. Rangers camp at Mogadishu airport.[83] While claims that bin Laden airlifted 3,000 fighters from Yemen to help Aideed's faction in Mogadishu are probably exaggerated[84]–testimony from former al Qaeda operatives indicates that it was only safe for Afghan Arabs with dark complexions to participate directly in the fighting in Mogadishu[85]–it is clear that al Qaeda was actively involved in fighting the U.S. and UN presence in Somalia "for one full year" before the eventual showdown of October 3.

U.S. WITHDRAWAL AND THE MARGINALIZATION OF UNOSOM II

The battle for Mogadishu presented the Clinton administration with some tough policy choices. In his memoirs, Clinton said Somalia "marked one of the darkest days of my presidency."[86] On the one hand, President Clinton faced immediate and tremendous pressure from the U.S. Congress to terminate American involvement in Somalia. The disturbing images of death and desecration in Mogadishu on October 3 outraged and astounded many Americans, particularly in Congress, where concerns had been mounting about the U.S.–UN operation for some time. Senator Byrd led the charge when he backed a Senate resolution on October 4 demanding an early withdrawal: "Americans by the dozens are paying with their lives and limbs for a misplaced policy on the altar of some fuzzy multilateralism ... This UN experiment on new world order nation-building, the new mission that neither the Congress nor the American people at large ever endorsed, ought to be shut down as far as U.S. involvement is concerned."[87]

Other voices in Congress added to the chorus of criticism. Senator Byrd argued that U.S. "credibility will not be exploded if we take our troops out of Somalia, because our strategic interests are not involved there." Senator Mitch McConnell (R-KY) observed that "creeping multilateralism died on the streets of Mogadishu,"[88] while McCain, a member of the Armed Services Committee and a former prisoner of war in Vietnam, simply said "Clinton's got to bring them [U.S. troops] home."[89] Moreover, early efforts by the Clinton administration to quell the crescendo of criticism in Congress failed miserably. Aspin and Christopher were dispatched to Capitol Hill, but they did not offer a defense of existing U.S. policy in Somalia, nor did they propose a new alternative policy. Instead, Aspin and Christopher invited members of Congress to help them find a policy, a gesture that only further undermined congressional confidence in the Clinton administration's handling of a major foreign policy crisis.[90] Clinton himself was left in no doubts about the mood in Congress on October 4 when he met with several members in the White House and most of them present demanded an immediate withdrawal of U.S. forces from Somalia.[91]

On the other hand, the Clinton administration was aware that the battle for Mogadishu was not a failure in strictly military terms. In Clinton's words, "Task Force Ranger had arrested Aidid's lieutenants by dropping into the middle of Mogadishu in broad daylight, executing its complex and difficult mission, and enduring unexpected losses with courage and skill."[92] While the losses shocked the United States, there was also strong evidence that General Aideed and his supporters were severely shaken by the level of casualties they had sustained in the seventeen-hour engagement. Local reports indicated that some of Aideed's strongest clan allies had fled the city, fearing an American counterattack. Aideed's arsenal of RPGs had been substantially depleted. Meanwhile, senior figures within the Habre Gedir sub-clan were sending peace feelers to the U.S. military in Mogadishu, offering to dump Aideed to ward off more bloodshed. Certainly, Admiral Howe and Major General William Garrison, the Commander of Task Force Ranger, as well as the U.S. troops that survived the battle of Mogadishu, were very keen to quickly resume the fight against Aideed's faction. According to Mark Bowden, they "believed Aideed had been struck a mortal blow and that it wouldn't take much more to finish the job."[93] As one American military observer put it: "Everyone on the ground who had seen the videos of our dead being dragged around seethed with anger. The American forces poised outside of Mogadishu were like an attack dog straining at the leash."[94] At the same time, President Clinton worried about the geopolitical fallout of being *seen* to withdraw immediately: "If we were to leave today, we know what would happen. . . . Our leadership in world affairs would be undermined at the very time when people are looking to America to help promote peace and freedom in the post-Cold War world. All around the world, aggressors, thugs, and terrorists will conclude that the best way to get us to change our policy is kill our people. It would be open season on Americans."[95]

Thus, the Clinton administration found itself confronted with a decision that would have "extraordinary ramifications" for America and the post–Cold War world. Indeed, Senator John Kerry (D-MA), the Democratic presidential candidate in 2004, claimed on October 6 that the "way we handle our involvement in Somalia will be the key to the ability of the United Nations to undertake peacemaking efforts in the future."[96] How then did Clinton respond to these conflicting policy pressures? Rather than make a decision to cut American losses and immediately withdraw or tough out the confrontation with Aideed, President Clinton settled for a compromise approach. On October 6, Clinton announced that the number of U.S. troops in Somalia would be more than doubled to 10,000, but in the next breath he said that all U.S. troops would be withdrawn from the country within six months. Despite coming off second best during the battle of Mogadishu, General Aideed's armed faction had been handed a major political victory by Washington. In the end, Clinton had decided, in David Halberstam's words, to "cut and run" after the Mogadishu showdown.[97] While the Clinton administration tried to project this decision as an orderly transfer of power to the UN ("we are going to get the UN to finally show up and take over"[98]), it had clearly decided that Somalia was an expendable commitment: "I didn't mind taking Congress on, but I had to consider the consequences of any action [in Somalia] that could make it even harder to get congressional support for sending American troops to Bosnia and Haiti, where we had far greater interests at stake."[99]

At a stroke, America's vision of a New World Order based on partnership with the UN had been jettisoned. In particular, the Clinton administration had aborted the UN's peace enforcement strategy in Somalia. Without U.S. muscle, there was little chance the UN could politically reconstruct Somalia without Aideed's cooperation. The return to traditional peacekeeping was duly codified in a revised UN Security Council mandate for UNOSOM II adopted on February 4, 1994. This explicitly precluded UNOSOM forces from intervening in interclan conflicts.[100]

Under the revised mandate, the main task of a slimmed down UNOSOM force, drawn largely from Asian and African countries, was to protect Somalia's principal seaports and airports and provide security for the main transport arteries for moving humanitarian supplies. Meanwhile, force protection became the main concern for the expanded U.S. troop contingent in Somalia. According to one U.S. military observer, "we basically withdrew into our armed camps and waited for March to come."[101]

In addition, the Clinton administration announced that there would be greater involvement of neighboring states in new efforts to implement the March 1993 peace accord. The hunt for Aideed was abandoned. Ironically, the former UNITAF envoy to Somalia, Oakley, was sent back to Mogadishu to make contact with General Aideed, and to demand the immediate and unconditional release of Mike Durant, the injured helicopter pilot captured by Aideed's militia on October 3. After Durant's release, Oakley opened negotiations with Aideed and achieved some sort of truce.

On November 18, 1993, the way was cleared for Aideed's political comeback when the Security Council decided to "suspend arrest actions against those responsible" for the June killing of twenty-four Pakistani soldiers.[102] In early December, in a move "that made the [U.S.] soldiers who had fought on 3 October cringe with disgust,"[103] U.S. military aircraft even flew Aideed to UN-sponsored informal talks at Addis Ababa with Ali Mahdi's Somali Salvation Alliance (SSA). Earlier, Aideed had refused a seat on a UN flight as unsafe. The talks ended in deadlock. Then, on March 25, 1994, as American troops were completing their withdrawal from Somalia, the UN announced with considerable fanfare that Aideed and Mahdi had signed a new ceasefire and agreed on a date for a national reconciliation conference. But the planned conference was postponed on at least four occasions as interclan fighting steadily escalated in Mogadishu and beyond.[104] Encamped in heavily fortified compounds and unable to respond except in self-defense, the UNOSOM force found itself powerless to deter such fighting. This violence, in the words of one UNOSOM military spokesman, was "an internal Somali affair."[105]

Thus, the U.S. disengagement in Somalia reduced the UN to something of a bystander. Because of the very real threat of kidnapping and attacks, a number of NGOs and UN agencies suspended their humanitarian operations. In July 1994, two agencies with an unbroken record in Somalia—Save the Children and the International Red Cross—were forced to retreat to Nairobi.[106] At the same time, UN peacekeepers remained targets for Somali gunmen.[107] Deprived of a security role in a stateless society, a much-weakened UN followed Oakley's example of cultivating the assistance of the warlords. Starting in early 1994, UNOSOM extended large sums of money to various individuals linked to the militias, including those opposed to the elected government of Ibrahim Egal, in the virtually autonomous and largely stable Somaliland Republic.[108] The big question that came to face the Security Council is whether or not Somalia would be better off without UNOSOM. The Clinton administration, which terminated its diplomatic presence in Mogadishu in September 1994, believed that it would. The UN Security Council agreed: Resolution 953 of October 31, 1994, called for a secure and orderly withdrawal of UNOSOM II by March 31, 1995. When the last UN troops deployed under UNOSOM II left Somalia, there was still no central government and no clear authority to assume control in the country.

AN ASSESSMENT

The U.S.–UN humanitarian intervention in Somalia clearly failed to live up to expectations. It has been variously described in the West as a "debacle,"[109] a "major setback,"[110] a "military misadventure,"[111] and "a major league CNN-era disaster."[112] President Clinton said he was "haunted" by the "battle of Mogadishu" and compared his experience with that of President Kennedy during the Bay of Pigs crisis of 1961.[113] Meanwhile, bin Laden and other senior al Qaeda figures have claimed credit, or at least part of it, for what they call America's "humiliation" and "shameful defeat" in Somalia, a landmark event which made America forget "all the hoopla and media propaganda . . . about being the world leader and the leader of the New World Order."[114]

But if the U.S.-led intervention in Somalia is widely seen as a failure, it is important to acknowledge that the degree of failure is disputed. In the United States, Somalia has often been viewed as a partial failure. This perspective has been expressed in several ways. First, there were observers like Bolton, Charles Krauthammer, and Richard Miniter, who have claimed that the Somalia intervention, after a very successful start, was derailed by the advent of the Clinton administration in January 1993. Unlike his predecessor, Clinton had little foreign policy expertise and gave priority to his domestic agenda—"it's the economy, stupid" was a key Clinton campaign theme—and to "big" foreign policy issues relating to Russia, Japan, China, Asia, and the world economy.[115] Consequently, it is contended no one at the highest levels of the Clinton administration paid much attention to Somalia until U.S. casualties began to mount in the summer of 1993. There is certainly some substance in this argument. Richard Clarke, who worked in the National Security Council under both the Bush and the Clinton administrations, confirmed that shortly after coming to office, the Clinton leadership shifted the coordination of the Somali operation from the White House to the State Department and its Bureau of African Affairs.[116] That arrangement remained in place until the Mogadishu confrontation of October 1993, when Clinton told Clarke and

Anthony Lake, his National Security Adviser, that he now wanted the White House to run the Somalia policy, "not the State Department or the Pentagon."[117] Moreover, during the first ten months of the Clinton administration, there was no high-level national security meeting to discuss U.S. military involvement in Somalia, and no one from a senior policy level in the Clinton administration visited the country. In fact, in a June 17, 1993, White House press statement, the president declared that the U.S. mission in Mogadishu was now "over."[118]

However, while President Clinton and Warren Christopher readily conceded in October 1993 they had not devoted enough attention to the U.S.–UN operation in Somalia,[119] such an explanation for U.S. policy failure is hardly convincing. For one thing, it is simply inaccurate to state that Operation Restore Hope "succeeded from the start."[120] It plainly did not. As will be demonstrated shortly, several momentous decisions made at the beginning of the Somali intervention by the Bush administration had a direct impact on the outcome of the U.S.–UN operation. In particular, the decision to hand over control of the operation to the UN as soon as possible and the decision *not* to systematically disarm the warlord groups and armed factions seriously compromised efforts to fulfill the mandate of the mission to create a secure environment for the distribution of humanitarian aid.

In addition, although President Clinton inherited the Somali operation and delegated quite a bit of the day-to-day management of U.S. policy in Somalia to an interagency committee composed of lower-ranking officials known as the "deputies committee," it would be wrong to presume—as some political opponents or supporters apparently did—that the Clinton White House relinquished its political control of policy formulation. It should not be forgotten that a close Clinton associate, then deputy National Security Adviser, Sandy Berger, chaired the aforementioned "deputies committee" and presumably reported to the president on its deliberations.[121] At the same time, President Clinton's foreign policy team was every bit as active in drafting Security Council Resolution 814 on the establishment of UNOSOM II as the previous Bush administration had been in drafting Security Council Resolution 794, which paved the way for UNITAF.[122] Both administrations, mindful of the need to satisfy the concerns of the Pentagon, drafted entire documents before sending them to the UN Security Council as a fait accompli.[123] Furthermore, Clinton's "hands-on" leadership style meant he was quite prepared to actively intervene even on "second tier" issues if he felt the political interests of his administration were at stake. For example, according to Clarke, President Clinton followed the Pentagon's advice rather than that of UN Special Representative of the Secretary-General (SRSG) Admiral Howe immediately after the killing of the twenty-four Pakistani peacekeepers in Mogadishu on June 5, 1993. That meant that Admiral Howe did not receive all of the military support he requested to pursue the hunt for General Aideed and his armed faction.[124]

A related but more widely held interpretation in America is that the UN was to blame for "moving the goalposts" in Somalia and "dragging" America into a UNOSOM II "nation-building" exercise that involved confronting the most formidable warlord, General Aideed, and his armed followers. This view was propounded in the aftermath of the battle of Mogadishu by the Clinton administration and by important members of Congress and the Pentagon. In this vein, President Clinton said he was "mystified" that the October 3–4 raid had occurred and in a subsequent interview with the *Washington Post* said, "I don't think we fully appreciated until several weeks ago just how much [the political process] . . . had been abandoned when we turned it [the command] over to the UN mission" in May 1993.[125] According to this cynical view, it was the expanded mandate of UNOSOM II, and the inability of the Clinton administration to keep a close eye on the UN-led operation, that put the United States and the UN on a collision course with Aideed's armed faction. Until the handover to the UN, Clinton, Powell and others maintained that the mission in Somalia had gone well. In his memoirs, Clinton notes that by the end of the UNITAF phase, "crops were growing, starvation had ended, refugees were returning, schools and hospitals were reopening, a police force had been created, and many Somalia were engaged in a process of reconciliation moving toward democracy."[126] Similarly, Powell claimed that by April 1993, "We had accomplished our mission [in Somalia] by ending the civil disorder that had disrupted the production and distribution of food and led to mass starvation."[127] Meanwhile, Halberstam also stressed the distinction between the U.S.-led and UN-led operations in Somalia: "American troops, sure of their mission, sure of when to fire back, accepted by the locals, post-Gulf War, for the singular military presence they represented, were being replaced somewhat haphazardly by UN troops."[128]

This account of what went wrong in Somalia is little more than a myth, albeit one that is widely believed in the United States. In the first place, it is simply untrue to assert that the United States had nothing to do with the expanded mandate of UNOSOM II. As related, the Clinton administration was heavily involved in the drafting of Resolution 814, which established UNITAF's successor mission in Somalia. According to Walter Clarke, it was not the UN but the Pentagon that inserted "nation-building" into the mandate of UNOSOM II.[129] Second, the claim by the Clinton administration and some members of Congress that the confrontation with Aideed was linked to the placing of U.S. troops under UN command is fanciful. As Bowden and others have pointed out, the U.S. government always retained direct operational control over the combat forces it contributed to UNOSOM II. While UN General Secretary Boutros-Ghali chose a Turkish general, Cevik Bir, as force commander, his American deputy, Army Major General Montgomery, could veto U.S. military participation in any UNOSOM II operation, and was also the direct tactical commander of the QRF, which conducted military operations against Aideed's faction after the killing of Pakistani peacekeepers in June 1993. Close to thirty other American officers were in key positions in UNOSOM II, including Admiral Howe, the SRSG in Somalia. It was Howe who was the single most forceful advocate for Task Force Ranger, which embroiled itself in the fateful firefight with Aideed's forces in early October 1993. And "Task Force Ranger was wholly an American production."[130]

Third, there is little hard evidence to support the repeated assertion that the situation in Somalia only declined after the U.S. handover to the UN in May 1993. Despite an initial lull in hostilities, the large but transitory U.S. military presence during Operation Restore Hope failed to establish stable and secure conditions in Mogadishu. The visit of President Bush to the city over the New Year was marked by sustained artillery, mortar, and machine gun exchanges just three miles north east of the American embassy.[131] By January 10, Mogadishu was gripped by the worst violence since the March 1992 ceasefire. However, UNITAF did not intervene. U.S. military officials dismissed such fighting as "internal" Somali incidents, outside the scope of the operation's mandate.[132] UNITAF's seeming neutrality on intra-Somali violence was perceived as weakness by the armed factions. Between February 25 and 27, U.S. troops fought running battles with thousands of rioters after Aideed publicly accused the United States of favoring a rival warlord, Siad Hersi Morgan, in Kismayo.[133] At the same time, armed robbery and extortion in Mogadishu took off. Relief aid workers and foreign journalists became favorite targets as the gunmen resumed control of large areas of the city. Certainly, Oakley readily conceded on the eve of his departure from Somalia in March 1993 that UNITAF had failed to control the "big problem" of Somali crime.[134]

Thus, much, though not all, of what went wrong in Somalia was the result of decisions made by U.S. officials. The U.S.-led humanitarian intervention was not wrong in principle, but it was flawed in both design and execution. In essence, there was a mismatch between a Desert Storm–style humanitarian intervention molded by the state-centric thinking of the Powell Doctrine and the long-term support necessary for reconstituting stateless Somalia, where prolonged civil war had turned a drought into a catastrophic famine. As noted, the Joint Chiefs of Staff and the Pentagon had been extremely reluctant to engage in a humanitarian intervention in Somalia, and only agreed to do so when President Bush, after his electoral defeat and rising pressures to act in Bosnia, accepted General Powell's terms for committing American troops. Operation Restore Hope, therefore, involved the adaptation, but not the abandonment, of the

Powell Doctrine. It attempted to treat only a limited and short-term aspect, mass starvation, of what really was a much wider and deeper problem: namely, lawless conditions flowing from the absence of any governmental authority in Somalia. In the words of one military participant, "none of us could have guessed that we were at the dawn of a new age."[135]

Despite the efforts of the Bush and Clinton administrations to minimize the scope of U.S. intervention and limit it to strictly humanitarian purposes, the arrival of a substantial international force could not but fundamentally alter the political landscape of Somalia.[136] Because the country had no national institutions and little infrastructure, UNITAF, at least in the eyes of many Somalis, became, in effect, the new de facto state. It was in this context that the application of the Powell model of intervention proved to be counterproductive. First, Powell's constant focus on an exit strategy for U.S. forces and handing over to UN control in Somalia "flavoured the whole operation as temporary."[137] The United States pursued what might be called the "sheriff's posse" approach to peacekeeping. According to Powell, UNITAF was "like the cavalry coming to the rescue, straightening things out for a while, and then letting the marshals come back in to keep things under control."[138] The short-term approach "kept forces from being deployed that were needed to secure the environment properly and did not allow the civil affairs units, the NGOs and the UN sufficient time to build a stable civil structure. . . . This was like a doctor going home once the cancer patient was sedated but before the tumor was removed."[139]

Second, Washington's insistence that UNITAF was a strictly humanitarian operation meant that it was not prepared to actively disarm the armed factions—Somalia's "tumor." That was a critical mistake. Several episodes highlighted this within the first week of Operation Restore Hope when the forces of the United States still overwhelmed and intimidated the Somali gunmen. U.S. marines discovered a large arms cache in a building owned by Osman Ato, General Aideed's then-financer and close aide, but were instructed not to remove the guns or their owners; U.S. marines confiscated weapons from gunmen only to discover that a batch of AK-47 machine-guns were subsequently returned to faction leader, General Aideed; and when French legionnaires seized weapons from some Somalis at road checkpoints, they were rebuked by the Americans for exceeding the UN mandate and were obliged to give them back to their owners.[140] Such incidents conveyed an image of weakness to the armed factions. Of course, by not attempting to confiscate weapons and disarm factions, UNITAF avoided the prospect of significant casualties. But such risk aversion destroyed any chance of breaking the power of the warlords and laying the foundation for the eventual restoration of stable governance in Somalia. Instead, UNITAF, much to the disgust of many Somalis, decided to work with the main warlords in the hope that these powerful warlords would agree to form a new sustainable political order. Such a hope proved illusory. As Bowden perceptively noted: "If you wanted the starving masses in Somalia to eat, then you had to outmuscle men like this Aidid, for whom starvation *worked*."[141]

Third, the Powell Doctrine's strong emphasis on the possession of an overwhelming force capability effectively centralized Operation Restore Hope in south Mogadishu. From a force structure standpoint, such a decision made logistical sense. After all, south Mogadishu contained the country's only major seaport and airport, as well as the large, walled U.S. embassy compound. But the concentration of the U.S.–UN operation in one place—one largely controlled by General Aideed's armed faction—became a trap once hostilities broke out in June 1993.[142] Bishop and Cohen were among those U.S. officials who had anticipated this problem. They had proposed to decentralize the U.S.–UN operation to at least four regions so as make it less dependent on conditions prevailing in Mogadishu. However, it was the Pentagon, not the State Department, that demanded the "sledgehammer" capability—and although this force structure design reflected the conditions for forging some sort of policy consensus in Washington, it was not strictly determined by the operational environment in Somalia.

Fourth, the high standing of the Powell Doctrine in Washington discouraged problem recognition in Somalia and thus reduced the prospect of correcting faulty policy. It is true that the deteriorating security situation in Mogadishu eventually jolted the UNITAF forces into some weapons seizures and a delayed concern with law and order. These measures, however, were improvised and did not form part of a comprehensive disarmament or civil affairs plan. Nor were they considered by the United States to be a central feature of UNITAF's mandate. Moreover, attempts to adjust U.S. policy to the security environment on the ground, both during UNITAF and UNOSOM II, were shackled by constant fears of "mission creep"—a perceived tendency to engage activities that are beyond the terms of the original mission. In the case of Somalia, in which there was such disconnection between U.S. policy and the situation on the ground, it was hard not to have some form of "mission creep."[143] Interestingly, even after the expanded mandate of UNOSOM II, President Clinton invoked the fear of "mission creep" as a reason for curtailing the military campaign against General Aideed's faction on October 3: "Arresting Aidid and his top men because the UN forces couldn't do it was supposed to be incidental to our operations there, not its main purpose."[144]

True, Aideed was not the sole creator of Somali violence or chaos, but he was the most successful exponent of it, and so he had to be dealt with in order to quell the activities of other warlords in what was a broken society. The Powell Doctrine had opposed dealing with the political causes of Somalia's humanitarian tragedy in the early stages of the intervention and thereafter remained an obstacle to getting fully to grips with the situation. The decision by President Clinton to call off the campaign against Aideed and his supporters on October 4 was a retreat to the full blown Powell Doctrine and was received with considerable bitterness by many of the U.S. military personnel on the ground who had survived the battle of Mogadishu.[145] They sensed that such a decision was a major strategic error. Osama bin Laden, for quite different reasons, agreed. For the al Qaeda leadership, the central lesson of Somalia "is that the Americans will leave if they are attacked."[146]

Chapter 4

What If? The Alternative History of Australian Involvement in Somalia

The fact that the U.S. operation in Mogadishu proved to be such a disappointment begs the question of whether things could have gone differently. For many observers, at the time and since, there was a fatalistic belief that the armed humanitarian intervention in Somalia was doomed to fail. It is clear that General Powell and some other senior figures in Washington had been lukewarm about the Somali operation at the outset and believed that subsequent events only justified their underlying skepticism. In late September 1993, when Powell's term as chair of the Joint Chiefs of Staff came to an end, he urged President Clinton to quit Somalia: "We can't make a country out of that place. We've got to find a way to get out and soon."[1] According to Powell, while "nation-building might have an inspirational ring . . . the Somali factions were ultimately going to solve their political differences their own way."[2] A similar strain of pessimism was evident in the views of Richard A. Clarke. Commenting on President Clinton's decision to abandon the campaign to arrest Aideed after the armed showdown of October 3, Clarke feared that such "self-restraint [would] reduce our deterrence" but admitted "I had no good idea about how to do anything about it . . . In retrospect, I doubt that there was anything that could have been done to deter al Qaeda [in Somalia]."[3] Sentiments of this kind were most fully captured by Robert Kaplan's counsel of despair in his influential 1994 article "The Coming Anarchy," in which the most that could be envisaged for the victims of civil wars like Somalia's was some amelioration of the symptoms of their suffering.[4]

But was the Mogadishu debacle really inevitable? Something of an alternative history for the Somali intervention is provided by the experience of Australian armed forces deployed as part of the UN intervention. In contrast to the American predicament in Mogadishu, the Australian contribution to the UNITAF operation was widely seen as a UN success story.[5] The Australian contingent in Baidoa fulfilled their primary mission of creating a secure environment for the distribution of humanitarian aid. This involved what might be described as a peace enhancement strategy that synchronized a tough stance toward the warring factions with a strong and credible peace-building program that included a policy of active disarmament, the establishment of a local police force, and the restoration of a fully functioning legal system. An important preface to an examination of the contrasting techniques and outcomes of Australian forces is the difference in size and scope of the respective commitments made by Canberra and Washington. At its full extent, U.S. deployment on the ground in Somalia totaled 26,000 troops, while Australian forces never exceeded 1,250. Nevertheless, even allowing for the differences in the scale of military commitment, and the differences in population size and clan composition between Mogadishu and Baidoa, an examination of the Australian deployment is illuminating.

AUSTRALIAN PEACE ENFORCEMENT IN BAIDOA

On January 17, 1993, the 1st Battalion of the Royal Australian Regiment (I RAR) took control of the Baidoa Humanitarian Relief Sector (HRS) from 700 U.S. marines and 142 French legionnaires.[6] Until the arrival of these troops on December 16, 1992, Baidoa was known as the "City of Death," because after Mogadishu it was the area worst affected by civil war and famine. Geographically, Baidoa HRS covered an area of nearly 17,000 square kilometers in central Somalia and comprised a total population of about 180,000.[7] Baidoa was the major population centre in the HRS, with 50,000 to 60,000 inhabitants, including 20,000 refugees. The Australian deployment, known as Operation Solace, lasted for just seventeen weeks but managed to create a stable situation in Baidoa in which relief agencies were able to freely operate and fulfill their work.

Although Australia did not have a history of close ties with Somalia, several factors prompted a positive response in mid-December 1992 to a U.S. request for assistance there. The Australian government led by Prime Minister Paul Keating believed that it was important to reinforce old ties with the United States at the dawn of the post–Cold War era. Linked by the Australia, New Zealand, United States Security Treaty (ANZUS) and the ABCA (America–Britain–Canada–Australia) cross-servicing arrangements, Canberra perceived that the interoperability of Australian and U.S. forces would minimize the operational risks of deployment under the leadership of the U.S. commander, Lieutenant General Johnston.[8] The Somali situation seemed almost an ideal testing ground for part of Australia's Operational Deployment Force (ODF). For five months prior to the Somali deployment, I RAR underwent intensive training in services protected evacuation exercises in northern Australia. These involved a strong emphasis on civil–military relations in conditions that bore a certain resemblance to the terrain in Somalia.[9]

However, the immediate security challenge facing the Australians in Baidoa was formidable. In many ways, the situation there followed the Mogadishu pattern. The arrival of U.S. and French troops in Baidoa at the outset of UNITAF initially had a calming effect. Quite a few heavy weapons, including "technicals," were neutralized, and many gunmen either buried their weapons or simply moved out. But by mid-January 1993, the gunmen began to re-assert themselves again. The U.S. marines became the target of Somali ambushes and hit-and-run shootings in Baidoa. On January 12, one U.S. marine was killed and another seriously wounded in separate incidents.[10] In retaliation for casualties taken, the marines assaulted several towns and villages in the Baidoa HRS. This heavy-handed response served only to increase tensions. On January 14, a marine patrol was stoned by a group of Somali youths. A day later, the first contingent of Australian troops to arrive at Baidoa was fired on at the airport.[11]

At the same time, humanitarian NGOs were subjected to increasing criminal harassment. Food and equipment were frequently stolen from NGO compounds. Relations between the aid agencies and the U.S. military became very strained. The NGOs, which paid enormous amounts to hired gunmen for "protection" against looters, were told they would not get U.S. security for their compounds or staff unless they requested it.[12] From the NGOs' standpoint, "the interest which the U.S. marines and the French troops displayed in their own security . . . often compromised the protection provided to the NGOs in Baidoa."[13] On January 15, a Swiss NGO employee of the International Committee of the Red Cross was robbed and murdered. Three of the six gunmen involved in the attack were Red Cross employees. This incident, and the looting of a Médecins Sans Frontières compound, convinced many in the NGO community that it was impossible for U.S. marines to stop such activity by "hiding behind sandbags at a heavily protected airport" or "riding around in a jeep."[14] For aid workers like Lockton Morrissey of CARE Australia, it was clear what needed to be done: "There is no way that the [Baidoa] operation could be successful in the long term unless the guns are taken out of circulation."[15] And the NGOs made it clear to Australian military officials that if there was not an improvement in Baidoa's security situation, they would all pack up and leave town.[16]

Aware that Operation Solace would fail unless a more secure environment was created, Colonel David Hurley, Commander of I RAR, developed a robust but clear-cut strategy. He donned the mantle of "military governor" of the Baidoa HRS and positioned the Australians above the armed clansmen in a counterinsurgency-style operation. This involved the "aggressive" protection of humanitarian work and the "domination" of the HRS through the use of static security positions, patrolling, and on-call quick reaction forces.[17] According to Australian military officials, Somali warlords and gunmen "only respected the realities of power"[18] and were quick to exploit perceived weakness. In such a "dog-eat-dog" environment, it was deemed psychologically important for Australian troops to "call the bluff" of Somali gunmen in any challenge to ensure local respect for the Australian presence. Failure to do so, it was believed, would produce an irreparable "loss of confidence" in the operation.[19] In an early "show of strength," the Australians engaged in a number of firefights with Somali gunmen. Overall, the Australians faced eleven major contacts. Five Somalis were killed and at least six were wounded. One Australian was killed.[20]

Disarmament was, in effect, part and parcel of the Australian strategy. Unlike the United States, Canberra adopted a broad interpretation of Security Council Resolution 794's mandate for the creation of a secure environment for the provision of humanitarian assistance. It was recognized that under U.S. military leadership there was no requirement to take guns and weapons from the Somali population. But while the Australian government openly acknowledged the potential risks to troops involved in active disarmament, it clearly indicated that it supported the UN's stand on the issue: "We believe that for there to be an effective long-term solution to Somalia we will have to disarm the people," said a spokesman for Australian Defense Minister, Senator Robert Ray. "And if we go ahead with disarmament . . . the risk factor will be high to very high."[21] But, as Australia saw it, the worst risk at this time was to refrain from taking any risks at all.

Certainly, the Rules of Engagement (ROE) under which UNITAF troops operated in Somalia were considered sufficient in scope to permit the application of force in certain situations beyond simple self-defense. UNITAF Commander Lieutenant General Johnston on January 8, 1993, issued a policy directive on weapons confiscation.[22] The directive allowed UNITAF Commanders in each HRS to confiscate weapons as the need arose. So from an early stage in Operation Solace the Australians served notice that arms would not be tolerated on the streets. Much of the heavy weaponry, such as "technicals," had been previously eliminated by the U.S. marines and French legionnaires. However, the Australians introduced a system of weapons registration. Under this scheme, Somalis working for the NGOs and performing other essential tasks in the HRS could retain their registered weapons. But all other unauthorized weapons in the township were confiscated on sight and destroyed.

Disarmament, though, was linked to a multifaceted peace enforcement operation. Four aspects stood out. First, the Australians guaranteed the distribution of humanitarian relief in the Baidoa HRS through escorting food convoys. By the end of Operation Solace, the battalion group had escorted a total of over 400 convoys carrying more than 8,000 tons of grain to more than 130 locations.[23] Second, the Australians provided security in the Baidoa township by maintaining a constant and visible presence. In response to the NGOs' dire need for protection, Australian troops occupied the compounds and other facilities of these humanitarian organizations to deter criminal activities by NGO guards.[24] Third, relentless patrolling was sustained throughout Operation Solace. Conducted by foot and by APC, this presence on the ground was seen by the Australians as the "bread and butter"[25] of the peace operation. It kept armed factions and bandits off balance and facilitated the enforcement of weapons reduction. Altogether, the Australians confiscated over 1,000 weapons during their stay in Baidoa. That constituted a sizeable proportion of the 2,250 small arms and heavy weapons seized by UNITAF forces as a whole during the first ninety days of the multilateral intervention.[26]

The fourth important operational dimension in the Baidoa HRS concerned civil–military relations. The civil military operations team (CMOT) was, according to Colonel Hurley, "one of the keys to the success of Operations Solace."[27] Its role was to provide an interface between the Australian military and the civilians with whom they needed to deal on a daily basis. As a starting point, the Australian army cultivated the NGO community in Baidoa. The relationship began before the arrival of Australian troops. Organizations such as CARE Australia and World Vision were consulted in December 1992 about local personalities and conditions in Baidoa.[28] These consultations, along with a demonstrated willingness to address the security concerns of the NGOs after deployment, forged a close bond between the Australian forces and aid workers. This relationship, as Colonel Hurley acknowledged, had wider implications for the Australians in Baidoa: "By winning the confidence and the trust of the NGOs, that then percolated down to the people. The NGOs who were feeding them, looking after them, educating them and so forth were giving them the message that the Australians were a competent and even-handed lot who could be dealt with. They could take their problems to us."[29] Having eased itself into the community through the NGOs, the Australians embarked on a process of "bottom-up" political reconstruction. This effort centered on frequent meetings with the clan elders, the semblance of civil authority left in Baidoa. "By establishing a good working relationship with them," noted Colonel Hurley, "we could also get our message down to the people about what we were trying to achieve."[30]

In March 1993, following two UN-sponsored peace conferences in Addis Ababa, arrangements were made to convene a National Congress at Baidoa. Several factions competed for power: the Somali Liberation Army (SLA), which was pro-Aideed; two wings of the Somali Democratic Movement (SDM); and the SDM Baidoa, a new third wing of the SDM. The Australians saw the latter as an authentic "grass-roots movement" that it "really wanted to foster." Such a stance caused some difficulty in Mogadishu between the Australians and the U.S. and UN leadership. The UN had a top-down approach to peace building that focused on the fourteen faction leaders, which meant the grassroots movements did not get much attention.[31]

The Australian approach proved effective. Upon arrival in Baidoa, the Australians discovered that the SLA ran a Mafia-style revenue gathering empire based on terror, intimidation, planned killings, and massacres.[32] The prime function of this external element was to raise funds to support Aideed's broader ambitions in Somalia. While the Australian army quickly faced down early challenges from SLA gunmen and bandits in a number of armed confrontations, the SLA soon realized they could covertly maintain their bandit empire without openly challenging the Australian troops. Indeed, the SLA tried to present itself as a legitimate political authority in Baidoa with whom the Australians should work in tandem.[33] But the "Mogadishu option" was resisted. Instead, CMOT, with the consent of UNITAF and considerable input from local clan elders, engaged in some nation-building and built up the law and order structure in Baidoa.[34] In Baidoa, Australian military police and a CMOT legal officer, Major Michael Kelly, as well as troops, were used to train the Somalis as police. By May 1993, a police force of over 200 had been recruited and deployed in Baidoa and outlying areas. Similarly with the judiciary, Australia went further than any other UNITAF partner in restoring a fully functioning legal system based on the 1962 Somali penal code.[35]

These measures helped rebuild local confidence in the rule of law and also encouraged surviving victims of the SLA's criminal organization to provide detailed information on its activities. As a consequence, the notorious and much-feared commander of the bandit empire known as Hussan Gutaale Abdul was arrested and brought to trial in Baidoa.[36] After appearances before the Regional Court and Court of Appeal, Gutaale was convicted of the murders of thirty-two people, as well as on related robbery charges, and was sentenced to death in accordance with the Somali penal code. According to Major Kelly, the execution of this "strong man" had dramatic results in Baidoa. The remnants of the SLA organization packed up and left town within days.[37] Something like seventy lesser-known figures were also arrested or fled Baidoa.

Meanwhile, the Australian troops were able to ensure that "there was no outside interference"[38] at the National Congress in Baidoa, and SDM Baidoa emerged as the major political force in the township. This outcome was a triumph for the "bottom-up" approach to reconstruction. By responding energetically to the elders' requests to reestablish a police force and judicial system, the Australians not only provided a model for the rest of the UN operation, but also consolidated local support for disarmament in the Baidoa HRS. It represented a radical departure from the "top-down" approach to peace building adopted in Mogadishu.

When the Australians left in May 1993, the situation in Baidoa was stable. Armed militiamen and their barricades had disappeared, and the surrounding villages were free of the terror once inflicted by armed gangs.[39] Such progress was possible because the Australians focused both on the humanitarian and sociopolitical symptoms of Somalia's civil conflict and on the material vehicles for perpetuating violence (like weapons and munitions). Operation Solace demonstrated that systematic weapons reduction can be a tool for promoting stability in conditions of little or no civil authority. Quite understandably, the Australians became very popular in Baidoa. And when the end of their operation approached, Canberra had to resist tremendous local and international pressure to extend the stay of the battalion group.[40] It is significant that the positive transformation of Baidoa's security environment was sustained by the 1,100 French UN troops that replaced the Australians and their successors, the Indians, both of whom also practiced "total immersion."[41] Baidoa remained a UN success until 1994 when it, too, succumbed to the violent turmoil that had reappeared in the rest of southern Somalia.

A COMPARATIVE ASSESSMENT OF MOGADISHU AND BAIDOA

At the beginning of the UN's humanitarian intervention, Mogadishu and Baidoa were both full of the sights and sounds of death and destruction. However, by the time UNITAF was replaced by UNOSOM II in May 1993, the security situation in the two locations had markedly diverged. Mogadishu saw a somewhat marginal improvement while Baidoa underwent a positive transformation. The difference in outcome was related to three factors.

1. Mission Definition

U.S. forces in Mogadishu constantly ran into difficulty over both the conception and duration of their commitment. From the outset, Washington stressed that UNITAF was a strictly humanitarian mission. According to President Bush, the United States did not intend to get involved in the political reconstruction of Somalia.[42] Furthermore, the U.S. government qualified its support for securing the environment for humanitarian relief. In this regard, General Powell said: "It is not a question on our part or on the subsequent UN part that we will guarantee a weapon-free and violence-free environment. But I think it will be an environment that is manageable . . . to ensure the continual delivery of humanitarian supplies to save lives."[43] As a consequence, the U.S. operation in Mogadishu did not look to establish a new transitional political authority, but adapted itself to "working with the major faction leaders." It maneuvered in the direction of maximum consent and tacitly accepted that active disarmament of the warring parties constituted an infringement of Somali sovereignty.

As events transpired, U.S. troops were drawn into limited disarmament when humanitarian work was impeded by general lawlessness and the level of violence in Somalia. But this belated response was too ad hoc and unsystematic to have any significant effect. Constant changes in the weapons policy[44] served to strengthen the resolve of the main warlords and diminished hopes entertained by NGOs and peaceful Somalis about a concerted U.S. disarmament policy. Puzzled and distressed by the gap between the United States' tremendous military capabilities and limited political will, many Somalis resigned themselves to the continuing power of the warlords: "Without disarmament, the Americans have missed the whole point. Unless they are going to disarm on a nationwide basis, they might as well pack their bags and go home."[45] The very slow efforts to reestablish a law-and-order system in the Somali capital also compounded that sense of disillusionment.

On the other hand, the Australians arrived in Baidoa with a reasonably clear counterinsurgency game plan.[46] The fact the Australians were deployed for a specified period of time was a distinct advantage. It facilitated a longer-term perspective on the UN mission in Somalia and the problems it faced. The Australians saw disarmament as a crucial but by no means exclusive element in creating a secure environment. Because Somalia was a heavily armed "failed state" with no effective civil authority, the Australians took the view there was no sovereignty to offend.[47] In asserting themselves as a local Leviathan, the Australians not only adopted a policy of forcible disarmament, but also signaled their determination to subdue any challenges from armed factions and criminals. Australian military officials believed that such firmness impressed both Somali gunmen and noncombatants alike.[48]

Unlike the Americans, the Australian battalion subscribed to an "arms spillover" security philosophy.[49] The belief was that if low-level armed crime or factional fighting was ignored or tolerated, similar copycat incidents would certainly follow, leading to a cycle of escalating violence and banditry. Massive displays of force alone, however, could not make much impact in a lawless society in which virtually everyone was armed.[50] Thus, the Australians deemed it necessary to take the initiative, intervene in intra-Somali violence, and confiscate weapons on a "street by street, block by block" basis until an environment of sustainable security was gradually created. It should be added that the Australians used force in a very disciplined fashion, which reflected the fact they had trained and prepared for a counterinsurgency style conflict prior to the Somali operation. According to one observer, the Australian troops "avoided firing automatically at anything suspicious . . . but returned high volumes of accurate fire when engaged."[51] Certainly, the number of violent incidents dropped significantly after the various fire fights in February 1993 and continued to fall in the following months.

But the Australian military leadership recognized that if any gains in security were to be preserved, it "was critical in Somalia to re-establish the law and order system quite quickly," because a large number of clans were moved by famine and civil war into areas traditionally held by other clans.[52] So the Australian military viewed nation-building not as some form of "mission creep" but as a necessary step in restoring security in a desperately fragmented society. In Baidoa, the restoration of the 1962 Somali Penal Code effectively paved the way for the removal of the pro-Aideed SLA organization from the town. Similar possibilities existed also in south Mogadishu. In 1991, General Aideed's Habir Gedir clan fought Ali Mahdi's Abgal followers and took control of much of the south side of the city, including Abgal homes and properties as well as the lucrative seaport and airport. However, the opportunity to use the Somali judiciary system to expel Aideed's foreign militia from south Mogadishu was soon lost when the Americans belatedly sought to restore law and order through the warlords in the Somali capital.[53]

2. Style of Peace Operations

The United States and Australia demonstrated contrasting styles of peacekeeping in Somalia. The U.S. approach was short-term, reactive, high-tech, crisis-oriented, and compartmentalized. At the other end of the spectrum, Australia exhibited a community-oriented style of peacekeeping. This was specific in time, purposeful, low-tech, integrated, and participatory. Overall, it was a "tough but tender" approach to peacekeeping.

In relation to disarmament, these differences in style added up to differences in substance. For one thing, there was the question of intelligence. To create a secure environment, UNITAF commanders needed to be able to detect the movement of opposing forces, to determine the location of hidden arms caches, and to anticipate the plans of those who might attach their forces or commit crimes. That required a sound information gathering system, but this proved elusive for the U.S. forces in Mogadishu.[54] To be sure, the intricacies of clan and factional loyalties in the Somali capital complicated the intelligence process at all times. Nevertheless, the uncertainties associated with the length of the U.S. deployment and the extensive use of advanced technology in a marginally developed country served to limit contacts with the local population.

The story in Baidoa, however, was quite different. Here, the Australians succeeded in establishing a useful community intelligence capability. Because it was clear that armed gunmen and bandits were blending into the community, the Australian troops, who lacked helicopter support, fostered the community as a source of human intelligence. A willingness to engage in the reconstruction of civil society helped Australian efforts in this con-text. A senior NGO official observed: "According to the UNOSOM direc-tives, the Australians were not required to rebuild warehouses or schools or jails, or help with the town's water supply. . . . The diggers did not have to build playground equipment for the orphanage. . . . But they did all of these things and more."[55] Such community involvement, along with regular con-tacts with the clan elders and the revival of a law-and-order system, were "critical" in providing "intelligence as to what was going on" in Baidoa.[56]

Relations between U.S. and Australian peacekeepers and NGOs also diverged considerably. It should be emphasized that humanitarian organ-izations such as Save the Children and CARE were confronting on a daily basis armed bandits and the "armies" of warlords to ensure that food reached the starving long before the UNITAF operation was launched. They did this without military training, the security of APCs, flak jackets, or backup force to call on if arrangements went wrong.[57] With one or two notable exceptions, the "sheriff's posse" style of U.S. peacekeeping alien-ated a significant number of NGOs in Mogadishu. The U.S. military were criticized for a tendency to treat aid workers as "bleeding hearts," largely ignoring their knowledge of local security problems in Mogadishu and putting the lives of NGO personnel at risk by constantly changing their policy toward the possession of arms in the city.[58] Against this, Australia's community-oriented peacekeeping nurtured a very good relationship with the various NGOs in Baidoa. Convinced they were engaged in a process of nation-building, the Australians stressed teamwork with the NGOs and the clan-elders. "What can we do for you?" and "How can we make your job easier?" were among the questions framing I RAR's dia-logue with these groups. As an upshot, the Australians developed a "product mix" that addressed local security concerns and provided a range of civilian assistance that went far beyond the U.S. preoccupation with convoy escorts for the delivery of relief aid.[59]

Third, the issue of patrolling was not given equal weight in the UNITAF operation. Because the U.S. commitment to a secure environ-ment in Somalia was limited, the American model of peacekeeping involved relatively few foot and mobile patrols in Mogadishu. Except for U.S. strongholds such as the UN compound and the international airport, most of the streets in south Mogadishu remained in the hands of armed factions and bandits. The United States occasionally contested this control but generally only responded to direct security challenges through rapid, "in-out" maneuvers (i.e., airlifting or transporting troops to a trouble spot on a temporary basis). The conspicuous absence of regular patrolling in Mogadishu undermined the United States' authority in Somali eyes and certainly compromised any disarmament efforts made there. By way of comparison, patrolling was the backbone of Australia's community-oriented peacekeeping in the Baidoa HRS. From the Australian perspective, a troop presence on the ground amongst the people was both a symbol of resolve and a prerequisite for achieving other humanitarian and security objectives, including disarmament. It gave, in the words of one senior Australian official, "a better outcome than having troops working remotely from the population."[60]

3. Cultural Respect

The Australian deployment in Baidoa highlighted the importance of cultural awareness. Despite a Cold War connection with Somalia, the U.S. military evidently found it difficult to adjust to the political culture of the country. Whether because of national insularity or peacekeeping inexperience, the United States made a series of culturally related blunders. These included UNITAF's persistent failure to recognize that dropping leaflets in Mogadishu was a poor way to shape public opinion in a largely oral culture, and the decision of Admiral Howe to offer a "Wild West"-style reward for General Aideed's arrest after the confrontation of June 1993—a decision that outraged even some of Aideed's enemies in Somalia.[61]

But the Australians had comparatively few problems relating to the population of Baidoa region. While the aforementioned willingness to engage in civil reconstruction certainly helped, the constant presence of Australian troops on the ground was also an important factor. Historically, the Somalis have been a fierce, nomadic, and proud people who eked out an existence from the land. In a harsh environment, particularly one that had descended into a completely lawless situation, presence was seen as culturally important for winning respect. At the same time, Australian troops gained a reputation for relating well to the local population, not least because they demonstrated a willingness to assist ordinary Somalis. By curbing the power of the warlords through a policy of active disarmament, the Australians pumped new life into the traditional social leadership of the clan elders and in doing so facilitated the restoration of some vestiges of civil society. While the leadership of the Australian battalion in Baidoa had few illusions about the potential for violence in that society, it took strong "administrative measures" against at least one of its troops when it became apparent that the individual concerned had behaved in a racially offensive manner.[62]

CONCLUSION

There was nothing magical about the effectiveness of peace enforcement in Baidoa. The Australians had a coherent strategy for dealing with both the humanitarian and sociopolitical symptoms of Somalia's civil conflict and the material means of perpetuating violence (such as weapons and munitions). The U.S. peacekeepers did not have a comparable program in Mogadishu and had to improvise within the constraints of the Powell Doctrine. Any extent to which the United States assisted in the rebuilding of the police and engaged in spasmodic disarmament was considered "mission creep."[63]

The Australian success had some important implications. First, it demonstrated that the failure of U.S. peace enforcement in Mogadishu was not a failure of humanitarian intervention per se but a failure to conduct a particular operation wisely and steadily in a society in which the state had collapsed. The debacle in Mogadishu was not inevitable. According to both American and Australian military officials, there was a clear relationship between Washington's initial reluctance to actively disarm the warring factions in Mogadishu and the absence of progress toward national reconciliation in Somalia.[64] Indeed, the first really serious attempt to implement a plan of voluntary disarmament only began in January 1993. But in a failed state like Somalia, in which no recognizable authority existed, the quest for disarmament by warlord consensus proved elusive. As an upshot, the United States' "arms control" approach proved unworkable in the chaos of Mogadishu and almost certainly, in the view of senior Australian military officials, set the scene for the period of confrontation in which UNITAF's much weaker successor, UNOSOM II, tried to enforce disarmament. It was a case of too little too late. Of course, Mogadishu was always going to be a harder nut to crack than Baidoa. But American military participants like Martin Stanton are convinced that a much more robust approach toward disarmament in Mogadishu would have worked:

> In the beginning, the United States and other nations overwhelmed and intimidated the Somalis. An ultimatum for disarmament of all sides backed by force would have been a concrete first step toward reestablishing civil order. It is true that some factions would have fought an effort to disarm, and others would have sought to avoid it. A clear and abrupt military defeat of one of the major clans at an early stage in the campaign would have had a tremendous effect on the remainder of the Somali factions. Disarmament would have taken months or perhaps even a year, but in the end it would have firmly established the international intervention forces (U.S.-led transitioning to UN-led) as the ultimate (albeit temporary) authority in Somalia.[65]

Second, the Australians demonstrated in Baidoa that in the "new wars" of the post–Cold War era, a measured willingness to use force is often the only way of restraining warlords or local "strong men" from practices that inflict massive human suffering on other citizens. In Somalia, a multi-sided civil war had destroyed any vestiges of central authority in the country and had converted a severe drought into a catastrophic famine. Armed clan-based fighting, not nature, was at the heart of the Somali crisis. In striking a balance between cultural respect and being prepared to use force to secure compliance with UN demands, the Australians gave themselves the chance to *learn* how to successfully adapt UNITAF's ROE to an Islamic environment complicated by the absence of state structures, the widespread use of khat, and a society that was armed to the teeth.[66] And while forcible disarmament was not by itself automatically tension-reducing, its application within the context of multifaceted civic action and nation-building, based on local legal and political practice, did win strong community support. That much was made clear by the Australians. However, the lessons of the Australian experience in Baidoa did not seem to register with the politicians in Washington, D.C.

Chapter 5

The Somalia Syndrome and the Rise of al Qaeda

The unhappy demise of the U.S.–UN intervention in Somalia had a profound and lasting impact on U.S. foreign policy in the post–Cold War era. The decision by the Clinton administration to withdraw all U.S. troops from Somalia effectively ended the international experiment with peace enforcement and culminated in the removal of all UN troops from the country in March 1995. The conditions that led to intervention in Somalia, civil war in a failed state, persisted.[1] When the UN left, Somalia still did not have a functioning, internationally recognized government. Nor would it have one in the years ahead. At the same time, new "Somalias" elsewhere appeared as intrastate strife displaced interstate war as the dominant pattern of conflict in the post–Cold War era.

The memory and "lessons" of what was known as the Somalia Syndrome were formally enshrined in the Clinton administration's Presidential Decision Directive (PDD) 25 of May 1994, which said the United States would henceforth only participate in UN peacekeeping operations if they were in the American national interest—something that largely depended on the extent to which conflicts were deemed by Washington to be a direct threat to international peace and security.[2] PDD 25 signaled a clear retreat from Bush's New World Order perspective, and what Clinton called initially called "Assertive Multilateralism," toward a reconfigured Powell Doctrine that emphasized the state-centric approach to international security. After Somalia, there was a fixation in Washington of not "crossing the Mogadishu line" and allowing engagement in intrastate conflict slide into nation-building exercises with the possible risk of U.S. casualties.[3]

It should be emphasized that the Somalia Syndrome marked the beginnings of a dangerous gap between the U.S. foreign policy posture and the transformed security environment of the post–Cold War world. According to Frankel, "perceptions, not detailed information, govern political behaviour."[4] Certain stimuli are noted or recognized, and others are de-emphasized or ignored; thus there will always be a sense in which the perception or image can be distinguished from "reality." But in the context of the Clinton and George W. Bush administrations, the discrepancy between American threat perceptions and the actual operational strategic environment of the post–Cold War era would prove to be critical. It played no small part in helping to facilitate the emergence of a transnational terrorist group like al Qaeda.

This chapter proceeds in six stages. The first part attempts to delineate the domestic political impact of the failed U.S.–UN operation in America. The second section explores the Somalia Syndrome concept and how it relates to the "Vietnam Syndrome" that preceded it. The third part examines how the Somalia Syndrome was formally expressed in policymaking terms through President Clinton's PDD 25 initiative. The fourth section considers the wider repercussions of the Somalia Syndrome for U.S. policy in a number of civil conflict situations during Clinton's first term. The fifth section charts the steady escalation of al Qaeda terrorist activities during this period. Finally, the concluding section shows how the Somalia Syndrome helped to create a dangerous gap between American threat perceptions and an increasingly globalized security environment of the post–Cold War era affording new possibilities for nonstate terrorist actors like al Qaeda.

THE POLITICAL FALLOUT AFTER THE BATTLE OF MOGADISHU

It is no exaggeration to say that the loss of American lives in Mogadishu in October 1993 was a deeply shocking event for Washington, and one that was to play a key part in framing U.S. foreign policy decision making for the rest of the 1990s and beyond. Many of the senior members of the Clinton administration were politically damaged by the domestic impact of the showdown in Mogadishu. That confrontation had cost the lives of eighteen U.S. Army Rangers, wounded more than eighty other American soldiers, killed more than 1,000 Somalis, produced thousands of hours of cable television news coverage and hostile congressional hearings, and, ultimately, resulted in the resignation of at least one high-level official in the Clinton administration. After the battle of Mogadishu, President Clinton drew parallels with another major U.S. foreign policy crisis: "I thought I knew how President Kennedy felt after the Bay of Pigs. I was responsible for an operation that I had approved in general but not in its particulars."[5] And, like Kennedy, Clinton was determined to learn from the experience of such a humiliating foreign policy setback. No senior member of the Clinton administration, and certainly not the president himself, wanted a repeat of the Mogadishu fiasco.

According to Clarke, President Clinton felt "the military had let him down"[6] in Somalia. In his autobiography, Clinton pointedly alluded to a slippage between the formulation and implementation of policy in Somalia: "What plagued me most was that when I approved the use of U.S. forces to apprehend Aideed, I did not envision anything like a daytime assault in a crowded, hostile neighbourhood."[7] While such comments may have been self-serving, it was also clear that President Clinton was exasperated that the battle of Mogadishu came just when the administration was beginning, in light of the disappointing UNOSOM II experience, to reconsider its policy toward assertive multilateralism. In a speech at Columbia University on September 20, 1993, Christopher said multilateralism was "warranted only when it served the central purpose of American foreign policy: to protect American interests. This country will never subcontract its foreign policy to another power or person."[8] Then, on September 21, Lake noted in a speech at Johns Hopkins University that only "one overriding factor can determine whether the United States should act multilaterally or unilaterally, and that is America's interests. We should act multilaterally where doing so advances our interests—and we should act unilaterally when that will serve our purpose."[9] At the same time, in his first speech to the UN General Assembly six days later, President Clinton warned that "the United Nations must know when to say no" if the United States were to maintain its support for UN peacekeeping. More specifically, Clinton put forward guidelines for U.S. involvement in multilateral peacekeeping operations.[10] The guidelines reflected the following questions: Is there a real threat to international peace? Does the proposed mission have clear objectives? Can an exit point be identified for withdrawing? How much will the proposed mission cost? Shortly afterward, the U.S. Ambassador to the UN, Madeline Albright, told an audience at the National Defense University in Washington, D.C., "UN peacekeeping cannot be a substitute for fighting or winning our own wars, nor to lessen our own military strength," especially when the UN organization was "overweight and out of shape."[11]

But if the Clinton administration believed it could regain the political initiative by announcing the withdrawal of all U.S. troops from Somalia by March 1994, it miscalculated politically. Concerns in Congress about Somalia had been steadily mounting for some time. From February 1993 to November 1993, over a dozen hearings and numerous briefings had been conducted in both the Senate and the House of Representatives regarding the Somali intervention. Furthermore, an estimated fifteen bills and resolutions had been introduced, many of them calling for a swift withdrawal of U.S. forces.[12] After the events of October 3, Capitol Hill was gripped by bipartisan expressions of outrage and panic. Explanations for the failed operation were publicly and repeatedly demanded. The Clinton White House found itself in a major political crisis made all the more embarrassing when the Pentagon, "eager to divert attention from its own miscues, leaked word that just three weeks before the administration had denied Montgomery's request for additional heavy armor."[13] Critics in Congress and in the media were quick to point out that with American-crewed Abrams tanks and Bradley fighting vehicles, American troops probably would have been able to quickly rescue the trapped Delta and Rangers forces. Having allegedly denied the military the resources they need to fight in Somalia, President Clinton "stood accused of being complicit in recklessly sending young Americans to their deaths."[14]

No matter what the administration did, it was not enough to mollify Congress. After President Clinton announced his plan for U.S. disengagement in Somalia, the debate shifted from congressional authorization to how soon American troops should withdraw. A number of senators supported what was called the McCain Amendment. Proposed by Senator McCain, this amendment contended that the deadline for pulling out from Somalia should be brought forward to January 31.[15] Speaking in support of the amendment, Senator Phil Gramm (R-TX) observed "that the President clearly did not learn anything from the mistake [in Somalia] because now he is asking us to give him 6 more months to stay in Somalia with no clearly defined mission."[16] Nevertheless, on October 15, the Senate eventually endorsed President Clinton's scheduled withdrawal from Somalia by March 31, 1994. However, the Clinton administration faced an even more intense struggle in the House of Representatives. On November 9, the House voted 224–203 in favor of withdrawal from Somalia by January 31, 1994. But one hour later, and after considerable pressure from the White House on those Democrats who had supported the Republican push for an earlier withdrawal deadline, the House of Representatives reversed itself and voted 226–201 in favor of Clinton's March 31 deadline.[17]

At the same time, Republican and Democratic members of Congress continued to voice strong criticisms of Clinton's handling of the Somali crisis. Senator McConnell said that Somalia was an "important learning experience . . . about how America should operate in the post-cold war period . . . We failed to define and protect U.S. interests. We allowed the UN to define the agenda using our troops to implement their plan."[18] Similarly, Senator William Roth (R-DE) said, "let us learn from history." Claiming that the U.S. humanitarian mission was already accomplished, Roth argued that U.S. involvement in Somalia "amounts to little more than an agenda set by the United Nations. It has nothing to do with America's strategic interests. It has nothing to do with our Nation's security."[19] Furthermore, Senator Kit Bond (R-MO) noted that President Clinton's "greatest error of judgment" was to agree "to put our troops under control of the United Nations and under command of foreign leaders. This is simply not acceptable."[20] Meanwhile, Senator Sam Nunn (D-GA) remarked: "We must remind ourselves that Somalia is devoid of any vital, strategic, or economic interest to the United States. It is one thing to place our military forces at risk on behalf of vital or strategic interests; on behalf of purely humanitarian interests, however, we should refuse to place them in significant jeopardy."[21] For Senator Bob Dole (R-KS), the Republican Party's nominee for president in 1996, the lesson of Somalia was that "if the United States is not in the drivers' [*sic*] seat at the United Nations, the United Nations will take us for a ride."[22]

To be sure, a number of Senators indicated that they did not support the very critical views of their colleagues. Senator Carol Moseley Braun (D-IL), for example, noted: "The Somalian conflict is probably typical of future conflicts in this post-cold war world . . . I believe that we should support the United Nations intervention when our core values are at stake, which touch on our long-term strategic interest."[23] Senator Jim Jeffords (R-VT) took issue with "panicked calls in this body for an immediate US withdrawal." He observed, "A collapse of the UN operation there would be devastating to our efforts to engage the wider international community, through the UN or other mechanisms, in the business of maintaining global stability and security. While the United States must retain the ability to act unilaterally when necessary, broader international commitment to peacekeeping and peacemaking can serve our interests by spreading the burden more widely."[24] In a similar vein, Senator Kerry maintained that "we have a national interest in ensuring that the United Nations fulfills its potential as a peacekeeping/peacemaking institution. Somalia is the first test of the UN in the post-cold war period. . . . I respectfully submit to my friends that should not create a 'Somalia syndrome' after spending 20 years to try and undo the Vietnam syndrome."[25] Moreover, Senator Carl Levin (D-MI) remarked: "The world after the cold war finally has a chance to act together, and Somalia is one of the first places that we are trying after the cold war—we must not be the first country that fractures that effort. . . . We should not be in every coalition, but we need coalitions to be created and we need coalitions to work."[26]

Nevertheless, Congress as a whole continued to give the Clinton administration a hard time. There were demands by both Republicans and Democrats for "housecleaning" of officials who had played a significant role in shaping and implementing U.S. policy toward Somalia. Almost immediately, Robert Gosende, U.S. Special Envoy to Somalia, lost his position, and Christopher was obliged to publicly concede that the Somali crisis stemmed principally from failings at the highest levels of the Clinton administration. "We were not sufficiently attentive," Christopher said.[27] But while Christopher managed to ride out demands for his resignation, Aspin did not. Confronted with a Congress demanding that heads should roll, President Clinton did little to protect his Secretary of Defense from his numerous critics on Capitol Hill. By December 1993, Aspin resigned for "personal reasons," although his disastrous meeting with Congress on October 5 had almost certainly played a major role in that outcome.[28]

Meanwhile, at the end of October 1993, legislative support for a continuing U.S. role in Somalia collapsed, and Congress canceled a proposed $175 million contingency fund set aside to cover immediate UN peacekeeping costs. Congress also abandoned a special payment planned by President Bush (Sr.) to cover existing arrears from the Somali operation and informed President Clinton that the U.S. share of peacekeeping costs should be cut from 31.7 to 25 percent. The House of Representatives rejected a Pentagon request for $10 million to strengthen the UN Situation Center in New York, which the Clinton administration had declared a priority.[29] In addition, the Pentagon's proposed Assistant Secretary was effectively derailed after congressional objections to the nominee. Congress also rejected several Defense Department peace operations budget requests and by 1996 developed legislation, the United States Armed Forces Protection Act, to make it more difficult for U.S. military forces to participate in international peacekeeping missions. Congressional resistance also meant that the Clinton administration fell further behind in its peacekeeping payments to the United Nations.[30]

So why did the Clinton administration, wherever possible, seek to accommodate its critics on Capitol Hill after the battle of Mogadishu? After all, President Clinton said he "had a lot of sympathy for General Garrison and the men [on the ground] who wanted to go back and finish the job" against Aideed.[31] He was also aware that some voices in Congress cautioned him against a "cut and run" strategy in Somalia. Ultimately, however, Clinton was not prepared to take on Congress over this issue, and this came down to a matter of political judgment. First, Clinton was anxious to minimize the losses of the Democratic Party in the November 1994 Congressional elections, and he did not relish a confrontation with Congress over America's role in Somalia in those circumstances. Second, Clinton felt that as president, he had to react to the anger and the sorrow that had been generated by the horrifying CNN footage of an armed Somali gang dragging the body of an American soldier through the streets of Mogadishu. It would be misleading, however, to believe that Clinton simply caved in to the "CNN Effect," with continuous and instantaneous television coverage having a major impact on U.S. foreign policy by forcing the President to do something (such as withdrawing from Somalia) that he would not have done otherwise. Contrary to claims by many in Congress and the media, public support for U.S. involvement in Somalia did not collapse immediately after the grim television pictures were shown. Polls taken by *ABC* and *CNN/USA Today* one day after the Battle of

Mogadishu showed that only 37 percent and 43 percent of the respondents, respectively, said they wanted the U.S. soldiers to withdraw immediately. In fact, much of the polling evidence taken at this time suggested that the American public favored increased U.S. military involvement in Somalia. Polls conducted by CNN/*USA Today* (55 percent), ABC (56 percent), and NBC (61 percent) indicated majority support for sending more U.S. troops after the October 3 showdown.[32] Rather than having a controlling effect on President Clinton's decision to withdraw U.S. troops, the "CNN Effect" served as a catalyst for accelerating already planned changes to Clinton's policy toward Somalia.

Third, and not unrelated, the Clinton administration seemed convinced that American tolerance for battlefield casualties had dipped further with the end of the Cold War. During the Cold War, many of the military operations that involved the United States were linked to the global struggle against communism and thus could be justified in terms of vital national interests.[33] In the post–Cold War world, however, U.S.–UN military intervention in civil conflicts like Somalia were less clearly related to U.S. national interests, and the Clinton administration believed that U.S. troop fatalities in such missions could only be endured at the risk of negative media commentary and damning political criticism. It is revealing that in the immediate aftermath of the Black Hawk Down episode, President Clinton bluntly instructed Lake and Clarke on this point: "No more US troops get killed, none. Do what you have to do, whatever you have to do."[34] Thereafter, American snipers were placed on the roofs and walls of U.S. compounds and were instructed to shoot on sight any Somali gunmen that entered these areas. When the United States left Somalia six months later, there had been no more American casualties.[35]

Fourth, because Somalia had become the "poster child" for the failure of UN peacekeeping on Capitol Hill, President Clinton sought to use Congressional antipathy toward the UN in a cynical attempt to limit the damage to his own administration. Even though the October 3 operation was solely an American one that did not involve any prior consultation with UNOSOM II officials, the Clinton administration was quick to make the UN a political scapegoat for U.S. policy failures. In a statement to Congress on October 14, President Clinton conceded it had been a mistake to let the "United Nations dictate a mission to us."[36] Meanwhile, Clinton's aides let it be known that the responsibility for launching the campaign against Aideed did not lie with the United States. Instead, it was claimed that Boutros-Ghali had waged a personal vendetta against Aideed's faction.[37] While the Clinton administration may have found it politically expedient to blame the UN after the events of October 3, such posturing only reinforced an already deep-seated mistrust of the UN within the U.S. Congress, with considerable long-term implications for U.S. security in the post–Cold War era.

THE ADVENT OF THE SOMALIA SYNDROME

Like the legacy of the Vietnam conflict before it, Somalia generated a U.S. foreign policy disposition that became known as a syndrome. Although there was a clear difference in the scale and circumstances of the Vietnam and Somalia conflicts, there was a considerable overlap in terms of the foreign policy orientations they engendered. The "Vietnam Syndrome" depicted a clear reluctance of the American public to accept military intervention, and the attendant risk of U.S. casualties, in wars where the strategic purpose of American involvement was deemed ambiguous. A major attempt to codify the lessons of the Vietnam War, in terms of national security, was the "Weinberger–Powell Doctrine" of 1984, which, as has been shown, specified six conditions for the proper use of military force by the United States. Moreover, the "Powell Doctrine" was essentially the "Weinberger–Powell Doctrine" with two refinements: if a military response was appropriate, (1) it should involve the use of overwhelming force, and (2) any military engagement should have a clear exit strategy.[38]

On the other hand, the Somalia Syndrome, a term closely associated with harrowing images of dead American soldiers being dragged through Mogadishu's streets, was characterized by a deep skepticism of multilateral intervention in civil conflict situations, especially when such interventions endangered American lives.[39] Thus, the bitter experience of the Somali misadventure sensitized the Clinton administration to the political dangers of putting U.S. military personnel at risk for UN-backed humanitarian missions. It was almost as if Somalia defined the moment in the United States when "pollyannish notions about intervening militarily to guarantee access to civilians caught in the throes of war, ethnonationalism, or massive human rights abuse were replaced by more-realistic assessments about the limits of such actions."[40] This did not mean a complete return to Cold War thinking about security. But it did signal a substantial refinement of the Clinton administration's early construction of the post–Cold War world.

According to Lake, the post–Cold War era was broadly characterized by growing international acceptance of "America's core concepts— democracy and market economics," the intensification of globalization and interdependence, and potentially destabilizing ethnic conflicts.[41] At the heart of the Clinton administration's initial strategic assessment was the assumption that American domestic interests and long-term economic prosperity were inextricably intertwined with global economic growth, and especially that of the democratic capitalist core. Consequently, the "domestic" and the "foreign" were seen as clearly linked. "American statecraft is not, in the first instance, about 'them;' it is about 'us.'"[42] The establishment of the National Economic Council (NEC) in 1993 symbolized President Clinton's determination to show that economic policy would feature strongly in American foreign policy after the Cold War.

Furthermore, "this political-economic nexus was understood to be the essence of U.S. security policy in an international system in which there were no plausible challengers to American security [as] traditionally conceived."[43] In a context in which the world's only superpower had an unrivaled amount of soft and hard power at its disposal, America's successor doctrine to containment was said to be "a strategy of enlargement"—that is, enlargement of the world's free community of market economies. But if the enlargement project required U.S. leadership, it also required U.S. engagement in institutions that could help maintain international peace and thus promote liberal globalization and the spread of democratic capitalism. Thus, in the early months of the Clinton administration, U.S. involvement in UN peacekeeping was characterized as assertive multilateralism,[44] a phrase that implied that such involvement advanced American strategic interests.

However, after the battle of Mogadishu, the Clinton administration effectively discarded the concept of assertive multilateralism. In testimony before the Senate Foreign Relations Committee shortly after the events of October 3, Albright questioned multilateralism as a policy tool for pursuing U.S. interests. Multilateral peacekeeping was still "potentially" significant, but in many situations it "may not impinge directly on the national security interests of America or its allies."[45] Somalia was regarded as an important learning experience by the Clinton administration. In the words of President Clinton: "After Black Hawk Down, whenever I approved the deployment of forces, I knew much more about what the risks were, and made much clearer what [military] operations had to be approved in Washington."[46] The Somali setback, it must be emphasized, did not challenge America's conception of global leadership based on a consciousness of enhanced military, political, and economic power arising from the attainment of sole superpower status in the post–Cold War world. The power to lead the world appeared to be self-evident to President Clinton when he formulated his response to the October 3 firefight: "We are also not gonna flatten Mogadishu to prove we are the big bad-ass superpower. Everybody in the world knows we could do that. We don't have to prove that to anybody."[47] Nevertheless, the Somali experience did change the way America discharged its responsibilities as "the indispensable nation" in the post–Cold War era.

The Clinton administration drew five precautionary "lessons" from the memory of Mogadishu. First, typical failed or failing states were simply not geostrategically important to the United States and could not by themselves be allowed to define the United States' broader strategy in the world. Second, multilateral institutions like the UN could not always be trusted when it came to matters of security, and certainly could not be allowed to exercise any constraining effect or veto on issues relating to American security. Third, Mogadishu seemed to show that in situations in which something less than vital national interests were at stake, America's willingness to take casualties was extremely limited. According to one American observer: "If I have to choose between pictures of starving Somalian babies or dead American soldiers being dragged through the streets of Mogadishu, well, I don't want to see any more dead Americans."[48] Fourth, Somalia demonstrated that the technological superiority of America's military could be neutralized by engaging in ground combat against a well-armed adversary that had a better knowledge of local conditions, especially in urban areas. Fifth, if the Clinton administration determined that a particular situation threatened the national interests of the United States or its global leadership, a distinctive new approach to applying U.S. military power—consistent with the aforementioned lessons of Somalia—would have to be employed. This new Clinton approach toward the use of force, fine-tuned in the post-Mogadishu period, manifested itself in a reliance on "distant punishment" through the application of air power and the use of local allies, rather than U.S. troops, to carry out much of the ground combat.[49] The first glimpse of this new military strategy appeared on June 26, 1993, when President Clinton, in retaliation for an alleged plot by Saddam Hussein's regime to assassinate former President Bush (Sr.), authorized a cruise missile attack on Iraqi intelligence headquarters in Baghdad.

Thus the "Vietnam Syndrome" and the Somalia Syndrome certainly shared some common ground. Both syndromes encompassed a perceived reluctance or aversion by the American public to accept the use of military intervention in circumstances that ran the risk of American military casualties. Diplomat Richard Holbrooke alluded to this connection after the battle of Mogadishu when he spoke of the emergence of a new "Vietmalia Syndrome."[50] But the major difference between the two syndromes stemmed from the global context in which they evolved. After Vietnam, Washington was anxious not to play into the hands of its Cold War superpower rival, the Soviet Union, by getting bogged down in bloody Third World conflicts in which Moscow only had limited involvement. After Somalia, the Clinton administration, conscious that the United States was now the world's only superpower with apparently no credible enemies, believed it could play down the threat posed by failed or failing states to minimize U.S. exposure to them without damaging American security interests or the broader sweep of its foreign policy in the process.

CODIFYING THE SOMALIA SYNDROME

The "lessons" of Somalia were formally enshrined in the Clinton administration's PDD 25 of May 1994. PDD 25 was released after a fourteen-month interagency review of U.S. policy toward multinational peace operations. While the review had begun well before the October 3 disaster, the traumatic impact of Somalia in Washington certainly played a substantial part in shaping the final wording of the document. Essentially, PDD 25 listed seven conditions that had to be fulfilled before Washington would approve any further UN-sponsored military operations, irrespective of whether U.S. troops were participating. These conditions were (1) the existence of a significant threat to international security, (2) a sudden interruption of established democracy or a gross violation of human rights, (3) a statement of clear objectives, (4) the availability of sufficient resources and troops, (5) a mandate that was appropriate to the UN mission, (6) a realistic exit strategy, and (7) the consent of the parties to a conflict, obtained before the deployment of the multinational force.

In many ways, PDD 25 was the functional equivalent of the 1984 "Powell–Weinberger Doctrine." Both formulations sought to apply limiting criteria for U.S. engagement in the wake of major foreign policy reverses in Somalia and Vietnam, respectively. But PDD 25 was much broader in scope, and potentially even more constraining. The most important result of PDD 25, which basically seemed to rule out U.S. involvement in UN-backed peace enforcement operations, was to promote a risk-averse approach to intrastate conflicts in the post–Cold War era. While the United States, in principle, could support UN peacekeeping operations if they advanced U.S. national interests, PDD 25 did not define such national interests.[51] So, as a guide to decision-making, it was never clear when there was a match between U.S. national interests and the specified conditions for U.S. participation in UN peacekeeping operations. What is clear, however, is that multilateral peace operations were considered by PDD 25 to be secondary to American national security concerns. PDD 25 thus signaled the emergence of a more unilateral approach to international security under the Clinton administration. Thus, in the wake of the Somali tragedy, there was a determination in Washington not to cross "the Mogadishu line" by engaging in UN peace operations that had the potential to expand into armed nation-building actions containing the associated risk of taking casualties.

THE IMPACT OF THE SOMALI SYNDROME ON U.S. FOREIGN POLICY

The broader international effects were momentous. Somalia was far from unique. With the end of the Cold War, the mix of factors affecting national security had changed. Issues dealing with norms, identities, political legitimacy, and cultures became more salient.[52] In the twelve-year period between 1989 and 2001, there were fifty-seven different armed conflicts in forty-five locations. All but three of these conflicts occurred within states.[53] These new conflicts were associated with mass killings, forcible resettlement, acts of terrorism, crime, and, almost by definition, major human rights violations.[54]

The first casualty of the Somalia Syndrome was Haiti. In June 1993, the UN Security Council had unanimously passed Resolution 841, which placed an arms and fuel embargo on Haiti in order to try to displace the military regime led by Lieutenant General Raoul Cedras that had overthrown the government of the democratically elected president, Jean-Bertrand Aristide, in 1991. These mandatory sanctions helped to produce the Governors Island Agreement whereby General Cedras would step down and Aristide would return, and UN troops and police would be deployed to oversee the political transition in Haiti. However, on October 11, just a week after the battle of Mogadishu, the first deployment of 200 U.S. and twenty-five Canadian troops aboard the USS *Harlan County* was unable to land at Port-au-Prince as previously agreed.[55] On the dock, more than 100 supporters of the military regime angrily protested against the deployment of UN troops and threatened America with another "Somalia!" Without even consulting the UN, the Clinton administration immediately ordered the *Harlan County* to leave Haitian waters and to return to the United States. A headline in the *New York Times* pinpointed the reason for the humiliating Clinton climbdown: "Policing a Global Village: As Peacekeeping Falters in Somalia, Foes of the U.S. Effort in Haiti Are Emboldened."[56]

As an upshot, the Governors Island Agreement collapsed, violence in Haiti continued with opponents of the Cedras military regime being targeted, and large numbers of Haitians sought to flee their country for the safely of the United States. It was a year before the Clinton administration took firm action to bring an end to the crisis in Haiti. In September 1994, confronted with the imminent threat of a U.S. invasion, Cedras's military junta finally agreed to step aside and permit the return of Aristide to resume democratic rule backed by a presence of U.S. troops.[57] While this outcome helped to restore some badly needed credibility to the Clinton administration, it could not erase the diplomatic damage that had been sustained in the interim. But the domino effect of the Somalia Syndrome would prove even more serious in Rwanda, where genocide began to unfold even as PDD 25 was issued.

Unwilling to do anything that might draw America in, the Clinton administration blocked the idea of an early deployment of 5,500 UN troops in Rwanda in the Security Council to halt the terror unleashed by ethnic Hutu extremists against the Tutsi minority, as well as Hutus considered supportive of the Tutsi. Requests from General Romeo Dallaire (the commander of UN forces in Rwanda to oversee the implementation of the Abuja Accords ending the war between the government and the Rwandan Patriot Front) were declined, and when the genocide duly began in earnest, all UN forces were quickly withdrawn.[58] It is likely, according to Alan Kuperman, in the wake of the Somalia debacle six months earlier, "that U.S. officials, consciously or otherwise, dismissed initial reports of large-scale violence in Rwanda because such information would have raised the prospect of another UN or US humanitarian intervention that they plainly did not want to contemplate."[59] Events in Rwanda were viewed in Washington through the prism of Somalia. The two situations were viewed as similar—both were seen as failed states.[60] As Klinghoffer noted, Rwanda's descent into genocide became blurred with Somali images of civil war and state failure so that the premeditation and directing role of the Hutu extremists was initially lost on Washington.[61] But if the Clinton administration could use PDD 25 to reject pleas for another Somalia-style humanitarian, its position bumped up against the distinctive reality that Rwanda, in the words of Philip Gourevitch, experienced "the most unambiguous genocide since Hitler's war against the Jews."[62] Confronted with the problem of the obligation to act against genocide under the Geneva Conventions, the Clinton administration refused to classify the slaughter in Rwanda as genocide until events had taken their course and more than 800,000 people had been killed in the most barbaric circumstances. The only response from the international community to the Rwandan genocide was a very late UN-authorized intervention by France.

As previously noted, it was partly the marked reluctance of the George H. W. Bush administration to become involved in the Bosnian conflict that had helped make intervention in Somalia in late 1992 a politically viable alternative.[63] However, the fact that an apparently much easier humanitarian operation in Somalia turned into a veritable nightmare only made the United States even more cautious toward the Bosnian conflict. During the 1992 election campaign, candidate Clinton had criticized Bush for failing to protect human rights in the Balkans, but after taking office, he showed no inclination to take a more active leadership role, even as the violence escalated and the world became aware that ethnic cleansing was being perpetuated on a major scale.[64] The standard line of the Clinton administration was that peace would only come to Bosnia when the warring parties chose it. But while the Clinton administration ruled out a military solution in Bosnia during its first two years and declined to participate in the UN operation overseeing the distribution of humanitarian aid in Bosnia, it also opposed a major diplomatic initiative for settling the conflict. Conscious of domestic concerns about crossing "the Mogadishu line" in Bosnia, especially in the Republican Party, the Clinton administration effectively vetoed the European Union (EU)–backed peace plan drawn up by former U.S. Secretary of State Cyrus Vance and former British Foreign Secretary David Owen. The Clinton administration said it opposed the Vance–Owen initiative because it was seen as conferring acceptance of state boundaries redrawn through the use of force.[65] But in the eyes of many of their European partners, the Clinton administration was seeking to exercise power in Bosnia without assuming responsibility for improving the situation. The perceived lack of U.S. leadership in relation to Bosnia caused serious strains in the trans-Atlantic relationship between 1993 and 1995. Something like 200,000 people had been murdered through ethnic cleansing since the Bosnian crisis had begun in 1991.

If Somalia had underlined to the Clinton administration the apparent dangers of straying from the national interest, Haiti, Rwanda, and now Bosnia highlighted that such conflicts were more than humanitarian tragedies; they could also be major international security problems. It became increasingly clear to the Clinton administration in 1995 that the price for continued inaction in the face of the worsening crisis in Bosnia would be a severe blow to U.S. leadership claims both in Europe and on the international stage generally. Indeed, Holbrooke warned the Clinton administration in a widely noted article in *Foreign Affairs* that Bosnia was "the greatest collective security failure of the West since the 1930s."[66] Moreover, as the flow of refugees out of Bosnia continued and reports of atrocities, largely attributed to the Bosnian Serbs, mounted, Serbian President Slobodan Milošević and his allies felt free to escalate their actions. In May 1995, the Bosnian Serb leadership began the systematic shelling of the Bosnian capital of Sarajevo despite international protests about the large civilian population located there; in July 1995, the Bosnian Serbs overran one of the UN-designated "safe zones" at Srebrenica in eastern Bosnia-Herzegovina and within hours had brutally murdered more than 7,000 Bosnian Muslim men captured in that assault; in August 1995, the Bosnian Serbs fired five mortar rounds into Sarajevo's Markale marketplace and killed thirty-seven shoppers as well as wounding around ninety others.[67]

The Markale marketplace attack was the final straw as for as the Clinton administration was concerned. Tacitly recognizing that a strict adherence to the PDD 25 policy in Bosnia actually threatened the strategic interests of the United States, President Clinton authorized Operation Deliberate Force, a North Atlantic Treaty Organization (NATO) program of air strikes—largely carried out by U.S. aircraft—directed at Bosnian Serb targets, ostensibly to establish some basis for a negotiated end to the Bosnian civil war. Significantly, the air campaign was opposed by many members of the U.S. Congress on the grounds that it exceeded the limits of presidential authority. But the Clinton administration did not rely solely on the coercive impact of air strikes in Bosnia. Several weeks before Operation Deliberate Force began, Washington gave the green light to a U.S.-trained and U.S.-equipped Croat army launching ground offensives to relieve Serb pressure on the western Bosnian city of Bihać and to annex the Krajina region from Serb control. These Croat operations proved to be successful and tilted the military balance against the Bosnian Serbs. Thus, the new Clinton approach toward Bosnia consisted of what Bacevich aptly called "gunboats and Gurkhas."[68] That is, the United States and its NATO allies looked to a combination of American air power and a U.S.-supported Croat army to bring the Serbs to the negotiating table.

The strategy seemed to work. U.S. diplomats subsequently pushed through the Dayton Accords in December 1995, which formally held Bosnia together as a single country; 60,000 heavily armed troops, mostly from NATO (20,000 from the United States), went to Bosnia and established a reasonably stable ceasefire. Furthermore, the Clinton administration also firmly supported the establishment of ad hoc tribunals charged with the indictment and prosecution of individuals accused of crimes against humanity and genocide in the former Yugoslavia and Rwanda. Thus, by the latter part of Clinton's first term, the administration had moderated its commitment to the PDD 25 criteria for international engagement, but its "gunboats and Ghurkhas" approach in Bosnia showed that it remained wary of crossing "the Mogadishu line."

In the meantime, the Clinton administration made it plain it wanted as little as possible to do with Somalia, the country responsible for the now debilitating syndrome in U.S. foreign policy. After withdrawing U.S. troops from the UN peacekeeping mission in March 1994 and providing military support to evacuate the remaining UN forces from Mogadishu in early March 1995, the Clinton administration effectively abandoned Somalia. There were no known visits by U.S. diplomatic or military personnel to Somalia between 1995 and 2001,[69] and America did not maintain any diplomatic representation in the country during this period. U.S. Special Envoy to Somalia Daniel Simpson and his staff had moved their offices to Nairobi in September 1994, citing security concerns. Administration officials said there was a limit to what Washington and its allies could do to help Somalia if the nation and its people were unwilling or unable to help themselves. Speaking before a House subcommittee in early March 1995, Christopher noted: "We went in there [Somalia] not to guarantee a result but to provide an opportunity. . . . They don't seem to have grasped their chance."[70] While Christopher argued that the United States "[left] the country in a lot better shape than when we went in"— the operation by some estimates saved up to 250,000 thousand lives in Somalia—officials made no attempt to hide their exasperation that Somali warlords and faction leaders had spurned the chance to make peace and form a government under U.S.–UN auspices. "It's their turn now," the U.S. Special Envoy to Somalia said. "I've told them categorically: You're out of time."[71]

After U.S. disengagement from Somalia, the most militant Islamist group, al Itihaad al Islamiya, consolidated its role as an active civil and military player in what was a stateless society. However, whereas other factions were essentially clan armies battling for territory and resources, al Itihaad's core objective was more ambitious: namely, to establish an Islamic state in the Horn of Africa. Al Itihaad advocated the establishment of a "Greater Somalia" through the unification of territories in Ethiopia, Kenya, and Djibouti inhabited by ethnic Somalis. The concept of a pan-Somali state was not new. A number of Somali governments since independence had, for example, tried without success to "liberate" the Somali-populated Ogaden region of neighboring Ethiopia. But the distinctive feature of al Itihaad's "Greater Somalia" drive was its vision of an Islamic caliphate for all Somalis.[72] For much of the period between 1993 and 1996, al Itihaad received training, materiél, and financial support from al Qaeda, other international jihadist groups, and states such as Iran and Sudan. This external support helped al Itihaad maintain a military presence in Mogadishu, a training camp on a small island near the coastal town of Ras Komboni, close to the Kenya–Somalia border, sustain an active al Itihaad presence in Ethiopia's Ogaden region, and establish a significant organizational base in the Gedo region from August 1992.[73]

It was in the Gedo districts of Bay and Bakol that al Itihaad, with al Qaeda assistance, began to construct structures for local governance. The organization attempted to fill the void left by the absence of central government by providing some of the basic civic needs of Somalis, including schools and hospitals, and enforcing *sharia* laws in areas under its control. While al Itihaad met some resistance from within the local population over its strict interpretation of Islam and its efforts to ban khat, the organization played an active part in the development of Somalia's Islamic Courts movement. Backed by a diverse range of interests in the business community, professional groups and clan elders, the courts were established to provide a framework of justice and order to the lawless streets of Mogadishu.[74] The ideological complexion of Mogadishu's Islamic Courts ranged from the Somali tradition of Sufi moderation to a Wahabist reformism with a pronounced jihadist orientation in courts organized by al Itihaad or associated groups. Later, the Courts movement extended beyond Mogadishu to other areas of southern Somalia.

It should be added that the Islamist militancy of al Itihaad contributed to a difficult and fluid relationship with the major armed factions in Mogadishu led by the warlords General Aideed and Ali Mahdi. Even though al Itihaad and al Qaeda provided critical assistance to General Aideed's faction in the October 1993 battle of Mogadishu, Aideed reportedly became suspicious of his Islamist allies and ended the association in 1994 in order to promote closer ties with a more traditional Islamic organization, in the Somali context, *Majima Al Ulama*. Interestingly, the military commander of al Itihaad, Hassan Dahir Aweys, responded by switching his organization's support to Aideed's great rival, Mahdi, whose stronghold lay in North Mogadishu. The new relationship led, among other things, to the establishment of an Islamic Court in North Mogadishu that upheld a harsh sharia punishment system, including amputations, for criminal offenders. However, by 1996, Mahdi had also become distrustful of al Itihaad and expelled its militia from territory under his control in North Mogadishu.[75]

Suspicions about al Itihaad within Somalia had been fuelled by its jihadist campaign against neighboring Ethiopia. With the departure of U.S. troops from Somalia, al Itihaad targeted what it saw as the "infidel" pro-American EPRDF government in Addis Ababa. Trained and supported in Gedo by a contingent of "Afghan Arabs," al Itihaad launched a series of small-scale armed actions in the Ogaden region of Ethiopia in late 1993. These incursions subsequently broadened into a campaign of terrorism inside Ethiopia. In January 1995, al Itihaad bombed a hotel in Addis Ababa; in May 1995, it detonated a bomb in Dire Dawa (Ethiopia's second-largest city) that killed eighteen people; in January 1996, al Itihaad bombed the government-owned Ghion Hotel in Addis Ababa; and in February 1996, it bombed the Ras Hotel in Dire Dawa. Moreover, al Itihaad claimed responsibility for the assassination of General Hayelom Araya, the head of operations of Ethiopia's Defense Ministry, and the attempted assassination of Abdulmejid Hussein, an Ethiopian Somali who was then Ethiopian Minister of Transport and Communication. These guerrilla attacks and terrorist actions, al Itihaad said, would continue until the Ogaden became independent of Ethiopia.[76] But many Somalis saw al Itihaad's military and terrorist attacks in Ethiopia as evidence that al Itihaad was simply implementing a regional strategy of Islamist expansionism on behalf of its foreign backers, particularly the National Islamic Front (NIF) government of Sudan and the lesser-known al Qaeda, which, until mid-1996, was based in Khartoum. Such a perception was further strengthened in late 1996, when the Sudanese charge d'affaires in Mogadishu, during a meeting with supporters of al Itihaad, publicly called for a jihad against Ethiopia.[77]

Not surprisingly, the task of combating jihadist activities of al Itihaad became a national security priority for Meles Zenawi's EPRDF government in Ethiopia. In August 1996, two months after pressure from the United States and Saudi Arabia effectively forced Osama bin Laden to leave Sudan for Afghanistan, Addis Ababa launched a military intervention in Somalia to seriously degrade the military and terrorist capabilities of al Itihaad. The initial move across the Somali border targeted the al Qaeda–supported al Itihaad camps in Luuq and Bula Hawa in the stronghold region of Gedo in the southwest of Somalia. After the rout of al Itihaad forces in this operation, Ethiopian troops thereafter intervened periodically in Somalia on an "as needed" basis. The Ethiopian interventions inside Somalia certainly impeded efforts by al Itihaad and al Qaeda to develop a strong Islamist presence in the Horn of Africa. Moreover, this set back probably compounded the effects of bin Laden's departure from the Sudan. Al Itihaad had lost the close support of a major ally and financer. While the Clinton administration tacitly supported Ethiopian attacks on al Itihaad, it declined to recognize the independence of Somaliland, a strategic ally of Addis Ababa after Eritrea's independence in 1993 had left Ethiopia landlocked. Such recognition would have incurred the anger of another U.S. ally, Egypt, and the United States apparently had no wish to take sides with regard to Somalia and generally preferred to stay clear of engagement.

THE EMERGENCE OF AL QAEDA'S GLOBAL JIHAD AGAINST AMERICA

There was a clear linkage between the Somalia Syndrome and the unfolding of a new and enigmatic threat to the United States from bin Laden's al Qaeda organization. Between 1992 and bin Laden's return to Afghanistan in May 1996, the al Qaeda leadership launched a major ideological offensive against the United States and its allies. Living in a large, well-guarded compound outside Khartoum, under the protection of a Sudanese military regime that at that time was allied to the radical Islamist leader, Hassan al-Turabi, the al Qaeda leadership, in a number of public statements, began to articulate the reasons for a "holy war" against the "Crusader-Jewish alliance." In a message to the "honourable scholars of the Arabian peninsula and Saudi Arabia in particular," bin Laden condemned what he said was "a calamity unprecedented in the history of our *umma* [community], namely, the invasion by the American and other foreign troops in the Arabian peninsula and Saudi Arabia, the home of the Noble Ka'ba, the Sacred House of God, the Muslim's direction of prayer, the Noble Sanctuary of the Prophet, and the city of God's Messenger, where the Prophetic revelation was received."[78] Moreover, all "this happened on the watch of the region's rulers, and with their active participation—in fact, these are the people actually implementing the plans of our *umma's* enemies. This invasion was financed by these rulers using our *umma's* wealth and savings."[79]

At the same time, the issue of Palestine featured strongly in bin Laden's rhetorical attacks against the United States and Israel. He denounced the 1993 Oslo Accords between Israel and the Palestine Liberation Organization (PLO) leadership "as a disaster for Muslims . . . which was praised and lauded by the prime minister of the Zionist enemy . . . [and] the traitorous and cowardly Arab tyrants." Bin Laden observed: "The legal duty regarding Palestine and our brothers there—these poor men, women and children who have nowhere to go—is to wage jihad for the sake of God, and to motivate our *umma* to jihad so that Palestine may be completely liberated and returned to Islamic sovereignty."[80] Thus, according to bin Laden, the Islamic world had no option but to confront the "terrible aggression" that it faced: "After the Crusaders' occupation of Saudi Arabia, the Jews' violation of Palestine . . . and the destruction and slaughter being meted out to Muslims in Chechnya today and Bosnia yesterday and throughout the world everyday, can matters get any worse?"[81]

On August 23, 1996, bin Laden publicly declared a defensive war or jihad "against the Judeo-Christian alliance which is occupying Islamic sacred land in Palestine and the Arabian peninsula." Bin Laden noted that after the Cold War, "America escalated its campaign against the Muslim world in its entirety, aiming to get rid of Islam itself."[82]

Consequently, "the defensive jihad against the US does not stop with its withdrawal from the Arabian peninsula; rather, it must desist from aggressive intervention against Muslims throughout the world."[83] It should be pointed out that bin Laden's formal declaration of a jihad against the U.S. government was issued after the Sudanese government, under intense American and Egyptian pressure, had requested that bin Laden—following various Saudi attempts to assassinate him—leave Khartoum. Nevertheless, it was plain that while al Qaeda perceived it had many enemies—Israel, the Mubarak regime in Egypt and the pro-Western Muslim countries as well as Christian states—the United States was the pivotal adversary as far as bin Laden was concerned, and had to be stopped.

So why did al Qaeda set itself the hugely ambitious goal of confronting the United States, the world's only superpower? The initial sense of confidence may have derived in part from the experience that Arab Afghans had in contributing to the defeat of another superpower, the Soviet Union, in Afghanistan during the late 1980s. Warriors of faith, according to bin Laden, "must rest assured that life is only in the hands of God," and Afghanistan did seem to demonstrate that the strength of a superpower was not necessarily limitless. However, the al Qaeda leadership surely recognized there were huge differences between the two superpowers in question; the overwhelming economic and military position of the world's only superpower, the United States, in the 1990s defied any easy comparison with a Cold War superpower like the former Soviet Union in the 1980s. It is more likely that the actual experience of the Somali intervention in 1992–1993, and particularly the Clinton administration's international reaction to its failure there, emboldened al Qaeda to target the United States. In an interview on al-Jazeera, bin Laden said the Somali experience was instructive: "Based on the reports we received from our brothers who participated in the Jihad in Somalia we learned that they saw the weakness, fragility, and cowardice of U.S. troops. Only eighteen U.S. troops were killed. Nonetheless, they fled in the heart of darkness, frustrated after they had caused great commotion about the New World Order."[84] In an internal al Qaeda communication, an analyst provided much greater insight on the strategic lessons that his Islamist organization learned from Somalia:

> The Somali experience confirmed the spurious nature of American power and that it has not recovered from the Vietnam complex. It fears getting bogged down in a real war that would reveal its psychological collapse at the level of personnel and leadership. Since Vietnam, America has been seeking easy battles that are completely guaranteed. It entered into a shameful series of adventures on the island of Grenada, then Panama, then bombing Libya, and then the Gulf War farce, which was the greatest military, political and ideological swindle in history . . . America wanted to continue this series of farces. It assumed that Somalia was an appropriate space for another ridiculous act. But the Muslims were there, so the great disaster occurred. They fled in panic before their true capabilities could be exposed.[85]

Certainly, it was true that al Qaeda's efforts to build and expand a largely self-supporting international insurgent organization that had the capability to seriously damage the United States or other perceived enemies of Islam gathered momentum after the Black Hawk Down episode. Having murdered three people at a CIA gatehouse in Langley, Virginia, in January 1993 and bombed the World Trade Center building in New York in February 1993, al Qaeda invested personnel and money in a jihadist operation in Bosnia between 1992 and 1994, ostensibly to support the Bosnian Muslims in their war with the Serbs. Furthermore, in January 1995, al Qaeda plots to assassinate Pope John Paul II and President Clinton were thwarted in Manila, Philippines, as were plans to bomb U.S. airliners flying the Pacific. In June 1995, an assassination attempt made by Islamic terrorists linked to bin Laden on a key American ally, Egyptian president Hosni Mubarak, narrowly failed in Ethiopia. But in November 1995, the headquarters of the U.S. military training mission to the Saudi National Guard in the Saudi Arabian capital of Riyadh was bombed by al Qaeda agents, killing five Americans. Then, in June 1996, a U.S. Air Force high-rise housing complex near Khobar, Saudi Arabia, was truck-bombed by bin Laden's followers. Nineteen Americans were killed in the devastating terrorist attack.[86]

THE DANGEROUS POLICY–SECURITY ENVIRONMENT GAP

Despite the clear pattern of an intensifying al Qaeda threat, the Clinton administration struggled to come to terms with it. The advent of the Somali Syndrome in Washington discouraged or even suppressed the idea of American military intervention in civil conflict situations. And that predisposition served, in turn, as a brake on the ability of the Clinton administration to learn about and recognize the threat presented by rising nonstate actors like al Qaeda. During Clinton's first term, the administration made only halting progress toward identifying the al Qaeda threat. In 1993–1994, certain analysts in the Federal Bureau of Investigation (FBI) and CIA identified bin Laden as a major financer of a terrorist grouping consisting of Afghan Arabs, but neither the FBI, the CIA, nor the Defense Department were able to verify al Qaeda as a terrorist organization, let alone connect it with violent events in Yemen, the World Trade Center, Mogadishu, and Bosnia during this period. Nevertheless, by 1994, the Clinton administration responded to the growing number of terrorist acts by publishing its formal counterterrorism policy, PDD 39.[87] While this policy was a step forward, it was hampered by patchy intelligence and a risk-averse U.S. military. Because Clinton was criticized as a Vietnam War draft dodger, he was limited in his ability to direct the military to engage in new antiterrorist operations that they did not wish to conduct.

It was only in 1995 that it became apparent to the White House that bin Laden might be much more than a bankroller of Islamic terrorism. In 1995, bin Laden's name appeared in the State Department annual publication *Patterns of Global Terrorism* for the first time. In January 1996, the CIA established Alec Station, an "interdisciplinary" intelligence unit whose sole brief was to track and monitor the activities of bin Laden. Shortly after its inception, the station began to accumulate an extraordinary amount of new information on the "character, direction and intentions of al-Qaeda," thanks in large part to the defection of al-Fadl, a senior member of the bin Laden network based in Sudan, in the spring of 1996. In April 1996, President Clinton warned the American people that "terrorism is the enemy of our generation, and we must prevail."[88] Thus, by the end of Clinton's first term, the president and a relatively small number of senior officials such as Clarke, John O'Neill, and Michael Scheuer became convinced that al Qaeda presented a clear and present danger to the United States, but this view was not widely shared in the federal government bureaucracy as a whole. The most frightening aspect of this new threat, therefore, "was the fact that almost no one took it seriously"[89] in the U.S. government.

Chapter 6

Too Little Too Late: Clinton's Growing Fears about al Qaeda and the Long Shadow of the Somalia Syndrome

During its second term in office, the Clinton administration steadily increased its efforts to address the threat of al Qaeda. By 1996, President Clinton and a small number of senior administration figures had recognized that al Qaeda was an ominous danger to the United States and its interests. This new threat perception indicated that the Clinton administration's thinking on security had partially developed beyond the narrow state-centric confines of the Somalia Syndrome it had embraced at the end of 1993. Such foreign policy learning, however, was a necessary—but not sufficient—condition for formulating an effective strategic response to the looming al Qaeda threat. From the mid-1990s, Clinton embarked on an active public campaign to explain that the terrorist threat was serious, an effort that grew in intensity after al Qaeda suicide bombers attacked the U.S. embassies in Tanzania and Kenya on August 7, 1998. While the Clinton administration swiftly retaliated with cruise missile strikes against al Qaeda targets in Afghanistan and Sudan, and secretly authorized the CIA to use all means necessary to neutralize Osama bin Laden and his associates, it did not make counterterrorism the top U.S. national security priority.

Despite the belief at the top levels of the administration that the United States was at war with al Qaeda, a number of factors served to blur the focus at the strategic policy level. These included more conventional foreign policy concerns like NATO enlargement and stability in Europe, stubborn resistance within the U.S. government bureaucracy, and a hostile domestic arena in which a Republican-controlled Congress questioned many aspects of Clinton's foreign policy, particularly when the president's warnings about the growing al Qaeda threat in 1998 coincided with the political fallout from the Lewinsky scandal. By the time Clinton left office, bin Laden was still free, but his administration had demonstrated "an evolving awareness"[1] of the al Qaeda threat. President Clinton had greatly increased funding for counterterrorism and publicly identified al Qaeda as a major enemy of the United States in the post–Cold War era, a point he strongly emphasized to President-elect George W. Bush during the political transition.

This chapter unfolds in five stages. The first part considers the changing nature of U.S. foreign policy during the Clinton administration's second term and its partial recognition of a new security environment, including the threat posed by al Qaeda. The second section explores the gathering momentum of al Qaeda's jihad against the United States. The third part examines the Clinton administration's response to the al Qaeda terrorist challenge. The fourth section shows that while the Clinton administration had moderated the Somalia Syndrome, it had not overcome it, and this limited the administration's ability to deal effectively with the increasing al Qaeda threat. Finally, the concluding section considers why the Clinton administration was politically reluctant to make the struggle against al Qaeda the new number one priority for U.S. national security policy. Amongst other things, the Clinton administration was wary of diminishing, in the eyes of a hostile Republican Congress, the national interest stipulation associated with its post-Mogadishu criteria for international engagement.

CLINTON'S "NEW THINKING" ON FOREIGN POLICY

With the winning of a second term, President Clinton began to embrace a more active and confident foreign policy. In some ways, the 1996 election victory was a vindication of the administration's softening stance toward the Somalia Syndrome. In Bosnia and Rwanda, the most important lesson learned by the Clinton administration was that America's failure to lead in such places not only contributed to international inaction but also damaged Washington's global standing in the process.[2] In Bosnia, the fact that it took bold military action by America and NATO in 1995 to finally stop the civil war only served to reinforce this lesson. At the same time, it did not escape the attention of the Clinton administration that intervention in Bosnia had divided the Republican Party—the Republican presidential nominee, Bob Dole, basically supported Clinton's approach to Bosnia during the 1996 election[3]—and so the domestic political benefits of forceful foreign policy leadership in some internal conflicts could not be underestimated.

There were other reasons for the second-term Clinton administration to be forward-leaning in the global context. By mid-decade, the information revolution, growth in global free trade, and the U.S. consumer-spending boom had transformed the recessionary economic context, which had affected the election of 1992.[4] "It's the economy, stupid!" had been Clinton's rallying slogan that year, and although his initial focus on domestic and economic issues in office sometimes led to presidential neglect of crucial foreign policy problems like Somalia in 1993, Clinton had consistently argued that America's ability to exercise global leadership depended on sustained economic recovery. International economic measures such as the North American Free Trade Agreement (NAFTA) in 1993 and the Mexican financial bailout package in 1995 seemed to gradually confirm what Clinton had always said—that globalization served the American national interest, because the huge American free-market economy would disproportionately benefit from the removal of trade blocks, tariff barriers, border controls, and other impediments to "openness."[5] With the retreat of economic decline talk in the United States, the Clinton White House seemed poised to promote its vision of the United States' role in the world.

In addition, significant changes to Clinton's foreign policy team after his reelection in 1996 foreshadowed an expanded presidential role. Madeleine Albright replaced Warren Christopher as Secretary of State. During her time at the UN, Albright had been critical of the Pentagon's lukewarm attitude toward humanitarian intervention, but had also successfully spearheaded an effort by the Clinton administration to oust Boutros-Ghali as Secretary General of the United Nations in 1996.[6] Sandy Berger, a close political associate of President Clinton, succeeded Anthony Lake at the White House as National Security Advisor. Meanwhile William Cohen, a retired Republican senator, replaced William Perry as Secretary of Defense, an appointment that was intended to maximize bipartisan support for Clinton's security policy in a Republican controlled Congress.

It was the concept of indispensable nation that most symbolized the newfound confidence and mood of the second Clinton administration in the international arena. Unlike some previous formulations used to conceptualize post–Cold War U.S. foreign policy under Clinton—"assertive multilateralism," "democratic enlargement," and "engagement and enlargement"—the term indispensable nation was both diagnostic and prescriptive. That is, the concept was a description of a world in which few international problems could be solved without the active participation of the sole superpower, the United States. It was also a calculus to rally Americans behind an activist global role that entailed responsibility and, at times, sacrifice.[7] The concept first surfaced during Clinton's 1996 presidential campaign and thereafter was used quite frequently by the president and Albright. It appeared to be a concept eminently suited to the age of globalization, a technologically driven process to reconfigure the international economic and political order in ways deemed consistent with the United States' national interests. According to Clinton, the likely result of deepening globalization was political liberalization: "In the new century, liberty will spread by cell phone and cable modem."[8] Thus, there

seemed to be a working presumption on the part of the Clinton administration that the United States "owned" globalization. For some inside and
outside the administration, it was tempting to think the indispensable
nation was also the independent nation. The United States might be
needed by others, but it did not need others for its own security.

But if Clinton believed America might be indispensable, he did not
believe America was invulnerable. By 1996, President Clinton took the
threat of al Qaeda to the United States seriously. He had read Benjamin
Barber's 1995 book on the twin challenges of *Jihad and McWorld* and saw
the emergence of transnational terrorist groups like al Qaeda as sympto-
matic of the basic tension between the competing forces of integration
and fragmentation in a fast globalizing world. Clinton told his aides:
"You can't have an integrated world without being vulnerable to organized assholes."[9] In August 1996, Clinton described international terrorism as "an equal-opportunity destroyer, with no respect for borders."[10] In
the same year, Clinton acknowledged "that while we can defeat terrorists, it will be a long time before we defeat terrorism. America will remain
a target because we are uniquely present in the world, because we act to
advance peace and democracy, because we have taken a tougher stand
against terrorism, and because we are the most open society on earth."[11]

In a sense, President Clinton was right. His administration had begun
to "toughen" its counterterrorism policy even before the second term com-
menced. But the policy had a lot of ground to make up. Osama bin Laden's
al Qaeda network had been targeting the United States since 1992. On
September 9, 1996, Clinton formally requested $1.097 billion from Congress
for counterterrorism. The request was approved the following month. The
largest single allocations in this package were made in the areas of baggage
screening, which was allocated $91 million to enhance detection technology
at U.S. airports, and Federal Bureau of Investigation (FBI) staffing (almost
$92 million).[12] In 1997, the Director of the CIA, George Tenet, claimed his
organization was "on a war footing" against al Qaeda.[13] At roughly the
same time, the Counterterrorism Security Group (CSG) was developing
plans to detain or "snatch" important terrorist figures such as bin Laden. In
1997, the CSG did succeed in snatching Mir Amal Kansi from Pakistan.
Kansi, it should be recalled, was the al Qaeda agent responsible for the
attack at a CIA gatehouse in Langley, Virginia, in 1993 that killed three people.[14] To intensify the effort against the al Qaeda leadership, the United
States and Saudi Arabia formed a joint intelligence committee to share
information on the activities and operations of bin Laden.[15]

Furthermore, the international terrorist threat obtained a new institutional expression within the Clinton administration. In May 1998, Clinton
issued two new PDDs (PDD-62 and PDD-63) on counterterrorism and
named Clarke America's national coordinator for security, infrastructure
protection, and counterterrorism.[16] In theory, Clarke's appointment as the

United States' "counterterrorism czar" would mobilize new bureaucratic resources as the U.S. government's effort against terrorism, sprawled over forty separate agencies, would now for the first time be coordinated by one person. Then, in the spring and summer of 1998, bin Laden was secretly indicted by a New York federal grand jury on charges of murdering Americans in Somalia in 1993 and in Riyadh in 1995.[17] Thereafter, the CIA was authorized by the U.S. government to conduct a snatch operation to put bin Laden on trial in New York. However, attempts by both CIA agents and local Afghans employed by the CIA to arrange an opportunity to snatch the al Qaeda leader came to nothing.

THE GATHERING MOMENTUM OF AL QAEDA'S JIHAD AGAINST THE UNITED STATES

Nevertheless, despite these new counterterrorist measures, the Clinton administration did not pursue a strategy that was commensurate with the growing threat that America faced from al Qaeda. During this period, Osama bin Laden repeatedly declared war against the United States. In an Arabic-language TV interview in February 1997, the al Qaeda leader said: "If someone can kill an American soldier, it is better than wasting time on other matters."[18] Almost exactly a year later on February 23, 1998, bin Laden issued another fatwa, which for the first time, publicly extended the military struggle against civilians. Amongst other things, the edict said: "The ruling to kill the Americans and their allies—civilian and military—is an individual duty for every Muslim who can do it."[19]

Then, in bin Laden's last war declaration before the 9/11 attacks, the al Qaeda leader gave a press conference in May 1998 at Khost, Afghanistan, in which he reiterated his determination to pursue a jihad against what he called "the Crusaders and the Jews." He discussed "bringing the war home to America" at the press conference and anticipated this campaign would "have a successful result in killing Americans and getting rid of them."[20] Bin Laden also confirmed at the Khost conference that al Qaeda's fatwa against the United States and its allies was backed by the International Islamic Front, a new organization that al Qaeda formed with other Islamist groups, including the Egyptian Islamic Jihad.[21]

Such rhetoric was backed by a steady escalation of violent attacks by al Qaeda or allied organizations. On September 18, 1997, *Gama'at al-Islamiyah* (IG), a terrorist group linked to al Qaeda, attacked a tour bus near a museum in Cairo and killed nine German tourists and one Egyptian.[22] Nearly two months later, on November 17, the IG organization launched its most deadly attack, at the Hatshepsut Temple near Luxor, Egypt. Altogether, the IG terrorists murdered fifty-eight foreign tourists and four Egyptians, and wounded twenty-six other tourists, in the assault. The IG terrorists left leaflets at the scene demanding the release of their spiritual leader, Sheikh Rahman, from his U.S. prison. Rahman had been imprisoned for his alleged involvement in the 1993 bombing of the World Trade building in New York.[23]

However, while the Clinton administration increased its efforts to address the al Qaeda threat, it did not make this effort a major foreign policy priority. In part, this was because American governments had never viewed terrorism as a first-tier threat, and consequently the country lacked the organization and the laws to deal with it in that way.[24] Moreover, the Clinton administration was probably wary of the political risks of emphasizing the al Qaeda threat at a time when there were apparently other important and often more conventional foreign policy issues to consider, and when a Republican-dominated Congress was quick to question President Clinton's foreign policy judgment.

Clinton believed that one of his most important foreign policy tasks was "to finish the unfinished business of leaving the Cold War behind."[25] That meant putting in place political arrangements in Europe to ensure that the continent would never again threaten the national security of the United States and its allies. As part of this agenda, the Clinton administration launched a major effort to enlarge NATO in July 1997 by inviting three former Eastern bloc states, Poland, Hungary, and the Czech Republic, to join the alliance in the face of considerable opposition from Boris Yeltsin's government in Russia and prominent U.S. critics. In many ways, NATO enlargement was Clinton's boldest foreign policy initiative. It certainly caused some controversy. Despite efforts to placate Russian opposition, the Yeltsin government essentially took the view that the Clinton administration was using NATO to entrench its own hegemony while simultaneously shutting Russia out from Central and Eastern Europe. George Kennan, the original architect of the American Cold War strategy of containment, was even more scathing. He argued that NATO expansion "would be the most fateful error of American policy in the whole post-Cold War era."[26]

But Clinton and his team saw an expanded NATO, with new members from behind the old Iron Curtain, as the vehicle for the creation of a peaceful, united, and democratic Europe. And many Eastern European states were very keen to join to permanently forestall the possibility of Russia's seeking once again to extend its influence over the region. Moreover, the idea of NATO enlargement won substantial Republican support in Washington. Senator Richard Lugar (R-IN) was an influential supporter, as were some former Bush officials, including the Secretary of State, James Baker. It was apparent to the Clinton administration that NATO enlargement had bipartisan appeal in Washington. The liberal internationalists in the Democratic Party liked using a multilateral institution to help anchor the fledgling democracies of Central and East Europe.[27] On the other hand, many hard-line conservatives, such as Senator Jesse Helms (R-NC), distrusted Russia and wanted NATO to consolidate what they saw as Cold War victory by extending security to the likes of Poland, the Czech Republic, and Hungary.

Another international issue that preoccupied the Clinton administration was its continuing confrontation with Saddam Hussein's regime in Iraq. Since Clinton had entered office, Hussein had been a constant problem for U.S. policymakers. He frequently challenged obligations placed on him by UN resolutions at the end of the first Gulf War in 1991 and sought to weaken, as best he could, the international support that had underpinned them. Confronted with this pattern of defiance, the Clinton administration opted for a policy of containment toward Hussein's "rogue" state. Over a period of five years, the U.S.–Iraq relationship was characterized by unending diplomatic conflict and periodic American military strikes. In September 1996, for example, President Clinton broke off from political campaigning to authorize a military assault, Operation Desert Strike, involving the use of forty-four missiles against Iraqi air defense sites and command-and-control facilities to the north and south of Baghdad after Hussein sent his troops against Kurdish dissidents in Irbil, the UN-endorsed sanctuary in northern Iraq.[28]

As Hussein's defiance continued, Clinton's containment policy became a subject for intense political scrutiny in the United States. A prominent critic was Paul Wolfowitz, formerly a senior Pentagon official during the Bush administration. In 1996, Wolfowitz said that Clinton's containment policy did little to address the international threat emanating from Hussein's unconventional weapons program, and contended that the only way to deal with this problem was to move from a policy of containment to one of regime change.[29] This hawkish view gathered impetus in 1997 with the formation of a new neoconservative think tank, the Project for a New American Century (PNAC).

The PNAC became highly influential within Republican circles during Clinton's second term and drew heavily on a Defense Planning Guidance (DPG) document written in 1992 by staff working for the then-Secretary for Defense Dick Cheney.[30] Among other things, the PNAC advocated the active pursuit of U.S. global primacy in the post–Cold War era and supported the use of preemptive military force against possible adversaries. In January 1998, the PNAC sent an open letter to Clinton on Iraq saying that the containment policy was "dangerously inadequate" and calling on the White House to embrace the idea of overthrowing Hussein's regime. If Hussein acquired weapons of mass destruction, the letter argued, he would pose a threat to American troops in the region, to Israel, to the moderate Arab states, and to the supply of oil to the West.[31] The signers of the letter included Donald Rumsfeld, Paul Wolfowitz, Richard Perle, and former Clinton CIA Director James Woolsey. In May 1998, the PNAC issued a second open letter on Iraq, calling on congressional leaders to use U.S. military power to force regime change in Baghdad. In autumn 1998, with Hussein showing few signs of being disciplined by containment, President Clinton, amid growing signs of Congressional disquiet, signed the Iraq Liberation Act, a measure that formalized the goal of regime change and authorized nearly $100 million in government funds to support the Iraqi opposition.[32]

In addition, and not unrelated to these foreign policy considerations, the Clinton administration was conscious that a largely hostile Republican Party dominated Congress. In the circumstances, there were political limits to how far the Clinton team was prepared to go in publicly redefining U.S. national security policy to counter the al Qaeda threat. Given the mood on Capitol Hill, the Clinton administration probably calculated that making counterterrorism its highest national security priority could be politically dangerous. And it was the need to maintain domestic support that best explains the continuation of policies that seemed to be at odds or contrary with Clinton's stated concerns about al Qaeda.

First, the Clinton administration's skeptical attitude toward the UN certainly did not help America mobilize international opinion against the threat of transnational terrorism. The days of a Republican U.S. president describing the UN as the center of a New World Order had long gone. For Clinton and his advisers, the UN had simply not lived up to expectations in the post–Cold War period. They continued to peddle the self-serving notion that the UN was somehow responsible for the U.S. failure in Somalia; and the experience of U.S. intervention in Bosnia in 1995 had only cemented the Clinton administration's inclination to look to NATO for multilateral support when it was required for peace operations.[33]

At the same time, the Clinton administration had few reservations about ousting Boutros-Ghali as UN Secretary and having Kofi Annan selected as his replacement in 1996. The Clinton administration also opposed or expressed caution about major UN human rights initiatives such as the 1997 Ottawa Treaty banning antipersonnel landmines and the establishment of the International Criminal Court (ICC) in 1998. Nor was the Clinton administration prepared to confront the U.S. Congress over paying America's arrears to the UN.[34] By the late 1990s, the country with the world's largest economy owed the UN nearly $1 billion, and the Republican Congress would not agree to pay off this debt unless the UN reformed itself. While Clinton's UN stance may have served the purpose of placating his domestic conservative opponents in Washington, many of whom viewed the UN as a major threat to U.S. sovereignty, it fueled a perception of "American heavy-handedness, arrogance and unilateralism" on the world stage.[35]

Second, Clinton's policy toward the Middle East seemed to be strangely divorced from his concern about the growing threat of al Qaeda.

Since the signing of the historic Oslo Accords at the White House in 1993, when the PLO and Israel formally recognized each other and embraced a "land for peace" deal, the Clinton administration virtually monopolized the role of "honest broker" in the search for a Middle East peace settlement. Officially, the Clinton administration viewed its role as helping facilitate the handover of occupied territories in the West Bank and the Gaza strip to Palestinian control. It also envisaged that Jerusalem would eventually be both the capital of both Israel and an independent Palestinian state. But in practice the Clinton administration combined the role of mediator with staunch support for one of the parties to this territorial dispute—namely, Israel.[36]

With an eye on the powerful Israeli lobby in the United States and mindful of their support in the 1992 presidential election, the Clinton team rarely voted against Israel in the UN or put pressure on Israeli governments to modify their policy of establishing thousands of new Jewish settlements in the occupied territories. The settlement policy, which accelerated during the time of Benjamin Netanyahu's coalition government (1996–1999), seemed to many observers to be a violation of the Oslo Accords. At the same time, the Clinton administration provided more than $2 billion in economic and military aid to Israel per annum. There was no comparable support for the Palestinians who lived under Israeli occupation. Not surprisingly, many Palestinians came to question the Clinton administration's credentials as an "honest broker" in the peace process. It seemed as if Washington were continuing to tolerate Israeli repression of Palestinians while paying lip service to the pursuit of Palestinian rights.[37] And al Qaeda was not slow to try and exploit the sense of outrage and perceived injustice that was common in the occupied territories. In interviews during 1997 and 1998, bin Laden said, amongst other things, that the United States had "committed acts that are extremely unjust, hideous, criminal, whether directly or through its support of the Israeli occupation of the Land of the Prophet's Night Journey [Palestine]."[38]

Third, despite mounting evidence that al Qaeda was active in Somalia, the Clinton administration showed no inclination that it wanted to get involved again in this failed state. While the Somaliland and Puntland regions in the north had obtained a semblance of stability, much of southern Somalia remained in the grip of localized violence, especially in and around Mogadishu, the former capital.[39] Various clan-based groups, as well as al Itihaad vied to extend their control in the country. Amid this turmoil, it was largely left to Ethiopia, a close ally of the United States, and a country directly affected by the jihadist activities of al Itihaad, to launch a number of incursions to reduce the threat of this Islamist group. Starting in August 1996, Ethiopian troops moved across the border to target al Qaeda–supported al Itihaad camps in southwest Somalia and then proceeded to occupy Dolo and Luuq in Somalia's Gedo region for most of 1997, and also Bula Hawa, in the same region, in August 1998.[40] In the course of these interventions, Ethiopia substantially eroded the military capabilities of al Itihaad and claimed to capture a number of "Afghan Arabs," financed by Osama bin Laden, who were serving with al Itihaad.[41]

But although al Itihaad suffered military reversals at the hands of Ethiopia, this did not end al Qaeda's role in Somalia. Thanks to information provided to the CIA by al-Fadl, a senior member of the al Qaeda network who defected in 1996, and a number of other sources, Washington now had available a much clearer picture of the al Qaeda–Somalia connection.[42] In a CNN interview with Peter Arnett in March 1997, bin Laden said: "With God's grace, Muslims over there [Somalia] cooperated with some Arab mujahidin who were in Afghanistan. They participated with their brothers in Somalia against the American occupation troops and killed large numbers of them. The American administration was aware of that."[43] Several years after the departure of U.S. and UN forces from Somalia, it was reported that al Qaeda's presence in the country had steadily risen to more than 400 fighters.[44] Moreover, after Ethiopia's cross-border raids against al Itihaad, bin Laden sent a number of his senior lieutenants to Somalia to "assess the situation."[45] Among those sent were Odeh, Ahmed Mohammed, and the IG's Mustafa Hamza, Saleh, and Khalfan. They arrived via Nairobi, which had been used as a support station for al Qaeda personnel going to Somalia since 1992. During a seven-month stay in Somalia in 1997, Khalfan assisted at an Islamist training camp at Gedo and later recalled "how he saw things similar to what he had seen in Afghanistan, the light weapons, handguns, rifles, surface to air missiles and rocket launchers."[46]

In the wake of the visits by senior al Qaeda operatives, the militarily weakened al Itihaad adopted a new strategy. Apparently on the recommendation of Osama bin Laden, al Itihaad joined with two other organizations—the Western Somali Liberation Front (WSLF) and the Somali Peoples' Liberation Front (SPLF)—to form an Islamist grouping called the United Front for the Liberation of Western Somalia (UF).[47] At the same time, Sheikh Aweys, the leader of al Itihaad, attempted to distance his organization from acts of terrorism in Ethiopia by announcing in late 1997 that henceforth al Itihaad would function as a political party.[48] Such a move was probably intended to make al Itihaad less a target of the Ethiopian army. In any event, Sheikh Aweys became a central figure of an Islamic court in western Mogadishu in 1998 that came to resemble less a court than a heavily armed military base. These measures, along with the provision of al Qaeda financial and military support for the UF, not only helped the Islamist groups in Somalia survive the Ethiopian onslaught but also ensured that they "regained their strength."[49] As an upshot, al Qaeda had consolidated and expanded its foothold in Somalia, and created a possible base for staging terrorist attacks in the wider Horn of Africa region.

CLINTON'S "LONG STRUGGLE" AGAINST AL QAEDA

The costs of the Clinton's administration's serious but limited response to the al Qaeda threat were soon made plain. On August 7, 1998—the anniversary of the arrival of American troops in Saudi Arabia in 1990—al Qaeda agents attacked the U.S. embassies in Nairobi, Kenya, and Dar es Salaam, Tanzania, with suicidal truck bombings within minutes of each other; twelve Americans died and seven were wounded, while 291 Africans were killed and nearly 5,100 were wounded. Osama bin Laden publicly praised the courage of the suicide bombers, describing them as "real men" who had "managed to rid the Islamic nation of disgrace. We highly respect them and hold them in the highest esteem."[50]

The terrorist attacks in Kenya and Tanzania involved years of careful preparation and were clearly linked to the al Qaeda presence in Somalia. It is striking that a number of the main players in the al Qaeda attacks on the U.S. embassies had either participated in the fighting against the United States and UN in Somalia in 1993 or provided significant training assistance to General Aideed's faction and al Itihaad both during and after the U.S.–UN operation in the country. The players in question included Odeh, Howaida, Fazul Abdullah Mohammed, Saleh, Khalfan Mohammed, Mustafa Fadhil, and Ali Mohammed. Somalia was an important link in the connection between al Qaeda and the 1998 terrorist attacks.[51]

Because al Qaeda wanted to target Somalia in the early 1990s, they decide to set up a support station in Nairobi. Having established an operational cell in Nairobi, al Qaeda had a network in place that would be used to target two U.S. embassies in East Africa. Planning for the 1998 attacks began when the United States was still involved in Somalia. A statement in a U.S. court by Egyptian Islamic Jihad (EIJ) operative, Ali Mohammed, was illuminating: "In late 1993, I was asked by bin Laden to conduct surveillance of American, British, French and Israeli targets in Nairobi. Among the targets I did surveillance for was the American embassy in Nairobi, the U.S. AID Building in Nairobi, the U.S. Agricultural Office Nairobi, the French Cultural Center and French Embassy."[52] Later, after Ali Mohammed returned to Khartoum with the photographs, "bin Laden looked at the picture of the American embassy and pointed to where a truck could go as a suicide bomber."[53]

Following the terrorist attacks in East Africa, the U.S. intelligence community soon discovered evidence that implicated al Qaeda in these bombings. Within days of the attacks, more than 300 FBI agents arrived in Nairobi. Forensic experts from the Bureau examined the rubble for bomb residue, while other FBI agents, working alongside their Kenyan counterparts, questioned hundreds of witnesses, including those in hospital beds in Nairobi—where Rashid Daoud al-Owali a Saudi national traveling on a false Yemeni passport, was located.[54] Suspected of being directly involved in the Nairobi bomb plot, al-Owali was flown to New York, where further questioning revealed links with the al Qaeda organization. This lead, along with additional evidence uncovered by the FBI and the CIA, convinced President Clinton "that these bombings were planned, financed and carried out by the organization bin Laden leads."[55]

On August 20, the Clinton administration decided to retaliate. Describing Osama bin Laden as "perhaps the preeminent organizer and financier of international terrorism in the world today," President Clinton ordered a cruise missile strike on al Qaeda training camps in Afghanistan and on a pharmaceutical factory in Sudan, associated with the bin Laden network, said to be "involved in the production of materials for chemical weapons." The U.S. military strikes were a kind of symmetrical response to the attacks of bin Laden's group on two American embassies. In a speech to the American nation justifying the attacks, Clinton said the "risks from inaction to America and the world would be far greater than action."[56] He acknowledged that the terrorism of the bin Laden network had a bloody history: "In recent years, they killed American, Belgian and Pakistani peacekeepers in Somalia. They plotted to assassinate the president of Egypt and the Pope. They planned to bomb six United States 747s over the Pacific." Clinton added that these terrorists also gunned down German tourists in Egypt. Thus, America's encounter with terrorism did not begin with the bombing of U.S. embassies in Africa. By striking at countries like Afghanistan and Sudan "that persistently host terrorists," the U.S. was taking "an uncompromising stand" in what Clinton said would be "a long, ongoing struggle" against "fanatics and killers who wrap murder in the cloak of righteousness."[57]

As well as taking retaliatory steps, President Clinton signed a confidential executive order on August 20 that expanded the authority of the CIA to use all means necessary to neutralize the bin Laden group. That was the first of a series of four presidential authorizations over the next three years that gradually enhanced the powers of the CIA to use lethal force against the al Qaeda leader and his lieutenants.[58] The administration also took steps to combat al Qaeda's financial network and subsequently extended some sanctions to the Taliban regime in Afghanistan for hosting the al Qaeda leadership. After the Africa embassy bombings, the Clinton administration, according to Berger, viewed al Qaeda "as the dominant threat"[59] to the United States and "was actively considering military strikes directed at Osama bin Laden and al Qaeda."[60]

Between 1998 and 2000, Berger held meetings with dozens of Principals, the group of officials responsible for policy recommendations to President Clinton, on al Qaeda. Meanwhile, Clarke requested three emergency meetings of the President and the Principals to consider cruise missile strikes on buildings in which bin Laden was believed to be located at the time. On each of these occasions, however, Tenet recommended that the intelligence was not of sufficient quality to be considered "actionable."[61]

At the same time, the Clinton administration pursued efforts on the law enforcement front. CIA agents went to Afghanistan and worked with local Afghan CIA operatives in a bid to arrange an opportunity to snatch the al Qaeda leader. But these efforts bore little fruit. One of the constraints as far as the CIA was concerned was the need to avoid killing noncombatants such as bin Laden's wives or his children in a snatch operation. Nor was the Pentagon, under the leadership of the Chairman of the Joint Chiefs of Staff, General Henry H. Shelton, keen on the idea of deploying U.S. Special Forces on the ground to snatch bin Laden. Concerned about the risk of military casualties, General Shelton opposed a Special Forces snatch operation unless it included a combat search-and-rescue capability.[62] The Pentagon's counterproposal was politically unattractive to the president and his senior staff because it would make the snatch operation much bigger and more expensive than they deemed appropriate.

That prompted the Clinton administration to look at another way of finding bin Laden. Rather than depending on human resources to find the al Qaeda leader, Clarke and the CSG endorsed the idea of surveillance by a new unmanned aircraft known as the Predator. The Predator had a long "dwell time" and provided real-time video, even when it was more than 10,000 miles away. While there was resistance to the idea from a number of government agencies, Berger "virtually instructed that the mission be carried out."[63] By September 2000, the Predator began flying over Afghanistan. The United States flew eleven missions and, according to Clarke, the camera eye of the Predator found bin Laden at least twice, although there were no U.S. military capabilities in place to detain or strike him during these clear sightings. By mid-October, weather conditions prevented further operations for the winter, but Clarke asked the U.S. Air Force to fast-track a plan to arm the Predator in preparation for the resumption of flights in late spring of 2001. This plan brought existing bureaucratic divisions over the use of the Predator to a head. Senior officers in the Air Force and CIA resented being instructed by Clarke in this matter and both had budgetary concerns about a project that neither would "own" in the organizational sense. Without the backing of these agencies, the Clinton administration found it was unable to sustain the Predator program against bin Laden. The Predator would not fly again over Afghanistan until September 2001.[64]

Meanwhile, at the end of 1999, the CIA became aware—following the arrest of thirteen members of an al Qaeda cell in Amman, Jordan, and the arrest of an Algerian terrorist at Port Angeles, Washington—of a plot by the bin Laden group to stage numerous simultaneous terrorist attacks in the United States and Jordan on or about the millennium rollover date. A massive CIA and FBI operation was put in place that lasted for about a month. It was worldwide. And it successfully thwarted al Qaeda terrorist attacks during the millennium. However, the experience of the millennium plot reinforced the view, long held by the likes of Clarke and John O'Neill, that there were al Qaeda sleeper cells in the United States. In a post-millennium after-action review commissioned by the Clinton administration, it was concluded that it was necessary to intensify law enforcement activities in the United States "in order to find, to root out and to prevent al Qaeda sleeper cells in the United States."[65]

Rhetorically, the top levels of the Clinton administration continued to press the case that the al Qaeda threat was serious. President Clinton told the UN General Assembly in September 1998 that "all nations must put the fight against terrorism at the top of their agenda." In an internal memo during the same year, Tenet said "we are at war [with al Qaeda]."[66] It was during this period in September 1999 that the U.S. Commission on National Security in the 21st Century identified mass-casualty terrorism on the U.S. homeland as an increasingly likely threat.[67] In early 2000, Clarke addressed all senior FBI supervisors from all offices in the United States, and he did not pull any punches: "Al Qaeda is a worldwide political conspiracy masquerading as a religious sect. . . . These people are smart, many trained in our colleges, and they have a very long view. They think it may take them a century to accomplish their goals, one of which is the destruction of the United States of America. . . . They are our number one enemy and they are amongst us, in your cities. Find them."[68]

Senior FBI officials like Dale Watson and John O'Neill shared Clarke's sense of urgency about the al Qaeda threat. And President Clinton continued to warn about the danger of terrorism. In January 2000, Clinton said: "I predict to you, when most of us are long gone but some time in the next ten to twenty years, the major security threat this country will face will come from the enemies of the nation-state, the narco-traffickers and the terrorists and the organized criminals."[69] By the end of the Clinton administration, spending on counterterrorism had quadrupled from $3 billion in 1993 to $12 billion.[70] Moreover, the reward for information leading to the arrest of bin Laden was raised to $5 million. At the time, it was the highest monetary amount permitted by U.S. federal law for a wanted person.

Thus, during Clinton's second term, it became apparent there was a group of people from the White House, the CIA, the FBI, the Treasury, and the State Department who were convinced that al Qaeda was a major threat to the United States. This group had grown from 1995 to 1998, but they still only constituted a "handful of people in each of these departments." According to Clarke, al Qaeda threat advocates "had a very hard time with . . . their internal audience." Many of them faced considerable opposition within their departments to their views on the al Qaeda danger. They "were accused of grandstanding. They were accused of exaggerating the threat. They were accused of empire-building, not playing with the team."[71] In short, as far as the al Qaeda threat was concerned, there were more skeptics than believers within the ranks of the U.S. federal government.

While the Clinton team understood that the threat was a serious one, it did not muster anything like the political effort that was required to build an interagency consensus around the idea that confronting al Qaeda was now one of America's top national security objectives. President Clinton appeared reluctant to exert that kind of leadership commitment on the al Qaeda issue. Despite the bombing of U.S. embassies in East Africa, the Clinton administration was either unable or unwilling to formulate an al Qaeda strategy that was commensurate with the level of concern increasingly expressed at senior government levels in Washington.

The dangers of this strategic mismatch were further highlighted on October 12, 2000, when two suicide bombers from al Qaeda launched an assault on the USS *Cole* in Yemen's Aden harbor. The attack left seventeen U.S. sailors dead and thirty-nine wounded in what was the most deadly attack on a U.S. warship since World War II.[72] The USS *Cole* was so severely damaged that it cost the U.S. taxpayer $250 million to make the necessary repairs to return the ship to active service. Among other things, the episode was an illustration of the patience and dogged determination of the bin Laden network to strike at the United States. Ten months earlier, at the beginning of 2000, two al Qaeda agents had made a similar but unsuccessful attempt to attack USS *The Sullivans,* stationed off the coast of Aden. On that occasion, the motorboat carrying the would-be suicide bombers was so laden with explosives that it sank before it could close within striking distance of its target.[73] However, the brutal attack on the USS *Cole* showed that al Qaeda was a terrorist organization that had the capacity to learn from its mistakes.

Nevertheless, the Clinton administration was not able to formulate a swift military response to this latest act of terrorism. At an emergency CSG meeting called in the White House Situation Room immediately after the USS *Cole* attack, there was deadlock on what to recommend to the Principals. The meeting was attended by Clarke, Michael Sheehan (the Coordinator for Counterterrorism in the State Department), Cofer Black (the CIA Director's Special Assistant for Counterterrorism), Brian Sheridan (Assistant Secretary of Defense for Special Operations), and Dale Watson (Head of Counterterrorism at the FBI). While Clarke and Sheehan had little doubt that bin Laden's network was behind the attack on the USS *Cole*, Black and Watson wanted to reserve judgment until more evidence was available.[74]

Later, Clarke and Sheehan attended a meeting with the Principals to discuss America's response to the USS *Cole* attack. Participants included William Cohen, George Tenet, Madeleine Albright, the Attorney General, Janet Reno, the Vice President's National Security Advisor, Leon Fuerth, and Deputy National Security Advisor, James Steinberg. To the immense frustration of Clarke, the Principals rejected his recommendation that the United States promptly retaliate by punishing the Taliban regime in Afghanistan and "blow up" the al Qaeda training camps in that country. Evidently, Albright and Reno, backed by the CIA and FBI, believed it would have been politically and diplomatically unwise to retaliate militarily without compelling evidence that al Qaeda was culpable for the attack. However, it seemed immediately clear to Clarke and Sheehan that bin Laden's network was directly implicated.[75] Among other things, U.S. intelligence knew that al Qaeda had an active presence in Yemen, it had attempted a similar assault on a U.S. warship in January 2000, and one of the suicide bombers, Abd al-Muhsin al-Taifi, was a Yemeni wanted in connection with the 1998 bombing of the U.S. embassy in Nairobi, Kenya. The CIA and the FBI did not reach a similar conclusion until after Clinton had left office.

Interestingly, Cohen opposed a retaliatory strike for slightly different reasons. The chief lesson that the Defense Department seemed to glean from the assault on the USS *Cole* was the need for much greater security for its ships or what was often called "force protection." According to Sheehan, Cohen's views were perfectly in tune with those of the top uniformed officers and Clinton's political appointees at the Pentagon. Clarke and Sheehan were exasperated and angered by what they saw as the Pentagon's weak response to the attack on the USS *Cole*: "What's it going to take to get them to hit al Qaeda in Afghanistan? Does al Qaeda have to attack the Pentagon?"[76] As an upshot, the Principals voted against Clarke's retaliation plan by seven to one. In the circumstances, the Clinton administration opted for a diplomatic response to the bombing of the USS *Cole* in Yemen. It was in the eyes of some administration officials a dangerously minimalist approach to a real and growing threat from al Qaeda.

When Clinton left office in January 2001, Osama bin Laden was still at liberty to continue his jihad against the United States. According to Richard Clarke, "the President didn't get what he wanted. The President wanted him [Osama bin Laden] dead."[77] Part of Clinton's frustration was due to the formidable obstacles facing the task of obtaining reliable intelligence about the whereabouts of bin Laden. First, al Qaeda was a decentralized organization, which made external analysis of its activities difficult. It was not as hierarchical as a nation-state institution or intelligence agency.

At the same time, al Qaeda cooperated with a number of other Islamist terrorist groups, a fact that sometimes complicated efforts by American intelligence organizations to assess precisely the extent to which al Qaeda was implicated in particular terrorist activities. Second, because al Qaeda was a fundamentalist but sophisticated and well resourced organization, it was very hard for any intelligence agent of the United States, or even of an allied country like Jordan or Israel, to penetrate the al Qaeda organization.[78] Third, U.S. intelligence organizations like the CIA or the FBI often lacked the linguistic capabilities to rapidly access intelligence derived by technical means. For example, Clarke noted that wiretap recordings of conversations of al Qaeda members or suspected al Qaeda members were sometimes not transcribed for weeks because of a shortage of Arabic, Farsi, or Pashto translators.[79]

But that was not the whole story. While the top levels of Clinton's administration had shown a growing awareness of the ominous danger al Qaeda posed, there had been a political unwillingness in the White House to reshape America's national security strategy to reflect this understanding. In other words, the Clinton team did not feel that it was in a position to take on al Qaeda in a no-holds-barred fashion. Let us now consider why the Clinton administration viewed the al Qaeda challenge in that way.

THE CONSTRAINTS OF THE SOMALIA SYNDROME

From what has been said, it is clear that al Qaeda's attacks on two U.S. embassies in East Africa in 1998 did not prove to be a turning point for American national security policy. In a way, this outcome was surprising. Since the Srebrenica massacre of 1995, the Clinton administration had moderated its "Mogadishu line" approach that failed states were strategically insignificant to the United States, and also increasingly recognized that a transnational terrorist organization, al Qaeda, had emerged as a major threat to the United States in the post–Cold War environment. Moreover, by 1997, the Clinton administration was aware of al Qaeda's involvement in the Black Hawk Down episode of October 1993 and publicly confirmed that connection in a nationwide address to the American people after the traumatic al Qaeda attacks in Nairobi and Dar es Salaam in August 1998.

But instead of seizing the chance to redefine America's security policy, the Clinton administration opted for an "uneasy amalgam" of quietly targeting the bin Laden network and adhering broadly to the so-called lessons of the state-centered Somalia Syndrome. It was a compartmentalized and, at times, contradictory approach that ultimately put domestic political concerns ahead of the urgent need to counter the al Qaeda problem. The fact that al Qaeda was able to launch a devastating attack on the USS

Cole warship two years after the terrorist attacks in East Africa served only to highlight this point.

The continuing imprint of the Somalia Syndrome was evident in a number of ways. First, while the Clinton administration had come to accept that civil wars and nonstate actors could be major international security problems, it maintained that such issues could not be allowed by themselves to determine the United States' broader strategy in the world. As the indispensable nation, the Clinton administration believed that the United States was uniquely placed in the 1990s to shape the international environment rather than simply being shaped by that environment. Thus, in the fall of 1998, when Saddam Hussein, after years of defiance, expelled UN weapons inspectors responsible for overseeing the disestablishment of Iraq's alleged development of weapons of mass destruction, the Clinton administration felt it had no alternative but to reassert its global leadership against a recalcitrant "rogue" state. Launched on December 16, Operation Desert Fox represented the biggest escalation since the first Gulf War.[80] Having formally backed the 1998 Iraq Liberation Act, the Clinton administration felt it was imperative to react vigorously, not least to counter criticisms in the Republican-controlled Congress that it was weak in the face of the Iraq challenge. In the course of four days, U.S. forces, supported by the British Royal Air Force (RAF), hit ninety-seven sites, including weapons research facilities, barracks of the elite Republican Guard, an oil refinery, and seven of Hussein's palaces. Yet Operation Desert Fox relied heavily on the "distant punishment" approach to the use of force that had been favored by the Clinton administration after the 1993 Black Hawk Down episode. Altogether U.S. combat aircraft flew more than 600 sorties; American warships delivered some 330 cruise missiles; and B-52 bombers dispatched another ninety. No American or British aircraft were lost during the operation. Nor were any allied military personnel killed or injured in the campaign.[81]

While the Clinton administration hailed the success of Desert Fox, this bombing seemed to make the Hussein dictatorship even more defiant. The regime in Baghdad refused to allow the return of UN weapons inspectors after the operation and announced that it no longer recognized the no-fly zones established immediately after the first Gulf War. What followed was a series of tit-for-tat exchanges in both the northern and southern no-fly zones. This war of attrition continued through the remaining two years of the Clinton administration. During this period, U.S. forces (sometimes supported by their British allies) deployed some 2,000 bombs and missiles against Iraqi targets. The campaign received little media attention, largely because Iraqi gunners failed to shoot down a single coalition aircraft. If Clinton's policy toward Iraq was a source of reassurance for those concerned about Hussein's regional ambitions, it provided an opportunity for al Qaeda to promote its own agenda. In a

1998 declaration, bin Laden roundly condemned "America's excessive aggression against the people of Iraq" using the Arabian peninsula "as a base" for military operations in Iraq, and claimed that the Americans had killed "over one million" people in the country.[82] Moreover, such actions served "the interests of the petty Jewish state." Bin Laden argued that the Clinton administration's "eagerness to destroy Iraq, the strongest neighbouring Arab state" reflected its desire "to guarantee Israel's survival" and facilitate "the continuation of the brutal Crusader occupation of the [Arabian] Peninsula."[83]

At the same time, Clinton's policy toward the Israeli–Palestinian conflict only served to boost al Qaeda's standing in the Middle East region. In particular, many Palestinians became exasperated and disillusioned with the stalled implementation of the Oslo Accords. The lack of progress reinforced the view among young Palestinians that the Clinton administration had morally failed to distinguish between the plight of the Palestinian victims of occupation and the rights of the Israeli occupying forces. According to Clarke, the Clinton administration understood that if it could "achieve a Middle East peace much of the popular support for al Qaeda and much of the hatred for America would evaporate overnight."[84] But in practice it was only in the middle of Clinton's last year in office that that the U.S. President pushed for a final settlement. On July 11, 2000, President Clinton hosted a Middle East Peace Summit at Camp David between Israeli Prime Minister Ehud Barak and Palestinian Authority Chairman Yasser Arafat.

It was ultimately an unsuccessful effort to negotiate a "final status settlement" to the Israeli–Palestinian conflict. Barak made what Clinton called a very generous offer to Arafat: to form a Palestinian state initially on 100 percent of the Gaza Strip and 73 percent of the West Bank (that is 27 percent less than the Green Line borders which Palestinian negotiators accepted at Oslo for the West Bank) with the prospect in ten to twenty-five years that the West Bank area under Palestinian control would extend to 90–91 percent. But Arafat rejected this offer. He wanted full Palestinian sovereignty over all of the West Bank and the Gaza Strip. The Palestinian negotiators maintained that UN Resolution 242 calls for full Israeli withdrawal from these territories, although Israel disputes that interpretation. In any event, Clinton publicly blamed Arafat for the impasse, a point that caused outrage within the Palestinian community. Shortly after the Camp David summit had collapsed, Ariel Sharon and a delegation of Likud politicians visited the Temple Mount area in Jerusalem, a small part of which includes the Al-Aqsa Mosque. Sharon's visit touched off a wave of violence known as the "second Intifada" which basically destroyed the Clinton administration's hopes for an Israeli–Palestinian peace settlement. Bin Laden praised the Palestinian uprising and observed in an interview the following year: "All that is going on in Palestine for the last 11 months is sufficient to call the wrath of God upon the United States and

Israel."[85] And, in a move that was designed to appeal disgruntled followers of Arafat, the al Qaeda leader vitriolically blamed America for the suffering of the Palestinian population: "You [America] have supported the
Jews in their idea that Jerusalem is their eternal capital, and agreed to
move your embassy there. With your help and under your protection, the
Israelis are planning to destroy the Al-Aqsa mosque. Under the protection
of your weapons, Sharon entered the Al-Aqsa mosque, to pollute it as a
preparation to capture and destroy it."[86]

In addition, the ambivalent response of the Clinton administration to
ethnic conflict in former Yugoslavia reinforced the al Qaeda perception,
held since the Black Hawk Down episode of 1993, that America was
essentially a precious superpower which lacked the ruthless determination to impose itself on its adversaries. According to bin Laden, al Qaeda
fighters in Somalia were "surprised" that after "a little resistance, the
American troops left after achieving nothing."[87] Six years later, President
Clinton's confrontation with the regime of Slobodan Milošević over the
Serbian repression of the largely Albanian population in Kosovo did not
altogether dispel this image.

Although the Dayton Accords had brought some stability to the central
Balkans, ethnic strife escalated in Kosovo, a province of former Yugoslavia
that had enjoyed considerable autonomy before Milošević came to power.
Milošević rescinded Kosovo's autonomy status and used force to quell the
push for independence in the province. This led to an escalation of violence
that had the potential to spread to neighboring countries in the Balkan such
as Macedonia and Albania. For more than a year, U.S. and European envoys
desperately tried to reach an agreement with Milošević under which
NATO troops would serve as peacekeepers, but eventually the Clinton
administration concluded that only force would work. In late March 1998,
the United States and its NATO partners began bombing Serbian air
defenses and other military targets. The bombing campaign was nominally
under NATO control, but was primarily an American operation directed by
a U.S. military commander. It was three months before Milošević capitu-
lated and agreed to accept a NATO peacekeeping force in Kosovo. By that
time, much of the infrastructure of former Yugoslavia was in ruins.

Following Milošević backdown, the Clinton administration could
rightly claim that it had achieved its overriding objective of ending
Milošević's tyranny over the Kosovar minority. In that sense, Washington
and its NATO allies had used military power for humanitarian purposes—
to end a sovereign government's suppression of its own citizens. But such
actions only constituted a partial rehabilitation from the Somalia Syndrome. Lessons from Somalia were very much in evidence in Kosovo. In
purely military terms, the Clinton administration's exclusive reliance on
an air campaign made the conflict with Milošević much harder to win,
particularly when it was signaled in advance to Belgrade. Without ground

forces, NATO could do little to stop Milošević's rampage against Kosovar civilians that had triggered a refugee crisis. In the words of two perceptive observers, it was as if "Kosovo's fate was important enough to go to war for, but not so valuable that the lives of US ground troops should be risked."[88] Certainly, bin Laden sought to capitalize on Washington's extreme reluctance to risk casualties. Commenting on Clinton's reaction to the 1998 East Africa terrorist bombings, the al Qaeda leader said: "This condemnation . . . is meaningless because it comes at a time when Muslim blood is spilled abundantly in Kosovo at the hands of the Serbian butcher, just like it was in Bosnia under the supervision of the United States and its allies."[89]

Two other aspects of the Kosovo campaign would have encouraged the al Qaeda leadership. For one thing, it reaffirmed that the Clinton administration did not trust the UN when it came to matters relating to international security and preferred to work through NATO, where it anticipated much greater freedom of action. Bypassing the UN Security Council certainly avoided the problem of Russia or China vetoing a U.S.-led air campaign against former Yugoslavia. However, by relying on NATO for support the Clinton team seriously weakened the legitimacy of the Kosovo operation in the eyes of the wider international community. In this vein, Lee Hamilton noted that the NATO mandate was no substitute for a United Nations Security Council resolution authorizing intervention. And given al Qaeda's hostility to the United Nations as well as the United States, the distance between these two international actors was a source of satisfaction for the bin Laden network.

Moreover, in the months following the conclusion of the Kosovo campaign, there was a very public disagreement between the United States and many of its European NATO allies over peacekeeping troop levels and who should pay for the reconstruction of the province. The fact that the EU provided over 70 percent of the troops and 80 percent of the budget for Kosovo's reconstruction showed that the Clinton administration still felt it had problems securing broad congressional support for American participation in a major international peace operation in an internal conflict situation. Continuing American concerns about "mission creep" were not lost on the al Qaeda leadership.

Furthermore, the emergence in the late 1990s of a strong consensus amongst conservatives within the Republican-controlled Congress in favor of missile defense buttressed a state-centric approach to international security. For conservative Republicans, President Clinton's public warnings about the growing threat of global terrorism missed the point. They believed that the most urgent threats to American security stemmed from a small number of ballistic missiles in the hands of "rogue" states. Convinced that senior Clinton administration officials and Democrats were ignoring a clear and present danger from regimes like Iran and

North Korea, the Republican Congress mandated two reviews of the intelligence community's work on this threat. The first review, chaired by former CIA Director Robert Gates, found no evidence that the intelligence community had underestimated the missile threat from "rogue" states. The second review, carried out by a nine-man commission headed by Rumsfeld and including Wolfowitz and Woolsey, produced a much starker assessment. It said that foreign assistance and widespread efforts to hide missile development programs from Western intelligence had established conditions under which North Korea, Iran, and Iraq could, with little or no warning, deploy ballistic missiles with ranges long enough to strike parts of the United States.[90]

Such assertions might have been ignored by the Clinton administration had it not been for the fact that shortly after the publication of the Rumsfeld Commission report, North Korea test-fired a missile, the Taepodong 1, that apparently traveled further than any launched by a developing country previously. Consequently, in late March 1999, the U.S. Congress overwhelmingly passed Republican-initiated legislation with a veto-proof majority calling for the deployment of a national missile defense system.[91] For the Clinton administration, the repercussions were significant. Missile defense began to dominate the national security agenda of the administration. In the summer of 1999, President Clinton made a decision on the specifications of the new missile system to be constructed, but he postponed formalizing the decision on construction for another year.

Suffice it to say that missile defense was another source of distraction and frustration for senior figures in the Clinton administration that had come to believe that al Qaeda was the biggest and most dangerous threat to American security.

THE POLITICS OF THE SOMALIA SYNDROME

A question remains. If the Clinton administration had a much better understanding of the al Qaeda danger , particularly after the East Africa terrorist bombings of 1998, why was it unwilling to jettison the constraints of the Somalia Syndrome in dealing with this transnational threat? During its second terms, the Clinton administration tried to combine an intensified covert campaign against the bin Laden network with a state-centered approach to security that was deemed broadly consistent with the "lessons" of Somalia.

From the standpoint of President Clinton, there were strong political reasons to maintain this mixed national security approach in the face of the looming al Qaeda threat. First, the Somalia Syndrome had significantly helped the Clinton presidency recover in domestic political terms from the trauma of Black Hawk Down in October 1993. By learning the 'lessons' of Somalia, the Clinton administration was to project itself internally as a more reliable defender of the American "national interest," and one that was prepared, if necessary, to stand up to international institutions like the UN that had purportedly compromised the country's good name in Somalia. Clinton was always mindful of domestic opinion and was wary, after Somalia, of embracing any foreign policy initiative that could not be robustly defended at home.

Second, the Clinton administration did not believe that it was necessary to abandon the Somalia Syndrome in order to combat the growing threat of bin Laden's terrorist organization. It already successfully moderated the post-Mogadishu criteria in order to deal with conflicts in failed states like Bosnia and Kosovo, and thus there appeared to be scope for covertly dealing with the al Qaeda challenge without the need for redefining the broad thrust of national security strategy.

Third, it would have taken very bold leadership for Clinton to make al Qaeda a top priority for U.S. national security during his second term. If the Clinton administration put into its intelligence estimates what it then knew about al Qaeda's role in the death of the American servicemen who were dragged through the streets of Mogadishu in 1993, it ran the risk of reopening the issue of whether the administration had reacted appropriately to those events. In particular, the Clinton administration probably worried that formally elevating the al Qaeda terrorist threat would further complicate its relations with a Republican dominated Congress. The search for a simple slogan or phrase that would characterize the country's new purpose to counter potential Republican criticisms proved elusive.[92] As it was, America's concerns about the embassy bombings in East Africa were largely overshadowed by the Lewinsky scandal in Washington and the impeachment process that engulfed the Clinton presidency. In fact, many Republicans criticized Clinton's cruise missile retaliation in Afghanistan and Sudan on August 20, 1998, as an attempt to divert domestic opinion in a "wag the dog" fashion. When Clinton told the United Nations in September 1998 "all nations must put the fight against terrorism at the top of our agenda" he conceded "all the television networks [in the United States] were showing the videotape of my grand jury testimony."[93] In the circumstances, Clinton was probably reluctant to push the al Qaeda issue too far because he anticipated he would incur the anger of a Republican Congress that believed supporting Israel, marginalizing Saddam Hussein, and establishing a national missile system were all far more important issues.

Fourth, Clinton's troubled relations with the U.S. military buttressed a conservative approach toward the al Qaeda threat. Because Clinton was criticized as a Vietnam War opponent without a military record, he believed he was limited in his ability to direct the military in his formal capacity as commander in chief. The fact that the Pentagon was extremely reluctant to participate in covert antiterrorist operations against al Qaeda certainly discouraged the Clinton administration from classifying al Qaeda as America's number-one adversary. According to Clarke, the Pentagon was not only skeptical of President Clinton's credentials, but also afflicted by what he termed a "risk-averse culture."

When Clinton requested that the Pentagon conduct a small Special Forces operation in Afghanistan to kill or snatch bin Laden, he encountered a favorite Pentagon tactic: a counteroffer with a proposed operation so large that the president and his senior staff backed down. In contrast, when the Pentagon employed a similar tactic when President Bush (Sr.) requested an armed humanitarian intervention in Somalia, the then-president called the bluff of the military by accepting their offer. The effects of a difficult relationship between President Clinton and the U.S. military on targeting al Qaeda were also compounded by general resistance to counterterrorism within the federal government bureaucracy. Too often, for example, middle-level personnel in the FBI and CIA interpreted the threat of al Qaeda through the lens of fighting jurisdictional turf wars in Washington, D.C.

In summary, by the end of Clinton's second term in office, the administration had learned to moderate its understanding of the "lessons" of Somalia. In the post-Mogadishu phase of U.S. foreign policy, it became apparent to the administration that intrastate challenges in places such as Rwanda, Haiti, and Bosnia could be major international security problems; that the United States could not be seen to do nothing in the face of such challenges; and that if the United States deemed it vital to intervene militarily, it would have to do it on the basis of the distant punishment doctrine. But the learning curve of the Clinton administration was limited. Although a number of senior figures in the administration had become convinced by 1998 that the bin Laden network was America's number-one enemy, the Clinton team was politically reluctant to redefine national security policy to reflect that assessment.

Instead, the Clinton administration opted for a mix of strategies that compartmentalized the targeting of al Qaeda from its other major policy concerns. This meant the administration not only pursued policies toward Iraq, the Israeli–Palestinian conflict, and Kosovo that at times boosted the bin Laden network, but also sometimes deliberately curbed its efforts against bin Laden in order not to do anything that might complicate other apparently more important initiatives such as Clinton's Camp David peace conference in 2000 or the intense air campaign against Milošević's regime in 1999. Moreover, it became clear what the Clinton administration had learned in the struggle with al Qaeda did not readily transmit to the new Bush administration of 2001.

Chapter 7

What Threat? Bush's Retreat to the Mogadishu Line and the Countdown to the 9/11 Attacks

Despite the increasing focus on the al Qaeda threat during the second Clinton administration, there was little sign in the months leading up to September 2001 that the new Bush administration shared that concern. In fact, George W. Bush's experienced foreign policy team had been critical of the Clinton administration's foreign policy. They rejected Clinton's embrace of globalization, belittled global interdependence as "globalony,"[1] and said that the Clinton administration was only too willing to send U.S. troops on "nation-building" operations that lay outside the scope of the national interest. For the first nine months of 2001, the mood in the administration was one of barely veiled triumphalism as President Bush confronted China, minimized the United States' multilateral obligations, and pressed for the establishment of an antimissile defense system to counter the alleged threat of ballistic missile attacks from "rogue" states.[2]

In essence, terrorism was not considered a priority by the Bush administration until 9/11. Yet there was little evidence that the al Qaeda's jihad against the United States was diminishing. From the moment it became apparent that George W. Bush would succeed Bill Clinton as president, the new president received numerous high-level warnings about the imminent danger presented by al Qaeda. These warnings intensified in the summer of 2001. Yet the Bush administration did not seem to be greatly moved by these expressions of alarm. It would be difficult, therefore, to imagine a greater shock for the Bush administration than the terrorist attacks of September 11. According to President Bush, the terrorist attacks on the World Trade Center in New York and the Pentagon in Washington, D.C., "changed the strategic thinking"[3] of the United States. However, the claim that 9/11 had suddenly transformed the international security environment was mistaken.

This chapter proceeds in five stages. The first part charts the foreign policy approach of the Bush administration. The second section examines the response of the new administration to immediate warnings about a deadly al Qaeda threat. The third part considers the continuing al Qaeda offensive against the United States in the pre-9/11 era. The fourth section evaluates the Bush administration's reaction to a second major round of warnings from U.S. intelligence and government agencies in the summer of 2001 about an imminent al Qaeda threat. Finally, the fifth section reflects on the origins of 9/11. The argument that develops in this chapter is that there was a clear casual linkage between the Somalia Syndrome and a permissive security environment for al Qaeda that helped make the events of September 11 possible.

BUSH'S EARLY PREOCCUPATION WITH STATE-CENTERED SECURITY

After eight years in power, the Clinton administration left office with a general sense of alarm about the continuing threat posed by al Qaeda to the United States. The Clinton leadership had gradually come to understand that globalization created enormous transnational security challenges. Yet while the Clinton administration had edged toward the realization in 2000 that interdependence meant that the United States could be "threatened more by another nation's weakness than by its strength,"[4] it had ultimately failed to provide the leadership, in terms of transforming national security policy, to effectively counter the growing threat posed by Islamic extremist groups such as al Qaeda. The Clinton team left the White House without codifying its new thinking about transnational terrorism.

In the 2000 presidential campaign, foreign policy played little part in the proceedings and the issue of terrorism, in particular, did not warrant a mention. Nevertheless, the Bush campaign was advised by a number of foreign policy veterans, and most of these advisers subsequently formed the spine of the foreign policy team that served the new Bush administration. The group included as Secretary of State, General Colin Powell, a former National Security Advisor and former chairman of the Joint Chiefs of Staff; Secretary of Defense Donald Rumsfeld, a former Secretary of Defense under President Ford; National Security Advisor Dr. Condoleezza Rice, a former National Security Council staffer in the first Bush administration; Assistant Secretary of Defense Paul Wolfowitz, a former Undersecretary of Defense for Policy; Assistant Secretary of State Richard Armitage, another former defense official; and Vice President Dick Cheney, former Secretary of Defense (1989–1993).[5] Thus, the Bush administration had considerable experience in the defense area, and it had within its ranks some of the most vociferous critics of Clinton's foreign policy.

To all appearances, the new Bush team seemed to be motivated by an "Anything But Clinton" foreign policy approach.[6] Under Clinton, U.S. foreign policy was deemed by the Bush leadership to be "overambitious" and prone to interventionism. In an article in *Foreign Affairs* in 2000, Dr. Rice said the Clinton administration had allowed the national interest to be superseded by "humanitarian interests" and that its "pursuit of, at best, illusory 'norms' of international behavior have become an epidemic."[7] On this view, the Clinton administration "had overused and under-resourced the armed forces, and sent them on missions which purportedly lay outside the scope of the [American] national interest."[8] For members of the Bush administration like Rice and John Bolton, the Undersecretary of State for Arms Control and International Security (2001–2005), the Somali debacle of 1993 epitomized the failure of Clinton's foreign policy. The fact that Somalia was an international commitment that Clinton inherited from a Republican president did little to shake the new Bush administration's belief that nation-building had no place in U.S. foreign policy: "I don't think our troops ought to be used for what's called nation-building. I think our troops ought to be used to fight and win wars."[9] To this end, George W. Bush pledged to end "open-ended deployments and unclear military missions."[10]

Such statements reflected a fundamental disagreement about the global role of the United States in the post–Cold War era. To Bush and many members of his administration, Clinton's embrace of globalization and his apparent belief in alliances, treaties, and international agreements were hallmarks of a rather naive approach to U.S. foreign policy. It was said to be a case of Prometheus playing pygmy on the international stage.[11] Perhaps because the Republicans had been out of power for eight years, the Bush people tended to play down the transformative impact of globalization, especially in the area of international security. Instead, they believed that U.S. allies and enemies alike would be influenced more by the example of raw American power than what were called "symbolic agreements of questionable value."[12] Thus, the first task of the new administration was to reassert American freedom of action in the international arena. It was evidently assumed that the benefits of reminding the world who had the overwhelming military power far outweighed the cost in terms of America's global popularity.[13]

When President George W. Bush took office in January 2001, there was a clear strengthening of unilateralist tendencies in U.S. foreign policy. Convinced that "power matters," and that security was still fundamentally determined by the military means of sovereign states, the new administration made it plain that it would pursue a "distinctly American internationalism."[14] In practice, this new assertiveness reduced the United States' multilateral obligations and upset both allies and potential adversaries of Washington. Prior to 9/11, the Bush administration renounced the Kyoto Protocol on climate change, "unsigned" the Rome Treaty creating an International Criminal Court, withdrew from the Anti-Ballistic Missile Treaty (ABMT) and rejected the Comprehensive Nuclear Test Ban Treaty (CTBT). At the same time, the early months of the Bush administration's foreign policy were focused on familiar national security priorities such as perceived mischief-making from Russia, strategic competition with China, managing Iraq, and countering the alleged threat of ballistic missile attacks from "rogue" states through the establishment of an antimissile defense system.[15]

It should be added that the Bush administration initially did not view US engagement in the Israeli-Palestinian conflict as a major strategic concern. Critical of what it saw as President Clinton's failure to impose peace on the two parties in 2000, the Bush administration said it would assist, but not insist on, a Middle East peace process. In the face of increasing violence between Israel and the Palestinians in the months prior to the events of 9/11, the Bush administration broadly adhered to a wait-and-see approach that confined itself to encouraging the parties to return to the path of negotiations.[16]

THE BUSH ADMINISTRATION AND EARLY WARNINGS ABOUT THE AL QAEDA THREAT

Before 9/11, there was little evidence to suggest that the Bush administration took the threat of al Qaeda terrorism seriously. According to CIA Director George Tenet, once the Bush administration arrived in Washington, there "was a loss of urgency" about the al Qaeda problem.[17] Certainly, there were numerous high-level efforts to alert the new Bush team to the fact that the bin Laden network represented an immense danger to U.S. security. In December 2000, in the traditional transitional meeting between leaders in the White House, President Clinton warned President-elect Bush that al Qaeda was a huge threat and was determined to strike inside the United States. To emphasize the seriousness of the situation, Clinton informed Bush that: "One of the great regrets of my presidency is that I didn't get him [bin Laden] for you, because I tried to."[18] Further, Sandy Berger also highlighted the al Qaeda threat during a meeting with his successor in the White House, Dr. Rice.[19] Then, about a week before Bush's inauguration, the President-elect, along with Cheney and Rice, attended a CIA briefing given by Tenet and James L. Pavitt, the Deputy Director for Operations (DDO), who headed the agency's clandestine service and covert operations. Tenet and Pavitt told Bush that bin Laden's al Qaeda group were a "tremendous threat" that was likely to target the United States in the near future, but they were unable to say when, where, or how.[20]

Shortly after Bush's inauguration, on January 24, 2001, Richard Clarke, who served as Clinton's National Counter-Terrorism Coordinator and who was initially retained in that capacity by the new Bush administration, sent a memo to Rice urgently requesting a Cabinet-level meeting to address "the imminent al Qaeda threat."[21] As a follow-up, Clarke briefed Rice, her deputy Stephen Hadley, Cheney, and Powell, on this request. But, with the exception of Powell, the response to Clarke's message was distinctly tepid. Rice made it clear that she viewed the NSC as a foreign policy coordination mechanism, not some place where issues of terrorism relating to the United States should be addressed. Clarke tried to explain the new importance of the terrorist threat in the post–Cold War era: "The boundaries between domestic and foreign have blurred. Threats to the US now are not Soviet ballistic missiles carrying bombs, they're terrorists carrying bombs."[22]

However, Rice was not entirely convinced by this argument. She made two significant decisions. First, Rice said the Principals could not discuss the al Qaeda threat until the issue had been framed by the Deputies.[23] That, in effect, postponed any discussion of Clarke's memo for months. Second, Rice deemphasized the threat of transnational terrorism by downgrading the position of National Coordinator for Counterterrorism from a Cabinet-level position to a staff-level role. Thus, the Bush administration demoted Clarke and reduced his leverage in the White House.[24]

Meanwhile, Tenet publicly echoed Clarke's deep concerns about the al Qaeda threat. In his February 2001 testimony to the Senate Intelligence Committee, he noted that al Qaeda was "the most immediate and serious threat" to U.S. national security. He added, "Terrorists are also becoming more operationally adept and more technically sophisticated in order to defeat counter-terrorism measures." More specifically, Tenet was worried that terrorist groups like al Qaeda "are seeking out 'softer' targets that provide opportunities for mass casualties."[25]

It was only in April 2001, three months after Clarke's urgent request, that the Bush administration finally held a meeting about the terrorist threat from al Qaeda. But the meeting did not involve the President or Cabinet. It was a meeting of the National Security Council deputies' committee, made up of the second-in-command in each relevant department and agency. If Clarke hoped that this meeting would generate quick action to confront al Qaeda, he was disappointed. Clarke's recommendation to target both the Taliban and the al Qaeda leadership was supported by Armitage but ran into strong opposition from Wolfowitz. Somewhat dismissively, Wolfowitz told Clarke: "You give bin Laden too much credit. He could not do all these things like the 1993 attack on New York, not without a state sponsor. Just because the FBI and CIA have failed to find the linkages does not mean they don't exist."[26] Given this split, the chair at the meeting, Stephen Hadley, opted for a bureaucratic compromise.

This approach treated al Qaeda terrorism and Iraqi state terrorism as part of a cluster of interrelated issues that had to be decided together after more research and more scheduled meetings over the next few months. Although the National Security Council deputies' committee did recommend that President Bush seriously consider arming the Northern Alliance in Afghanistan, divisions over al Qaeda, and the Bush administration's focus on other apparently more important foreign policy issues, effectively ruled out any swift implementation of the measure proposed.[27]

INDICATIONS OF A GROWING AL QAEDA THREAT

For Clarke, Tenet and a number of experienced officials, the exasperating thing was not just the failure of the new Bush administration to seriously address the al Qaeda threat, but also that the threat itself appeared to be growing. In February 2001, bin Laden had virtually acknowledged responsibility for the devastating terrorist attack on the USS *Cole* in Yemen in October 2000. In a poem that was televised and broadcast widely in the Middle East, bin Laden did not conceal his satisfaction with the outcome. He said the USS *Cole* "sails into the waves flanked by arrogance, haughtiness, and false power. To her doom she moves slowly. A dinghy awaits her riding the waves. In Aden, the young men stood up for holy war and destroyed a destroyer feared by the powerful." Bin Laden's poem also hinted that further attacks on the United States would follow: "your brothers in the East [have] readied their mounts . . . and the battle camels are prepared to go."[28] This was not an empty threat. In April 2001, Italian and German authorities used information seized in Frankfurt, Germany, to arrest five bin Laden-associated Islamists near Milan in Italy, while the German police simultaneously arrested another bin Laden operative in Bavaria. Those arrested were reported to have been targeting the U.S. embassy in Rome, and also the 2001 G-8 Economic Summit in Genoa, Italy.[29]

Then, on May 29, 2001, four al Qaeda agents—Wadiha el-Hage, Mohammed Sadiq Odeh, Rashid Daoud al-Owali and Khaffan Khamis Mohammed—were convicted in a New York federal court of 302 counts ranging from murder to perjury for their roles in the bombings that destroyed the American embassies in Kenya and Tanzania in August 1998.[30] Each of the four operatives was imprisoned for life. These sentences followed what had been to date the most comprehensive overseas investigation ever conducted by the U.S. government. The three-month-long trial generated thousands of pages of documents and the testimony of dozens of witnesses who had some knowledge of bin Laden's al Qaeda network. Among other things, the trial revealed that al Qaeda was actively seeking to acquire weapons of mass destruction, that the training of bin Laden's operatives in al Qaeda camps in Afghanistan was fairly rigorous, and that bin Laden's organization was a transnational one, drawing its membership from four continents.[31]

At the same time, the early months of the Bush administration coincided with a significant consolidation of the strategic alliance between al Qaeda and the *Taliban* leadership in Afghanistan. In a statement to an estimated 500,000 delegates that attended the International Conference of Deobandis, held at Peshawar, Pakistan, between April 9 and 11, 2001, bin Laden urged Islamic unity to fight the forces of "global unbelief" (led by the United States) and said that it was the duty of all Muslims to pledge loyalty to "the Islamic Emirate of Afghanistan under the leadership of the Commander of the Faithful Mullah Muhammad Omar." Indeed, bin Laden went out of his way to emphasize the link between the Taliban leadership and his organization: "I assure you and Muslims across the world that I submit to God on the duty of allegiance to Mullah Muhammad Omar, and that I have taken my oath of allegiance to him."[32]

In addition, there were signs that al Qaeda was deepening its involvement in stateless Somalia. After more than a dozen failed peace initiatives in the 1990s, Djibouti hosted a reconciliation conference in 2000 that resulted in the creation of the Transitional National Government (TNG) and a three-year mandate to establish a permanent national Somali government.[33] Thereafter, a 245-member transitional parliament and a new President of Somalia, Abdulkasim Salat Hassan, maintained a limited presence in Mogadishu. While the TNG became the first Somali political initiative since 1991 to achieve a degree of international recognition, the majority of the country's militia factions opposed it.[34] Denied any special status in the Djibouti sponsored negotiations, Somalia's warlords and faction leaders were concerned that the TNG would challenge their hegemony and help entrench the growing Islamic Courts movement. Such fears were linked to the fact that a militant Islamist group like al Itihaad, with its international jihadist rhetoric and ties to al Qaeda, had rebranded itself as an Islamic Court in the late 1990s and had used its militia to expand the movement.[35] In October 2000, for example, the Islamic courts took military control of Marka, an important Indian Ocean port facility. Moreover, diverse Arab backing for the TNG, and the announcement by the TNG in June 2001 that it was "nationalizing" the Mogadishu Islamic Courts network, reinforced the perception among warlords and some observers that the TNG was "harbouring militant Islamist sympathizers."[36]

However, the new Bush administration exhibited little interest in the Somali situation. It was firmly opposed to the idea of American participation in nation-building, and was thus even more determined than the second Clinton administration to keep out of places like Somalia. In the absence of U.S. engagement, it was left to neighboring Ethiopia, a traditional adversary of Somali nationalism and an ally of Washington, to broker a warlord coalition against the TNG and the Islamic courts. In March 2001, after several meetings in Addis Ababa, Hussein Aideed and a number of other factional leaders established a rival organization, the Somali Reconciliation and Restoration Council (SRRC).[37] While the faction leaders and their Ethiopian backers saw the SRRC as an important counterweight to the TNG, the continuing failure to establish a functioning government in Somalia also helped to perpetuate the very conditions of crime and lawlessness that had helped foster the rise of militant Islam in the country.

Thus, the early months of the new Bush administration were characterized by a distinct downplaying of the threat presented by al Qaeda. President Bush would later acknowledge that bin Laden's network was not his focus, or the focus of his national security team before 9/11. According to Bush, "I knew [bin Laden] was a menace. . . . I knew he was responsible or we felt he was responsible for the [previous] bombings that killed Americans. . . . But I didn't feel that sense of urgency, and my blood was not nearly as boiling."[38] This sense of detachment was certainly reflected in policymaking. Upon coming to office, the Bush administration authorized a review of how America was organized on terrorism, homeland security, and cybersecurity.[39] In May 2001, the counterterrorism portfolio was split from the cyberterrorism portfolio, a development that coincided with the aforementioned demotion of the position of National Coordinator for Counterterrorism. And while President Bush appointed Vice President Cheney to head a task force to "combat terrorist attacks on the United States," the task force apparently never met.[40] The Bush administration also requested a policy review of al Qaeda, but the leisurely pace of this review was such that its findings would not be finalized by the principals until the first week of September 2001.

So why was the Bush administration initially reluctant to take the threat of al Qaeda seriously? Several factors contributed to this. First, the Republicans had been out of power since 1992.[41] Consequently, they did have not the chance to work on complex new security issues such as transnational terrorism and to learn how deepening globalization had created a new security environment in which the pattern of conflict moved beyond the protection of the state. According to Clarke, many of the new Bush officials were still operating with an old Cold War paradigm when they came to the White House in January 2001: "It was as though they were preserved in amber from when they left office eight years earlier. They came back. They wanted to work on the same issues right away: Iraq, Star Wars. Not new issues, the new threats that had developed over the preceding eight years."[42]

Second, the Bush administration was slow to recognize the *need* for fresh thinking in global security. The new Bush team prided itself on its deep experience in the security sphere, and the Bush leadership essentially believed that military power was still the major determinant of foreign policy. They also saw the Clinton record in the area of defense and security as one of unmitigated disaster. The Bush leadership was not inclined to take lessons or advice about transnational terrorism from the Clinton administration or from public officials like Clarke or Tenet who worked for it. According to one observer, "The notion that nonstate actors, failed states, and civil conflicts should dominate America's attention was simply not accepted by the Bush team. They found it inconceivable that a bin Laden could threaten the mightiest power in world history. They couldn't imagine it, so they didn't prepare for it."[43]

THE BUSH ADMINISTRATION AND THE SECOND ROUND OF AL QAEDA WARNINGS

By June 2001, the CIA and the NSC's CSG became convinced that a major terrorist attack from al Qaeda was imminent.[44] During that summer, U.S. intelligence detected a strikingly high level of Internet "chatter" amongst various bin Laden associates—there were thirty-four specific communications intercepts—that included declarations such as "zero hour is tomorrow" or "something spectacular is coming."[45] According to Clarke, the last time the CIA had picked up a similar level of chatter was on the eve of the millennium rollover date in December 1999, when President Clinton ordered his Cabinet to go to "battle stations," or high alert. Among other things, that response helped prevent a major attack on Los Angeles International Airport after an al Qaeda operative was stopped at the Canadian border driving a car full of explosives.[46]

The sudden increase in the level of al Qaeda "chatter" prompted fears in the CIA that a terrorist operation was being planned against U.S. embassies abroad, or at locations with concentrations of American tourists. Furthermore, the CSG did not rule out the possibility of multiple simultaneous attacks, some overseas and some inside the United States.[47] Consequently, from early June 2001, the CIA issued a series of terrorist threat warnings to all U.S. embassies and all U.S. military facilities abroad. At the same time, the CIA Director warned the White House in his daily briefings to the president that a major al Qaeda attack was going to happen against the United States somewhere in the world in the weeks and months ahead.[48] It was the basis of this information that the Federal Aviation Administration (FAA) issued a general warning on June 22 to all U.S. airports and airlines.[49] Then on July 2, the FBI also warned of a possible terrorist attack. On July 5, Clarke summoned all domestic security agencies—the FAA, the Coast Guard, Customs, the Immigration and Naturalization Service, and the FBI—and told them to intensify their security procedures in light of an impending al Qaeda attack.[50] The FAA issued further warnings of a possible terrorist attack on July 18 and July 31, and the FBI gave another warning on August 1.[51]

Despite all these warnings, President Bush did not hold a meeting on the subject, or order his National Security Advisor to hold a Cabinet-level meeting on the subject during this period. But Hadley strongly rejected the charge that President Bush was indifferent to the looming al Qaeda threat: "The president heard those warnings. The president met daily with . . . George Tenet and his staff. They kept him fully informed . . ."[52] The problem with the intelligence chatter relating to al Qaeda was said to be that it was quite general in nature, and that it did not specifically pinpoint when or where the attacks would occur. Still, according to Hadley, President Bush did not rule out the possibility of a threat to the U.S. homeland and thus put his administration "on battle stations" during summer 2001.

However, there appeared to be little evidence to support Hadley's claim. While Mr. Bush spoke of terrorism as one "the threats of the 21st century" in a speech in Alabama on June 22, 2001, he used the word "terrorist" to describe rogue nations like Iran that provided assistance to groups like Hezbollah and Hamas, and thus to rally domestic support for his administration's new National Missile Defense policy.[53] The speech showed little recognition that nonstate terrorist organizations like al Qaeda could also, by their own efforts, harm or threaten the United States. In July, the National Security Council deputies' committee held a follow-up meeting to their previous April session on the al Qaeda threat. The committee recommended to the Principals a comprehensive plan not only to eliminate al Qaeda, but also to destabilize the Taliban in Afghanistan.[54] But it was not until September 4, 2001, that the Principals Committee meeting that Clarke had "urgently" requested on January 25 finally met. Ironically, the Principals quickly approved a plan to give the CIA $125 to $200 million a year to arm the Northern Alliance.[55] No one at the meeting disagreed with the concerns that Tenet and Clarke had been struggling to raise about al Qaeda since George W. Bush took office. By September 10, Condoleezza Rice had a National Security Presidential Directive (NSPD) ready for the president to sign. The NSPD was numbered 9, which meant eight other matters had been formally assessed, vetted, agreed upon, and signed off on as policy by the president before the al Qaeda issue was dealt with.[56]

It was not just the slowness of the Bush administration's response to the al Qaeda threat that belied Hadley's claims. It was also the fact that the intelligence warnings on the al Qaeda threat persisted in August 2001 and, in some cases, became quite specific. On August 6, the CIA sent President Bush an intelligence briefing that was titled "Bin Laden determined to attack inside the US." Amongst other things, the briefing document said the CIA had "detected patterns of suspicious activity in this country consistent with preparations for hijackings."[57] Yet no one in the Bush administration acted on this report. Then, on August 16, the FAA issued yet another terrorist threat warning.[58] In a sign of mounting desperation over the failure of Bush administration to take the threat of terrorism more seriously, Clarke sent Rice a letter on September 4 that asked "policymakers to imagine a day after a terrorist attack, with hundreds of Americans dead at home and abroad, and ask themselves what they could have done earlier." But this letter failed to stir the White House. In a comment that echoed previous responses by the Bush administration to warnings about the al Qaeda threat, Rice later said Clarke's note was not "specific" and could only therefore be considered a "generic warning."[59]

In the circumstances, it is safe to say that the Bush administration was stunned by the terrorist attacks of September 11. In the space of one day, an administration that prided itself on its "national security realism"[60] saw its world turned upside down. The most military capable nation in the world was powerless to prevent attacks on its soil against the very symbols of American economic and military power and prestige by a transnational terrorist group, al Qaeda. For officials like Clarke and Tenet, the events of 9/11 confirmed their worst fears about the long-term and deadly threat posed by al Qaeda to the United States. Confronted with attacks on the Twin Towers and Pentagon, Clarke immediately thought of "the 1998 simultaneous attacks on the American embassies in Kenya and Tanzania."[61] Equally, the first reaction of Tenet, informed of the attacks during a breakfast engagement with former Senator David Boren (D-OK) on September 11, was to declare that "this has bin Laden all over it."[62]

THE SOMALIA SYNDROME AND THE MARCH TO 9/11

For the president and many Americans, 9/11 seemed to have changed everything. As President Bush put in an address to a joint session of Congress on September 20: "All of this was brought upon us in a single day—and night fell on a different world."[63] The new conventional wisdom in Washington, D.C., was that the events of September 11 had suddenly transformed the international security environment. Such a response assumed the traumatic events of 9/11 came out of a clear blue sky. Indeed, members of the Bush administration argued that the United States had little or no impact on the international circumstances that shaped the advent of 9/11. But that claim was profoundly mistaken. President Clinton was certainly aware by 1996 that al Qaeda was targeting the United States. And, as has been shown, President George W. Bush received regular warnings about the al Qaeda threat, beginning from the time he became President-elect.

The Causal Nexus

What September 11 did was force Mr. Bush to face disconcerting realities that he and his predecessor had failed to address properly or had simply wished away. The global security environment had been radically changing since the end of the Cold War, and 9/11 can—and perhaps must—be seen as part and parcel of longer-term patterns of al Qaeda opposition to the enhanced power position of the United States in the post–Cold War period. Yet, if we concede that al Qaeda's terrorist campaign against the United States did not appear overnight, a major issue remains: how was it possible for al Qaeda since 1992 to intensify its terrorist attacks on the United States to the extent that it could launch 9/11? The main answer lies in the distorting impact that the Somalia Syndrome had on America's conception of international security in the post-Cold War era after 1993. But, to be plausible, this causal connection must be substantiated. It is important here not to confuse correlation and causation. Without supporting evidence, it would be wrong to presume one development (the rise of al Qaeda) that largely followed another event (the Somalia Syndrome) occurred as a necessary result of the preceding development. So what is the evidence for the connection posited here? For the remainder of the chapter, four types of causal association[64] between the Somalia Syndrome and the rise of al Qaeda will be identified.

Consistency of Association

With the end of the Afghan War in 1989 and the subsequent disintegration of the Soviet Union, bin Laden had established al Qaeda to pursue jihad against what he saw as the new major enemy of Islam: America. The first al Qaeda attack occurred at the beginning of the U.S.–UN intervention in Somalia in December 1992. The Somali crisis proved to be a landmark event for the development of al Qaeda in the 1990s. To a large degree, strife-torn Somalia exemplified the changing context of international security after the Cold War. Above all, the Somali crisis demonstrated that weak or failed states were now the main source of threat and instability in the world,[65] and that the capacity of the international community to respond to such challenges would largely depend on the stance of the United States, the sole superpower.

But if the Somali problem was a paradigm of the new security environment, the Clinton administration struggled to adjust to it. Although it was not apparent to Washington at the time, the stiff resistance of General

Aideed's militia in Somalia was linked, in part, to military assistance provided by bin Laden's multinational insurgent organization, al Qaeda, and the involvement of some of bin Laden's fighters in the Black Hawk Down episode that eventually prompted Clinton to withdraw U.S. troops from the country.

The Somalia Syndrome, as it became known, found formal expression in the Clinton administration's PDD 25 of May 1994. This measure signaled the return of a more traditional state-centric approach to international security, and a clear retreat from the idea that the United States had a national interest in participating in multilateral intervention in failed states. The advent of the Somalia Syndrome marked the emergence of a gulf between U.S. security policy and the transformed security environment of the post–Cold War era. Between 1993 and 2000, American interests and personnel or those of allies were on the receiving end of steadily escalating terrorist attacks from al Qaeda in places such as Somalia, the United States, Ethiopia, Saudi Arabia, Kenya, Tanzania, and Yemen.

To be sure, the Clinton administration moderated its adherence to PDD 25 criteria by the mid-1990s and gradually intensified its efforts after 1996 to address the threat of al Qaeda. But although President Clinton had come to recognize that globalization created enormous transnational security challenges for the United States, he was reluctant, for political reasons, to re-define US national security policy to squarely address these new challenges, which included the threat of Islamic terrorism. Among other things, Clinton did not want to further alienate an already hostile Republican Congress that generally regarded terrorism and the troubles of failed states as a bit of a strategic sideshow.[66] So while Clinton was prepared to use apparently low-risk force through the application of air power and the use of local allies to deal with problems like genocide, ethnic conflict, and terrorism emanating from weak or failed states, he was distinctly unwilling to place U.S. troops at risk in such situations. Thus, the United States' Somalia Syndrome was refined, not abandoned, when it bumped against the underlying political and strategic realities of a globalizing security environment in the second half of the 1990s.

Moreover, the new Bush administration did much less than its predecessor to dissuade groups like al Qaeda from waging jihad against the United States. Convinced that the real lesson of the Black Hawk Down disaster was that it had highlighted the dangers and limits of intervening outside the realm of the American national interest, the Bush White House in effect offered a reinvigorated Somalia Syndrome that strongly rejected the idea of nation-building, reaffirming the traditional view that security was fundamentally determined by the military means of the sovereign state. Hence, there was a conceptual reluctance within the Bush administration to even recognize that nonstate terrorist groups like al Qaeda could seriously threaten the United States.

Strength of Association

The Somalia Syndrome had a profoundly precautionary impact on U.S. foreign policy in the post–Cold War era. It not only sensitized the Clinton administration to the political dangers of putting U.S. military personnel at risk for UN-backed humanitarian missions in civil war or failed state scenarios, but it also helped to reinforce a risk averse doctrine of military force that relied heavily on "distant punishment" to face down perceived challenges to U.S. interests. Force protection became a constant concern for the White House and the Pentagon after Somalia.[67] Despite these constraints, the Clinton administration and the Bush team, conscious of America's overwhelming preeminence, remained convinced, albeit to differing degrees, that the United States could prevail internationally on its own terms.

To the al Qaeda leadership, the Somalia Syndrome appeared to reveal a significant chink in the otherwise enhanced position of the United States after the Cold War. Such a perception must have inspired a forward-leaning attitude within the al Qaeda network. After the Cold War, bin Laden noted: "America escalated its campaign against the Muslim world in its entirety, aiming to get rid of Islam." Two factors loomed large in bin Laden's call for a "holy war" against the "Crusader-Jewish alliance." First, he condemned what he said was "a calamity unprecedented in the history of our *umma* [community]"[68]—namely, the stationing of American and other foreign troops in the Arabian Peninsula during the first Gulf War. Second, the plight of the Palestinians living under occupation featured strongly in bin Laden's rhetorical attacks against the United States and Israel, especially after the Oslo Accords in 1993.[69]

Specificity of Association

Although the U.S. response to Saddam Hussein's invasion of Kuwait confirmed America as the main enemy in bin Laden's eyes, it was the Somalia Syndrome, more than anything else, that convinced him that a global jihad against the United States was viable. The al Qaeda leadership apparently believed that America had experienced a setback of global proportions in Somalia. Although the United States had enormous structural power in military and economic terms in the post–Cold War international system, the Somalia Syndrome seemed to suggest to al Qaeda leaders that the superpower's political resolve to protect its interests was limited when the going got tough. Mindful of the uproar on Capitol Hill after the Black Hawk Down incident, the al Qaeda leadership probably calculated that after Somalia, Washington would show greater restraint in international conflicts and crises. More specifically, because some al Qaeda operatives were involved in the Mogadishu showdown in early October 1993, the al Qaeda leadership probably believed it had actually helped create the Somalia Syndrome.

Somalia also seemed to reinforce a lesson that had been learned by the Arab Afghans in Afghanistan. The clout of a superpower was not limitless. The Soviet Union had not prevailed in Afghanistan, and events in Somalia seemed to suggest to bin Laden and other al Qaeda leaders that the United States was not even as tough as the Russians when it came to fighting, despite their considerable material advantages. According to bin Laden, warriors of faith "must rest assured that life is only in the hands of God," and in that sense, a struggle against America was seen as winnable. The change of the presidency in 2000 did little to disturb bin Laden's conviction that the United States remained the principal adversary and had to be confronted. If anything, that conviction grew with the advent of a president whose family had close links with the ruling regime in Saudi Arabia,[70] and who seemed even less interested than his predecessor in the plight of the Palestinians.

Coherence of Association

There was a definite connection between the Somalia Syndrome and al Qaeda's journey to 9/11. After the Somali debacle, a new foreign policy disposition emerged in Washington that deemphasized the strategic significance of failed or failing states to U.S. national security and helped elevate a new doctrine of military force that sought to minimize the role of U.S. ground forces when it was determined that American strategic interest were at stake.

The Somalia Syndrome had a marked effect on the leadership of al Qaeda. America's semidetached attitude toward the UN and its reluctance to get involved in messy civil conflict situations emboldened the bin Laden network and gave it the time and the space to build and expand a multinational insurgent organization in the 1990s with links to more than sixty countries. These links enabled al Qaeda to steadily escalate its violence globally against the United States as the 1990s unfolded.

While the Clinton administration gradually came to recognize the deadly threat posed by al Qaeda, it was always playing catch-up in this regard. Despite some energetic covert efforts to weaken the bin Laden network, the Clinton presidency was unable or unwilling to build a political consensus that would realign U.S. national security policy to directly and publicly confront the al Qaeda threat. The fact the George W. Bush administration largely ignored the al Qaeda danger, despite repeated high-level warnings, made 9/11 all but inevitable. Ultimately, then, the terrorist attacks in Washington and New York were more about a failure of policy than about the limitations of America's intelligence agencies or the laxity of its airport security. The roots of this policy failure lay in the emergence of the Somalia Syndrome in 1993–1994.

CONCLUSION

The Somalia Syndrome substantially contributed to the permissive international environment between 1994 and 2001 that enabled al Qaeda to grow to the point where it was capable of mounting the devastating terrorist attacks of 9/11. The idea that 9/11 suddenly heralded a new security environment was false. The environment had been radically changing since the end of the Cold War. But until 9/11, policymakers in Washington were generally either reluctant, or unable, to grasp the nature of this change. Thus, a dangerous gap formed in the wake of the Somalia debacle between the reinvigorated national security emphasis of the United States and a transformed security environment wherein the pattern of conflict went well beyond the state.

While it is unrealistic to claim that the Somalia Syndrome was the sole cause of al Qaeda's global offensive against America—bin Laden's organization already had the United States in its sights by the time of the Persian Gulf War of 1990–1991—it did serve as a major catalyst in promoting the development of a transnational terrorist organization that had both the self-confidence and the capability to seriously damage the United States. The evidence of a causal relationship between the Somalia Syndrome and the rise of al Qaeda was substantial. This association was expressed in terms of its consistency, strength, specificity, and coherence. Such a finding reveals that 9/11 was a manifest symptom rather than a starting point of a "new strategic era."

Chapter 8

Conclusion: America's Strategic Shortfall

This book is concerned with the origins of 9/11. Rejecting the widely held view that 9/11 marked a "new" strategic era in global politics, it is argued here that the unsuccessful U.S.–UN intervention in Somalia in 1992–1993 was a pivotal event for both U.S. foreign policy and the evolution of the post–Cold War security order. The Somali crisis was important because it was one of the first major international efforts to deal with the complex economic, political, and security challenges posed by globalization. These trends included: the diminished primacy of the Westphalian state-centric structure because of the proliferation of non-state actors ranging from multinational corporations to terrorist groups in the international system: the dramatic rise in irregular warfare, involving insurgency, warlordism, and new forms of terrorism,[1] because weak or failing states had become major sources of threat and instability in the world; the social impact of the information revolution shaped these new conflicts because both state and non-state combatants utilized new communication technologies on the battlefield[2]; and the capacity of the international community to address such trends depended, in large measure, on the stance of the United States because it was the world's sole superpower.

If the Somali intervention had succeeded, the history of many parts of the world might have been quite different. But it did not succeed, and that outcome dashed the hopes of those observers who saw Somalia as a possible model for dealing with the disorder and conflicts of the new era[3]. Instead, the intervention generated a reaction in the United States—the Somalia Syndrome—that actually made US national security policy less relevant to a globalized security environment. The memory and lessons of the Somalia Syndrome, formally distilled in PDD 25 in May 1994, signaled a clear retreat from the first Bush administration's vision of a "New World

Order" in favor of a reinvigorated Powell Doctrine of national security in which the security role of the sovereign state remained paramount, and war was seen as essentially the instrument of state policy.[4] On this view, it was not necessary for America to learn how to fight Somali-style conflicts since it was the job of the president, the Commander-in-Chief, to politically determine which wars were in the national interest of the country, and satisfied the criteria of having a clear mission objective that was morally sound and achievable

Between late 1993 and 9/11, the Somalia Syndrome shackled American thinking about the "new wars" of the post–Cold War period. There was a constant preoccupation in Washington with not crossing "the Mogadishu line" and allowing multilateral intervention in civil conflict situations, especially if such operations endangered the lives of American troops. After Black Hawk Down, the Clinton administration and, to an even greater extent, the second Bush administration embraced the view of the skeptics or realists that globalization had not fundamentally weakened the security role of the sovereign state. And as the most powerful state in the international system, it was believed America could respond selectively to the challenges of the post-Cold War security environment. The other Western countries more or less followed the United States' lead.

But there was nothing inevitable about the failure of the U.S.–UN operation in Somalia. In the early stages of the armed humanitarian intervention in Somalia, several momentous decisions were made that had a direct bearing on the outcome. Two of the most serious ones were the decision to hand over control of the peacekeeping operation to the UN at the earliest possible time and the decision by Washington not to disarm the warlord groups and political factions that were active in the country. Ironically, the military muscle of the United States and other nations initially frightened and intimidated the Somali warlords and their followers. Although it is true some armed factions would have resisted disarmament efforts, a clear and decisive military defeat of one of the major factions at an early stage of the international intervention would have had a tremendous effect on the other Somali factions.

A clear glimpse of what might have happened in Mogadishu was provided by the Australian military in Baidoa. That city had been the scene for some of the worst fighting in the civil war outside of Mogadishu. In January 1993, the 930-strong 1st Battalion of the Royal Australian Regiment arrived in the Baidoa area and quickly achieved a remarkable transformation in the security environment there. Unlike the Americans in Mogadishu, the Australians took a robust approach toward implementing UNITAF's mandate in their part of Somalia. From the beginning, the Australian operation was conducted like a no-nonsense counterinsurgency campaign. It involved the armed protection of relief convoys and the domination of the Baidoa region through the confiscation of all nonauthorized weapons on the streets, constant day and night patrolling, and the cultivation of extensive links with the NGOs, and with the local population via their clan elders. At the same time, the Australians helped reestablish a functioning police force and a judicial system. By the end of the Australian deployment in May 1993, Baidoa was stable and remained so until 1994, when it too became engulfed by the violent turmoil that reappeared in the rest of southern Somalia.

As well as having a profoundly precautionary impact on America's post–Cold War foreign policy, the Somalia Syndrome added impetus to the rise of an Islamist transnational terrorist group, al Qaeda. Composed primarily of "Arab Afghan" veterans, al Qaeda was formed at the end of the Cold War by Osama bin Laden to confront what was seen as the new major enemy of Islam: namely, the United States. Certainly, the decision by the Clinton administration to effectively "cut and run" after the Black Hawk Down episode in October 1993 made a strong impression on the al Qaeda leadership. In particular, three aspects of the Somalia Syndrome that took shape after the U.S. withdrawal served to embolden the al Qaeda leadership. First, Washington's new conviction that failed or failing states were not strategically vital to the United States must have strongly encouraged the bin Laden network. It is not difficult to see why. Such states were deemed to be absolutely vital to the strategic interests of a transnational terror network like al Qaeda. A stateless society like Somalia, for example, offered al Qaeda the prospect of a potential sanctuary or base for terrorist activities against perceived enemies in the Horn of Africa region. The fact that the United States after 1994 paid little attention, in policy terms, to Somalia and other "Somalias" like Afghanistan until the events of September 11 provided al Qaeda with some leeway to pursue its global terror campaign against the United States.

Second, the cynical attempt by the Clinton administration after Somalia to limit the role of the UN in matters relating to American security was a welcome development as far as al Qaeda was concerned. While Clinton won domestic support on Capitol Hill by blaming the UN in the aftermath of the Somalia debacle, it was probably interpreted by the al Qaeda leadership as a sign that Washington was reluctant to "punch its weight" on the international stage. Given its long-range goal of establishing a global Islamic order under the leadership of one Caliph, the bin Laden network was sensitive to the relationship between the world's only superpower and the world's most prominent interstate organization, the UN. It was certainly aware that the United States was the most influential player in the UN after the Cold War and sometimes depicted the UN's role in the post–Cold War era in places like Somalia as "a tool with which the plans of global unbelief against Muslims are implemented."[5] In other words, there was an implicit recognition by the al Qaeda leadership that the UN was an asset to the United States internationally, serving as a source of legitimacy for U.S. foreign policy. The fact that Clinton compromised the United States' relationship with the UN after the Somali setback did not impress the al Qaeda leadership, and probably encouraged them to believe that Washington lacked the political ambition to assert itself internationally against faith-driven challengers.

Third, the Somalia Syndrome tended to reinforce partisanship in the United States' approach to the Israeli–Palestinian dispute. Historically, successive administrations in Washington found it difficult to step outside of themselves and what was a close strategic partnership with Israel when judging Palestinian aspirations for self-determination and statehood. However, the Oslo Accords of September 1993 appeared to offer a breakthrough in the Israeli–Palestinian relationship, and provided America with an unprecedented opportunity to broker the implementation of the peace process. Nevertheless, the new emphasis on vital national American interests after the disappointment of nation-building in Somalia effectively curbed the Clinton administration's willingness to take a more even-handed position in relation to the Israeli-Palestinian conflict. More often than not, the Clinton administration sided with Israel at critical junctures during negotiations with the Palestinians after 1993, and the new Bush administration was even less inclined to drive the Middle East peace process in the period before 9/11. All of this left many Palestinians convinced that the United States was not interested in an Israeli–Palestinian peace deal unless such a deal was on Israel's terms. The inability of the Clinton and Bush administrations to grasp the urgency of the Palestinian issue effectively played into the hands of extremists such as Osama bin Laden who argued that America was at war with Islam and thus indifferent to the desperate plight of the Palestinians living under occupation.

Taken together, these aspects of the Somalia Syndrome had a significant impact in the eyes of the al Qaeda leadership in fostering a security environment that was favorable to the growth and development of the bin Laden network. Moreover, it is now known that the connection between the Somalia Syndrome and the rise of al Qaeda was even more direct than these repercussions suggest. Because al Qaeda's covert involvement in the traumatic Black Hawk Down incident, it is highly likely that al Qaeda leaders believed they had actually helped create the Somalia Syndrome that had proven so beneficial to their organization. Having claimed the credit for bringing about the defeat of one superpower in Afghanistan, the Soviet Union, bin Laden's organization apparently believed after 1993 that an escalated terrorist campaign against the sole remaining superpower, the United States, would keep Washington on the defensive and force it to retreat from longstanding positions in the Middle East and elsewhere. In that sense, the events of September 11 were the culmination of al Qaeda's efforts in this direction, and a graphic illustration of the failure of U.S. security policy to come to terms with this looming threat.

A question remains: if there was a connection between the Somalia Syndrome and the emergence of al Qaeda's global offensive against the United States during the 1990s, why did the Clinton and Bush administrations fail to realize this and make the necessary policy adjustments to address the growing al Qaeda threat? After all, America is a democratic superpower that would seem, on the face of it, to have a built-in capacity to address new challenges, such as the al Qaeda threat, rising from the globalization of the security environment. Moreover, by 1996, key individuals in the Clinton administration, including the president himself, recognized that al Qaeda's terrorist campaign constituted a clear and present danger to American citizens and interests worldwide.

Three factors help to explain this strategic shortfall. First is the powerful influence of tradition on American military identity. The terms "national security" or "national security interests," which were repeatedly invoked after the promulgation of PDD 25 by the Clinton administration, assumed that American security fundamentally relates to the military dimensions of interactions between nation-states.[6] Threats from nonstate terrorist groups, by definition, tended to be almost overlooked in this conception. "Notwithstanding all of the changes that have taken place in the world," Powell noted at the beginning of the Clinton administration, "we have a value system and a culture system within the armed forces of the United States. We have this mission: to fight and win the nation's wars. That's what we do . . . We're warriors."[7] As an upshot, there was a startling lack of attention given by many military professionals in the United States to the rise of irregular warfare in 1990s, an omission that was probably linked to America's unhappy past encounter with unconventional war in Vietnam[8].

Early efforts by the Clinton administration to downsize the Pentagon's budget encountered resistance from interested parties like defense contractors and interest groups, defense bureaucrats and members of Congress. The Pentagon's "Bottom-Up Review" of 1992–1993, for example, effectively preempted large-scale military reorganization by stipulating that U.S. forces must maintain the ability to fight two major regional conflicts (MRCs) simultaneously.[9] Clearly, managing the power and the actions of other states and their leaders, rather than focusing on failing states or on nonstate actors, remained the priority. As an upshot, the military budget of the Pentagon, which averaged about $270 billion per year during the 1990s, contained many longstanding Cold War weapons systems.

Second, although U.S. policymakers and federal government employees recognized in the abstract that the Cold War was over, it was not immediately clear what the new security paradigm might look like. With respect to the intelligence community, for example, Clarke said that "it was difficult to figure out how you take an institution whose whole existence was predicated for 50 years on the Cold War and change the way they do business and the way they think at the operator and analyst level."[10] Besides, many Americans, especially those working in the security sector, felt that the existing national security infrastructure had proved itself by "winning" the Cold War against the Soviet Union and thus assumed, as the world's sole superpower, that the United States was on the right side of history and would shape, rather than be shaped by, the emerging post–Cold War security environment. After the Somali crisis in 1993, the first instinct of a rather shaken Clinton administration was thus to fall back on a familiar Cold War conception of national security rather than to directly engage with the new transnational security threats of the post–Cold War period. That reflex diminished during Clinton's second term in office, but the continued emphasis on "force protection" in the Pentagon as the White House tried to grapple with the al Qaeda threat highlighted the limits of strategic change.

Although counterinsurgency and stability operations received relatively little military attention in the United States in the 1990s, defense secretaries and Pentagon spokesmen frequently spoke of the need for a revolution in military affairs (RMA) in order to meet the new challenges of a post–Cold War environment. However, there was a gap between the rhetoric and the substance of U.S. military policy. As Bacevich pointed out, the U.S. military establishment of 2000 bore a striking resemblance, in organizational terms, to its Cold War predecessor.[11] It continued, for instance, to maintain four distinct air forces, with the Air Force, Army, Navy, and Marine Corps each maintaining separate fleets of aircraft. It also continued to field two distinct and formidable land armies—the Army and the Marine Corps—consisting of 169,800 troops, a figure larger than the entire armies of middle-range powers like Britain, France, or Italy. And despite Pentagon claims that the military budget contained "no Cold War relics," there was still a suspicion in some quarters that the services had persisted in buying military hardware best "suited for war in Europe with the defunct Soviet Union."[12]

Third, the end of the Cold War and the process of deepening globalization enhanced the impact of domestic politics in the making of U.S. foreign policy. Because the United States had no real geopolitical competitors in sight, and because it was located in an increasingly interconnected world in which foreign policy increasingly affected domestic affairs, President Clinton found that the U.S. Congress demanded a greater say in foreign policy than had generally been the case during the Cold War, especially when the policy appeared to be in trouble. After the disturbing TV images of death and desecration in Mogadishu on October 3, 1993, President Clinton faced immediate and tremendous pressure from the U.S. Congress to terminate American involvement. Within days, Clinton bowed to such pressure, subsequently adopting PDD 25 in a further bid to quell pressure from Congress. While the advent of the Somalia Syndrome worked in domestic political terms for Bill Clinton—he was reelected in 1996—it critically slowed the administration's recognition of the al Qaeda threat, and then shackled an effective response by reinforcing risk-averse tendencies within the CIA and the military.

In summary, the Somalia Syndrome was responsible for a major shortfall in America's national security policy between late 1993 and 2001. Unable or unwilling to recognize that the global security environment had been radically transformed since the end of the Cold War, policymakers in Washington reacted to Black Hawk Down by reaffirming that national interest would be the critical determinant of America's commitment to international engagement. As a result, a significant gap developed between the advent of a more unilateral approach to international security under the Clinton administration and a globalized security environment where the pattern of conflict went beyond the confines of the state. This mismatch not only emboldened al Qaeda to intensify its global offensive against America after 1993, but also contributed to a fateful misreading in Washington of transformative strategic trends in the post-Cold War security environment. Ultimately, the terrorist attacks of 9/11 were more about a failure of policy than the limitations of America's intelligence agencies or the imperfections of its airport security. The roots of that strategic policy failure lay in the advent of the Somalia Syndrome.

Notes

Preface

1. Barack Obama, quoted in Jeff Zeleny, "Obama Looks to Shift Focus of Campaign To Economy," *New York Times*, September 17, 2008.

2. Warren Christopher, quoted in Eric Smith, "Somalia's First Lesson for Military is Caution," *New York Times*, March 5, 1995.

Chapter 1

1. G. John Ikenberry, "Illusions of Empire," *Foreign Affairs* 83, no. 2 (2004): 144.

2. Terence Taylor, "Security Policy in a World of Complexity," in *Overcoming Indifference: Ten Key Challenges in Today's Changing World*, ed. Klaus Schwab (New York: New York University Press, 1995), 66–67.

3. John Groom, "The End of the Cold War; Conceptual and Theoretical Implications for the Study of International Relations" (Paper, University of Otago, Dunedin, New Zealand, July 4, 1995), 1.

4. Daniel Yergin, *Shattered Peace: The Origins of the Cold War and the National Security State* (Harmondsworth, UK: Penguin, 1977), 5–6. See also Michael Hogan, *A Cross of Iron: Harry S. Truman and the Origins of the National Security State 1945–54* (Cambridge, UK: Cambridge University Press, 1998); Marcus G. Raskin, *Essays of a Citizen: From National Security State to Democracy* (Armonk, NY: M.E. Sharpe, 1991).

5. President Harry Truman, cited in Ernest R. May, "National Security in American History," in *Rethinking America's Security: Beyond Cold War to a New World Order*, eds. Graham Allison and Gregory F. Treverton (New York: W. W. Norton, 1992), 99.

6. Robert G. Patman, *The Soviet Union in the Horn of Africa: the Diplomacy of Intervention and Disengagement* (Cambridge, UK: Cambridge University Press, 1990), 25.

7. Mohammed Ayoob, "The Horn of Africa: Regional Conflict and Superpower Involvement" (Faculty Working Paper 18, Strategic and Defence Studies Centre, Australian National University, Canberra, 1978), 11.

8. Patman, *The Soviet Union in the Horn of Africa*, 118.

9. "Somalia: Sending Moscow a Message," *Newsweek*, August 29, 1977, 16.

10. Patman, *The Soviet Union in the Horn of Africa*, 204–254.

11. Zbigniew Brzezinski, *Power and Principle* (London: Weidenfield and Nicolson and Son, 1983), 187–189.

12. *Africa Research Bulletin*, May 1987, 8837

13. President George Bush, State of the Union Address, *United States Department of State Dispatch* 3, no. 1 (February 1992), 73.

14. Ronald Reagan, *An American Life* (New York: Simon and Schuster, 1990), 548–549.

15. Archie Brown, *The Gorbachev Factor* (Oxford: Oxford University Press, 1996), 317.

16. Elizabeth Teague, "Current Developments in the Soviet Empire" (Lecture, 11th International Summer School, Institute of Security Studies, Christian-Albrechts University, Kiel, Germany, July 28–August 16, 1991).

17. Robert G. Patman, "Reagan, Gorbachev and the Emergence of 'New Political Thinking,'" *Review of International Studies* 25, no. 4 (1999): 578–579.

18. William D. Jackson, "Encircled Again: Russia's Military Assess Threats in a Post-Soviet World," *Political Science Quarterly* 117, no. 3 (2002): 375–376.

19. Jan Scholte, "The Globalization of World Politics," in *The Globalization of World Politics: An Introduction to International Relations*, eds. John Baylis and Steve Smith (Oxford: Oxford University Press, 2001), 1.

20. Ian Clark, *Globalization and Fragmentation* (Oxford: Oxford University Press, 1997), 15.

21. David Held and Anthony McGrew, *Global Transformations* (Cambridge, UK: Polity Press, 1999), 4.

22. Ibid., 8.

23. Nigel Haworth, "Multinational Corporations and State Sovereignty," in *State and Sovereignty: Is the State in Retreat?* eds. G. A. Wood and L.S. Leland Jr. (Dunedin: University of Otago Press, 1997), 80–88.

24. Francis Fukuyama, "The End of History?" *The National Interest*, no. 16, (1989), 4–19.

25. Ibid.

26. Michael Scheuer, *Through Our Enemies' Eyes: Osama bin Laden, Radical Islam and the Future of America*, rev. ed. (Washington, D.C.: Potomac Books, 2006), 115; Lee Ann Matzinger, "The American Connection: United States Foreign Policy and Terrorism in Somalia" (Master's Thesis, Alliant International University, San Diego, 2002), 31.

27. Michael Dennis and Vaughan Shannon, "Osama bin Laden and the 'Myth of Superpowers': Reputation and Lessons of History in Lebanon, Afghanistan, and Somalia" (Paper, Annual Meeting of the *International Studies Association*, Le Centre Sheraton Hotel, Montreal, Quebec, Canada, March 17, 2004).

28. Scheuer, *Through Our Enemies' Eyes*, 95–128.

29. Theodore S. Dagne, "Ethiopia: New Thinking in US Policy" *CRS Report for Congress*, no. 91-489F (June 1991), 3.

30. Mohamed Sahnoun, *Somalia: the Missed Opportunities* (Washington, D.C.: United States Institute of Peace Press, 1994), 15–16; Jonathan Stevenson, "Hope Restored in Somalia?" *Foreign Policy*, no. 91 (1993): 143.

31. Patman, *The Soviet Union in the Horn of Africa*, 46.

32. *The Guardian*, September 5, 1992.

33. Theodore Dagne, "The Horn of Africa: A Trip Report," *CRS Report for Congress*, no. 91-823F (November 1991), 15.

34. Ioan Lewis, *Making History in Somalia: Humanitarian Intervention in a Stateless Society, Discussion Paper 6* (London: Centre for the Study of Global Governance, 1993), 5.

35. John Drysdale, *Whatever Happened to Somalia?* (London: Haan Associates, 1994), 27–28.

36. Ioan Lewis, "Misunderstanding the Somalia Crisis," *Anthropology Today*, no. 9 (1993): 1.

37. Gregory A. Pirio, *The African Jihad: Bin Laden's Quest for the Horn of Africa* (Trenton, NJ: The Red Sea Press, 2007), 46–49.

38. "Somalia's Islamists" *International Crisis Group*, Africa Report, No. 100, December 12, 2005, 4.

39. Peter Woodward, *US Foreign Policy and the Horn of Africa* (Aldershot, UK: Ashgate, 2006), 61–62.

40. Khat is a recreational drug used widely in Somalia.

41. Lewis, *Making History in Somalia*, 3; Ken Menkhaus and Terence Lyons, "What Are the Lessons to Be Learned From Somalia?" *CSIS Africa Notes*, January 1993, 3.

42. Rakiya Omaar, "Somaliland: One Thorn Bush at a Time," *Current History*, no. 93 (1994): 232.

43. Senate Resolution 115—Regarding the Emergency Humanitarian and Political Situation in Somalia (Senate—April 25, 1991), 55311, *Congressional Record*: http://thomas.loc.gov/home/r111query.html. See also Michael Clough, "The United States and Africa: The Policy of Cynical Disengagement," *Current History* 91, no. 565 (1992): 194.

44. David Shinn (Ambassador, Director for East African Affairs, Department of State), discussion with the author, January 1994.

45. Quoted in Daniel Volman, "Africa and the New World Order," *Journal of Modern African Studies* 31, no. 1 (1993): 7.

46. Drysdale, *Whatever Happened to Somalia?* 24.

47. *The Observer*, August 2, 1992.

48. Mohamed Sahnoun, "Preventing Conflict: The Case of Somalia" (Presentation, Secretary's Open Forum, Washington, D.C., January 12, 1994).

49. James Jonah, quoted in Thomas J. Callahan, "Some Observations on Somalia's Past and Future," *CSIS Africa Notes*, March 1994, 3.

50. Testimony of L'Houssaine Kherchtou, *U.S. v. Usama bin Laden, et al.*, S (7) 98, Cr. 1023 (2001), 1426-33.

51. *U.S. v. Usama bin Laden, et al.*, S (7) 98, Cr. 1023 (2001), 281-2, 1173, 1645, 649, 4933.

52. Peter Woodward, *US Foreign Policy and the Horn of Africa*, 60; Pirio, *The African Jihad*, 46.

53. Lewis, "Making History in Somalia," 14.

54. Drysdale, *Whatever Happened to Somalia?* 39–40.

55. Ibid.

56. Lewis, "Making History in Somalia," 9; Menkhaus and Lyons, "What Are the Lessons to Be Learned from Somalia," 3–4.

57. Drysdale, *Whatever Happened to Somalia?* 42.

58. Lewis, "Misunderstanding the Somali Crisis," 2.

59. Sahnoun, "Preventing Conflict: The Case of Somalia."

60. Samuel M. Makinda, *Seeking Peace from Chaos: Humanitarian Intervention in Somalia* (Boulder: Lynne Rienner, 1993), 62.

61. Stevenson, "Hope Restored in Somalia?" 145.

62. Drysdale, *Whatever Happened to Somalia?* 53.

63. Elisabeth Lindenmayer (Department of Peacekeeping Operations, United Nations), discussion with the author, New York, NY, January 1994.

64. Makinda, *Seeking Peace from Chaos*, 63.

65. *Otago Daily Times*, July 29, 1992.

66. *Guardian*, November 27, 1992; *Observer*, October 11, 1992.

67. Lindenmayer, discussion with the author.

68. R. Marchal et al., "Globalization and Its Impact on Somalia," *Somalia Watch*, February 4, 2004, www.somaliawatch.org/archive/000204601.htm.

69. Ibid.

Chapter 2

1. In November 1992, Sahnoun said: "In view of the human tragedy which Somalia is facing, it's very difficult to stick to rules which certainly are obsolete in the post cold war period." *The Guardian*, November 14, 1992. However, Sahnoun subsequently claimed he opposed the U.S.–UN intervention in December 1992. See Mohamed Sahnoun, "Preventing Conflict: The Case of Somalia," presentation, Secretary's Open Forum, Washington, D.C., January 12, 1994, 6–11.

2. *UN Security Council Resolution 794* (December 3, 1992).

3. George Bush, quoted in United States Information Agency, "Substantial American Force Ordered to Somalia," *East Asia/Pacific Wireless File*, December 4, 1992, 7.

4. Colin Powell, *My American Journey* (New York: Ballantine, 1995), 568.

5. James L. Woods (Ambassador, former Deputy Assistant Secretary of Defense for African Affairs, December 1986–April 1994), discussion with the author, Washington, D.C., January 6, 2000.

6. Dr. Philip Johnston, former President of CARE, discussion with the author, October 25, 1999.

7. Peter Beinart, "Tough Love," *The New Republic*, August 1993, 15.

8. Alberto R. Coll, "For U.S., Hidden Risks in Somalia's Feudal Chaos," *Wall Street Journal* (Eastern edition), September 7, 1993, A16.

9. Herman J. Cohen (Ambassador, former U.S. Assistant Secretary of State for African Affairs), discussion with the author, Washington, D.C., November 4, 1999.

10. Cohen, discussion with the author.

11. Ibid.

12. Ibid.

13. Ibid.; Terence Lyons, "The Transition in Ethiopia," *CSIS Africa Notes*, August 1991, 5.

14. Ioan Lewis and James Mayall, "Somalia," in *The New Interventionism 1991–94: United Nations Experience in Cambodia, former Yugoslavia and Somalia*, ed. James Mayall (Cambridge, UK: Cambridge University Press, 1996), 108.

15. James L. Woods, "US Government Decisionmaking Processes during Humanitarian Operations in Somalia," in *Learning from Somalia: the Lessons of Armed Humanitarian Intervention*, eds. Walter Clarke and Jeffrey Herbst (Boulder: Westview, 1999), 152; Herman Cohen, "Intervention in Somalia," in *The Diplomatic Record, 1992–1993*, ed. Allan E. Goodman (Boulder: Westview Press, 1994), 54.

16. Harry Johnston and Ted Dagne, "Congress and the Somalia Crisis" in *Learning from Somalia*, 192.

17. Cohen, discussion with the author.

18. Woods, "US Government Decisionmaking Processes," 153.

19. Herman J. Cohen, "An Exit Interview with Hank Cohen," *CSIS Africa Notes*, April 1993, 2.

20. Robert Houdek (Ambassador, Deputy Assistant Secretary of State for African Affairs, 1991–1993), discussion with the author, Washington, D.C., November 5, 1999; James Bishop (Ambassador), discussion with the author, Washington, D.C., November 5, 1999; Jon Western, "Sources of Humanitarian Intervention," *International Security* 26, no. 4 (2002): 112–113.

21. Powell, *My American Journey*, 550.

22. George F. Kennan, *New York Times*, September 30, 1993.

23. Powell, *My American Journey*, 293.

24. Ibid., 292.

25. Ibid., 293.

26. Cohen, discussion with the author.

27. Peter Woodward, *US Foreign Policy and the Horn of Africa* (Aldershot, UK: Ashgate, 2006),, 62.

28. Bishop, discussion with the author.

29. Cohen, discussion with the author.

30. *New York Times*, January 2, 1992.

31. Lawrence Eagleburger, quoted by Cohen, discussion with the author.

32. Cohen, discussion with the author.

33. Smith Hempstone, *Rogue Ambassador: An African Memoir* (Sewanee, TN: University of the South Press, 1997), 212.

34. Walter Kansteiner (former Director for Africa, National Security Council), discussion with the author, Washington, D.C., November 8, 1999.

35. Hempstone, *Rogue Ambassador,* 212.

36. Thomas J. Callahan, "Some Observations on Somalia's Past and Future," *CSIS Africa Notes*, March 1994, 3.

37. General Brent Scowcroft, former National Security Adviser in the first Bush administration, discussion with the author, November 30, 1999.

38. Kansteiner, discussion with the author.

39. Bishop, discussion with the author.

40. Senator Nancy Kassebaum, quoted in Reed Kramer, "Somalia Rescue Begins," *Africa News*, August 1992, 1–2.

41. Kansteiner, discussion with the author.

42. William Shawcross, *Deliver Us from Evil: Warlords & Peacekeepers in a World of Endless Conflict* (Bloomsbury, London, 2000), 65–66.

43. Houdek, discussion with the author.

44. Ambassador Frank Wisner, former Under Secretary of State for International Affairs, discussion with the author, New York, November 1, 1999.

45. Cohen, discussion with the author.

46. Cohen, "Intervention in Somalia," 60.

47. *Christian Science Monitor*, August 6, 1992.

48. Cohen, discussion with the author.

49. Woods, discussion with the author.

50. Ibid.

51. Powell, *My American Journey*, 550.

52. Woods, "US Government Decisionmaking Processes," 157.

53. Bishop, discussion with the author.

54. John L. Hirsch and Robert B. Oakley, *Somalia and Operation Restore Hope: Reflections on Peacemaking and Peacekeeping* (Washington, D.C.: United States Institute of Peace, 1995), 31.

55. *The Washington Post*, December 6, 1992.

56. Jon Western, "Sources of Humanitarian Intervention," *International Security* 26, no. 4 (2002): 135.

57. General Colin Powell, quoted in Shawcross, *Deliver Us from Evil*, 66.

58. *New York Times*, October 4, 1992.

59. Powell, *My American Journey*, 548.

60. Robert Gallucci (former Assistant Secretary of State for Politico-Military Affairs in the first Bush administration), discussion with the author, Washington, D.C., November 9, 1999.

61. Ibid.

62. Lewis and Mayall, "Somalia," 110.

63. Houdek, discussion with the author.

64. Ken Menkhaus with Louis Ortmayer, "Key Decisions in the Somalia Intervention" (Pew Case Studies in International Affairs, Institute for the Study of Diplomacy Publications, School of Foreign Service, Georgetown, D.C.), 6.

65. Shawcross, *Deliver Us from Evil*, 66.

66. Houdek, discussion with the author.

67. Colonel Kevin M. Kennedy, former Chief of Staff, Operation Provide Relief, Mombassa, 1992, telephone discussion with the author, November 11, 1999.

68. Houdek, discussion with the author.

69. Hirsch and Oakley, *Somalia and Operation Restore Hope*, 43.

70. Admiral David Jeremiah, quoted in the *Washington Post*, December 6, 1992.

71. Wisner, discussion with the author.

72. Cohen, discussion with the author.

73. Houdek, discussion with the author.

74. General Brent Scowcroft, quoted in Western, "Sources of Humanitarian Intervention," 137.

75. Admiral David Jeremiah, former Vice-Chairman of Joint Chiefs of Staff in the first Bush administration, discussion with the author, Burke, VA, November 3, 1999.

76. Ambassador Brandon Grove, former Director of Somalia Task Force in Washington, D.C., in 1992–1993, discussion with the author, November 6, 1999.

77. Houdek, discussion with the author.

78. Woodward, *US Foreign Policy and the Horn of Africa*, 64; Wisner, discussion with the author.

79. Scowcroft, discussion with the author.

80. Wisner, discussion with the author.

81. Hempstone, *Rogue Ambassador*, 230.

82. Smith Hempstone, former U.S. Ambassador to Kenya, December 1989–March 1993, discussion with the author, Washington, D.C., November 5, 1999.

83. Ibid.

84. Jeremiah, discussion with the author.

85. President John F. Kennedy, quoted on the flyleaf of Graham Allison, *Essence of Decision: Explaining the Cuban Missile Crisis* (Boston: Little, Brown and Company, 1971).

86. Hirsch and Oakley, *Somalia and Operation Restore Hope*, 42.

87. Woods, discussion with the author.

88. Jeremiah, discussion with the author.

89. Gallucci, discussion with the author.

90. Grove, discussion with the author.

91. Kansteiner, discussion with the author.

92. Jeremiah, discussion with the author.

93. Ibid.

94. Kennedy, discussion with the author.

95. Grove, discussion with the author; Johnston, discussion with the author; Kansteiner, discussion with the author.

96. Gallucci, discussion with the author.

97. Scowcroft, discussion with the author.

98. Grove, discussion with the author.

99. Walter Clarke, former Deputy Chief of Mission at the U.S. Embassy in Mogadishu, Somalia, in 1993, telephone discussion with the author, January 6, 2000; Bishop, discussion with the author.

100. *UN Security Council Resolution 794* (December 3, 1992).

101. Dick Cheney and Colin Powell, "US Mission to Somalia Is Necessary and Clear," *East Asia/Pacific Wireless File*, December 4, 1992, 2.

102. Ken Menkhaus, "Getting Out vs Getting Through: US and UN Policies in Somalia," *Middle East Policy* 3, no. 1 (1994): 155.

103. George H. W. Bush, quoted in Terrence Lyons and Ahmed I. Samatar, "Somalia: State Collapse, Multilateral Intervention, and Strategies for Political Reconstruction" (Brookings Occasional Paper, Washington, D.C., The Brookings Institution, 1995), 34.

104. Brandon Grove Jr., *Oral History* (Arlington Hall, VA: Institute for Diplomatic Studies and Training, 1998), 469–470; Walter Clarke, discussion with the author.

Chapter 3

1. Ismat Kittani, "UN Peace Efforts in Somalia" in *UN Peacekeeping at the Crossroads*, eds. Kevin Clements and Christine Wilson (Canberra: Peace Research Centre, Australian National University, 1994), 135.

2. *Reuters*, December 14, 1992.

3. *The Independent*, December 15, 1992.

4. *The Age* (Melbourne), December 15, 1992.

5. *Reuters News Service*, December 12, 1992 and December 15, 1992.

6. *The Age* (Melbourne), December 15, 1992.

7. *The Evening Standard* (London), December 22, 1992.

8. *Reuters News Service*, December 15, 1992; *The Evening Standard* (London) December 22, 1992; *The Guardian*, December 24, 1992.

9. George Bush, quoted in United States Information Agency, "Substantial American Force Ordered to Somalia," *East Asia/Pacific Wireless File*, December 4, 1992, 2.

10. *The Evening Post* (Wellington), December 30, 1992.

11. *The Independent*, December 15, 1992.

12. *Reuters*, December 17, 1992.

13. *The Times*, December 15, 1992.

14. *The Age* (Melbourne), December 15, 1992.

15. Clement Adibe, *Managing Arms in Peace Processes: Somalia* (New York: United Nations Institute for Disarmament Research, 1995), 60.

16. *BBC News*, first broadcast December 9, 1992, by the BBC.

17. Walter S. Clarke, "Testing the World's Resolve in Somalia," *Parameters* 23, no. 4: 43.

18. Thomas J. Callahan, "Some Observations on Somalia's Past and Future," *CSIS Africa Notes*, March 1994, 6.

19. Stephen Shalom, "Gravy Train: Feeding the Pentagon by Feeding Somalia," *ZMag*, February 1993, www.argumentations.com/Argumentations/StoryDetail_2907.aspx.

20. *The Guardian*, December 12, 1992; *Africa Research Bulletin (ARB)*, December 1992, 10834.

21. Mohammed Sadiq Howaida, quoted in Michael Scheuer, *Through Our Enemies' Eyes: Osama bin Laden, Radical Islam and the Future of America*, rev. ed. (Washington, D.C.: Potomac, 2006), 149.

22. Testimony of L'Houssaine Kherchtou, *U.S. v. Usama bin Laden, et al.*, S (7) 98, Cr. 1023 (2001), 4359-60.

23. Ibid., 4359; U.S. State Department, "Press Release on the Indictment of Bin Laden and Atef," news release, November 4, 1998.

24. *U.S. v. Usama bin Laden, et al.*, 4360 and 4924; Richard Miniter, *Losing Bin Laden: How Bill Clinton's Failures Unleashed Global Terror* (Washington, D.C.: Regnery Publishing, 2004), 1–5; Richard A. Clarke, *Against All Enemies: Inside America's War on Terror* (New York: Free Press, 2004), 88.

25. Abu Shiraz, "May 1998 Interview with Bin Laden Reported," *Pakistan*, February 20, 1999, quoted in Michael Scheuer, *Through Our Enemies' Eyes*, 147.

26. David Shinn (Ambassador, Director for East African Affairs, Department of State), discussion with the author, January 24, 1994.

27. Clarke, "Testing the World's Resolve in Somalia," 48.

28. "The World Today" (includes interview with Alex de Waal), *BBC World Service Radio*, August 14, 1993.

29. Daniel Campagnon, "The Lack of Consideration for Internal Political Dynamics in the International Intervention in Somalia" (Paper, International

Colloquium on Integration and Regionalism, Talence, Bordeaux, France, April 27–30, 1994), 19.

30. Ioan Lewis, "Making History in Somalia: Humanitarian Intervention in a Stateless Society" (Discussion Paper 6, Centre for the Study of Global Governance, London, 1993), 12.

31. Martin Stanton, *Somalia on $5 a Day: A Soldier's Story* (New York: Ballantine, 2001), 113; Scott Peterson, *Me against My Brother: At War in Somalia, Sudan, and Rwanda* (Routledge: London, 2001), 61.

32. Samuel M. Makinda, *Seeking Peace from Chaos: Humanitarian Intervention in Somalia* (Boulder: Lynne Rienner, 1993), 71.

33. Shinn, discussion with the author.

34. Lewis, *Making History in Somalia*, 9; *ARB*, February 1–28, 1993, 10904.

35. *The Guardian*, January 12, 1993.

36. *ARB*, February 1–28, 1993, 10904.

37. *The Guardian*, January 2, 1993.

38. *ARB*, May 1–31, 1993, 11018.

39. Clarke, *Against All Enemies*, 76–79.

40. Osama bin Laden told *ABC News* in 1998, "America will see many youths who will follow Ramzi Yousef," quoted in Miniter, *Losing Bin Laden*, 38.

41. Scheuer, *Through Our Enemies' Eyes*, 146.

42. *U.S. v. Usama bin Laden, et al.*, 1433 and 4924; Scheuer, *Through Our Enemies' Eyes*, 148; US State Department, "Press Release on the Indictment of Bin Laden and Atef."

43. *U.S. v. Usama bin Laden, et al.*, 5255.

44. Ibid., 5260.

45. Scheuer, *Through Our Enemies' Eyes*, 148; Miniter, *Losing Bin Laden*, 52.

46. Hamid Mir, "Interview of Osama Bin Laden," *Pakistan*, March 1997.

47. *US Department of State Dispatch*, April 1993, 240–243.

48. Peter V. Jakobsen, "The Four 'Ws' of UN Collective Military Peace Enforcement in the New World Order: Why, When, (By and Against) Whom?" (Paper prepared for Workshop 10, Military Security and Its Controversial Dimensions, at the Second European Peace Research Conference in Budapest, November, 12–14, 1993), 12.

49. Walter Clarke and Jeffrey Herbst, "Somalia and the Future of Humanitarian Intervention," in *Learning from Somalia: The Lessons of Armed Humanitarian Intervention*, eds. Walter Clarke and Jeffrey Herbst (Boulder: Westview, 1997), 241.

50. Peterson, *Me against My Brother*, 74–75; William Shawcross, *Deliver Us from Evil: Warlords and Peacekeepers in a World of Endless Conflict* (London: Bloomsbury, 2000), 98–99.

51. Michel Couton (Colonel, Department of Peacekeeping Operations, United Nations, New York), discussion with the author, January 1994.

52. A confidential source in the State Department's Bureau of Intelligence said that the attack on the Pakistani peacekeepers was "not a surprise."

53. *International Herald Tribune*, April 1, 1994.

54. Relief aid worker quoted in *The Times*, June 7, 1993.

55. John Drysdale, *Whatever Happened to Somalia?* (London: Haan, 1994), 16–17.

56. Patrick J. Sloyan, "Somalia Mission Control: Clinton Called the Shots in Failed Policy Targeting Aideed," *Newsday*, December 5, 1993.

57. Ken Menkhaus, "Getting Out vs Getting Through: US and UN Policies in Somalia," *Middle East Policy* 3, no. 1 (1994): 157.

58. Clarke, *Against All Enemies*, 85.

59. Peterson, *Me against My Brother*, 92–93.

60. Ibid., 76–80.

61. Shawcross, *Deliver Us from Evil*, 100; Peterson, *Me against My Brother*, 20–122.

62. Shawcross, *Deliver Us from Evil*, 100.

63. David Halberstam, *War in a Time of Peace: Bush, Clinton, and the Generals* (New York: Touchstone, 2001), 260.

64. Drysdale, *Whatever Happened to Somalia?* 199.

65. Arab Press Service Organisation, "Aideed Under Islamic Banner," *APS Diplomat Recorder*, July 31, 1993.

66. Senator Robert Byrd, quoted in Callahan, "Some Observations on Somalia's Past and Future," 8.

67. Shawcross, *Deliver Us from Evil*, 100.

68. *The Guardian*, July 17, 1993.

69. *The Guardian*, August 16, 1993.

70. Miniter, *Losing Bin Laden*, 41–44.

71. *Lying to a U.S. Senator*, 103rd Cong., 1st sess., *Congressional Record* 139 (September 9, 1993): S11267.

72. Halberstam, *War in a Time of Peace*, 261.

73. Shawcross, *Deliver Us from Evil*, 101; Peterson, *Me against My Brother*, 110.

74. Herman J. Cohen, "Somalia and the United States: A Long and Troubled History," allAfrica.com, 2002, allafrica.com/stories/printable/200201210455.html.

75. Shawcross, *Deliver Us from Evil*, 101.

76. Ibid.; Peterson, *Me against My Brother*, 137–138.

77. Miniter, *Losing Bin Laden*, 68.

78. Chris Wallace, "Transcript of President Bill Clinton's Interview," *Fox News Sunday*, September 22, 2006, http://thinkprogress.org/clinton-interview.

79. Miniter, *Losing Bin Laden*, 51.

80. Mark Bowden, *Black Hawk Down* (London: Corgi, 2000), 167–168; Peterson, *Me against My Brother*, 140.

81. *U.S. v. Usama bin Laden, et al.*, 5458; Miniter, *Losing Bin Laden*, 52.

82. *New York Times*, December 23, 2000; Scheuer, *Through Our Enemies' Eyes*, 148.

83. Testimony of James Francis Yacone, *U.S. v. Usama bin Laden, et al.*, 4459-69.

84. Ann M. Lesch, "Osama bin Laden's 'Business' in Sudan," *Current History*, May 2002, 205.

85. *U.S. v. Usama bin Laden, et al.*, 4791-99.

86. Bill Clinton, *My Life* (London: Arrow, 2005), 550.

87. *Carnage in Somalia*, 103rd Cong., 1st sess., *Congressional Record* 139 (October 4, 1993): S12876.

88. *Department of Defense Appropriations Act of 1994*, 103rd Cong., 1st sess., *Congressional Record* 139 (October 14, 1993): S13447.

89. John McCain, quoted in Bill Clinton, *My Life* (London: Arrow, 2005), 551.

90. Halberstam, *War in a Time of Peace*, 263–264.

91. Clinton, *My Life*, 552.

92. Ibid.

93. Bowden, *Black Hawk Down*, 452.

94. Stanton, *Somalia on $5 a Day*, 291.

95. Bill Clinton, "Address to the Nation on Somalia, Presidential Document 2022," *Public Papers of the Presidents* (October 1993).

96. *Somalia*, 103rd Cong., 1st sess., *Congressional Record* 139 (October 7, 1993): S13235.

97. Halberstam, *War in a Time of Peace*, 264.

98. Bill Clinton, quoted in Clarke, *Against All Enemies*, 87.

99. Clinton, *My Life*, 552.

100. Menkhaus, "Getting Out vs Getting Through," 147.

101. Stanton, *Somalia on $5 a Day*, 291.

102. *ARB*, November 1993, 11242.

103. Stanton, *Somalia on $5 a Day*, 291.

104. Michael Maren, "The UN Provides Somalis the Incentive to Fight," *SNU* [electronic mail] 3, no. 20, July 11, 1994.

105. Chris Budge, quoted in "New Fighting in Mogadishu," *SNU* [electronic mail] 3, no. 18, June 26, 1994.

106. *The Guardian*, August 4, 1994.

107. *Teletext*, News International, August 23, 1994.

108. "UNOSOM and the Price for Peace" *SNU* 3, no. 23, September 14, 1994.

109. Shawcross, *Deliver Us from Evil*, 102.

110. Sloyan, "Somalia Mission Control."

111. Peterson, *Me against My Brother*, 161.

112. Halberstam, *War in a Time of Peace*, 262.

113. Clinton, *My Life*, 552.

114. John Miller, "Exclusive Interview with Osama Bin Laden: Talking with Terror's Banker," *ABC News*, May 29, 1998, *abcnews.com*; al Qaeda operative, Mohammed Sadiq Howaida, quoted in Khamran Khan, "Palestinian Unveils Osama's International War against US; Bombing Suspect Says His Men Hit Targets from Somalia to the Philippines," *News*, August 19, 1998.

115. *Washington Post*, October 17, 1993.

116. Clarke, *Against All Enemies*, 85.

117. Ibid.

118. Elizabeth Drew, *On the Edge: The Clinton Presidency* (New York: Simon & Schuster, 1994), 319.

119. *The Financial Times*, October 18, 1993.

120. Colin Powell, *My American Journey* (New York: Ballantine, 1996), 551.

121. *The Washington Post*, October 17, 1993.

122. David D. Laitin, "Somalia: Intervention in Internal Conflict," *Center for International and Security Studies at Maryland*, October 12, 2001, www.cissm.umd.edu/papers/files/Somalia.pdf.

123. Clarke and Herbst, "Somalia and the Future of Humanitarian Intervention," 241.

124. Clarke, *Against All Enemies*, 86.

125. Bill Clinton, quoted in *The Washington Post*, October 17, 1993.

126. Clinton, *My Life*, 550.

127. Powell, *My American Journey*, 565.

128. Halberstam, *War in a Time of Peace*, 255.

129. Walter Clarke, "Failed Visions and Uncertain Mandates in Somalia," in *Learning from Somalia*, eds. Walter Clarke and Jeffrey Herbst, note 19, 18.

130. Bowden, *Black Hawk Down*, 487.

131. *The Times*, January 1, 1993.

132. *The Sunday Times*, January 1, 1993.

133. *The Dominion* (Wellington), February 25, 1993.

134. Robert Oakley, quoted in *The Guardian*, March 3, 1993.

135. Stanton, *Somalia on $5 a Day*, 57.

136. Terrence Lyons and Ahmed I. Samatar, "Somalia: State Collapse, Multilateral Intervention, and Strategies for Political Reconstruction" (Brookings Occasional Papers, The Brookings Institution, Washington, D.C., 1995), 37.

137. Stanton, *Somalia on $5 a Day*, 113.

138. Colin Powell, quoted in U.S. Information Agency, "US Mission to Somalia Is Necessary and Clear," *East Asia/Pacific Wireless File*, December 1992, 17.

139. Stanton, *Somalia on $5 a Day*, 113.

140. *Otago Daily Times* (New Zealand), December 12, 1992; Couton, discussion with the author; *Evening Post* (Wellington) December 26, 1992; *The Guardian*, December 15, 1992.

141. Bowden, *Black Hawk Down*, 58.

142. Menkhaus, "Getting Out vs Getting Through," 155.

143. Stanton, *Somalia on $5 a Day*, 166.

144. Clinton, *My Life*, 553.

145. Bowden, *Black Hawk Down*, 478.

146. *U.S. v. Usama bin Laden, et al.*, 5400.

Chapter 4

1. Colin Powell, *My American Journey* (New York: Ballantine, 1996), 572.

2. Ibid., 565.

3. Richard A. Clarke, *Against All Enemies: Inside America's War on Terror* (New York: Free Press, 2004), 88–89.

4. Robert D. Kaplan, "The Coming Anarchy," *The Atlantic Monthly*, February 1994, 44–76.

5. The Australian forces were the only army in the UN operation to receive a letter of commendation from the NGO community in Baidoa. See Peter Kieseker, "Relationships Between Non-Government and Multinational Forces in the Field," in *Peacekeeping: Challenges for the Future*, ed. Hugh Smith (Canberra: Australian Defence Force Academy, 1993). There was also great national and international pressure for the Australians to extend their stay in Baidoa beyond May 1993. This point was made by Gerry Carradine (Rear Admiral, Australian Defence Force Academy), discussion with the author, January 20, 1995, and Bill Mellor, "The Australian Experience in Somalia," in *Peacekeeping*, ed. Hugh Smith, 64.

6. Robert Breen, *Through Aussie Eyes: Photographs of the Australian Defence Force in Somalia* (Canberra: Department of Defence, 1994), 13.

7. Commonwealth of Australia, Joint Standing Committee on Foreign Affairs, Defence and Trade, Defence Subcommittee, 37th Parl., 1st sess. (April 8, 1994), 530–531.

8. Mellor, "The Australian Experience in Somalia," 66; Commonwealth of Australia, Joint Standing Committee on Foreign Affairs, Defence and Trade, Defence Subcommittee, 37th Parl., 1st sess. (October 12, 1994), 51.

9. David Hurley, "An Application of the Laws of Armed Conflict: Operation Solace," in *The Force of Law: International Law and the Land Commander*, ed. Hugh Smith (Canberra: Australian Defense Force Academy, 1994), 180.

10. Ibid., 14.

11. Ibid., 15.

12. *The Guardian*, December 17, 1992.

13. Kieseker, "Relationships Between Non-Government Organisations," 71.

14. Ibid.

15. *The Times*, December 15, 1992.

16. Breen, *Through Aussie Eyes*, 15.

17. Hurley, "An Application of the Laws of Armed Conflict," 180.

18. Philip McNamara (Brigadier, Queenscliff Military Training College), discussion with the author, January 23, 1995.

19. Michael Kelly, "Legal Regimes and Law Enforcement on Peace Operations," in *The Force of Law*, ed. Hugh Smith, 202.

20. Bill Mellor, discussion with *Pacific Research* 6, no. 4 (1993); Breen, *Through Aussie Eyes*, 53.

21. *The Age* (Melbourne), December 29, 1992.

22. F. M. Lorenz, "Weapons Confiscation Policy during the First Phase of Operation 'Restore Hope,'" *Small Wars and Insurgencies* 5, no. 3 (1994): 415.

23. Mellor, "The Australian Experience in Somalia," 62–63.

24. Kieseker, "Relationships Between Non-Government Organisations," 72.

25. Hurley, "An Application of the Laws of Armed Conflict," 185.

26. Breen, *Through Aussie Eyes*, 79; Lorenz, "Weapons Confiscation Policy," 424.

27. Hurley, "An Application of the Laws of Armed Conflict," 181.

28. Mellor, "The Australian Experience in Somalia," 60; Kieseker, "Relationships Between Non-Government Organisations," 67.

29. Testimony of Colonel David Hurley to Joint Standing Committee (April 8, 1994), 536.

30. Ibid., 536.

31. Mellor, discussion with *Pacific Research*.

32. Kelly, "Legal Regimes and Law Enforcement," 199–200.

33. Commonwealth of Australia, Joint Standing Committee on Foreign Affairs, Defence and Trade, Defence Subcommittee, *Australian Participation in UN Peace Operations*, 37th Parl., 1st sess. (1993), 17.

34. Commonwealth of Australia, Joint Standing Committee (April 8, 1994), 546.

35. Robert Shoebridge (Colonel, Department of Defense), discussion with the author, January 25, 1995.

36. Kelly, "Legal Regimes and Law Enforcement," 201.

37. Submission of Major Michael Kelly, *Australian Participation in UN Peace Operations*, 18.

38. Mellor, discussion with *Pacific Research*.

39. Breen, *Through Aussie Eyes*, 110.

40. Carradine, discussion with the author.

41. *The Otago Daily Times*, November 23, 1993.

42. United States Information Agency, "Substantial American Force Ordered to Somalia," *East Asia/Pacific Wireless File*, December 4, 1992, 2.

43. Colin Powell, quoted in United States Information Agency, "US Mission to Somalia Necessary and Clear," *East Asia/Pacific Wireless File*, December 4, 1992, 19.

44. Commonwealth of Australia, *Australian Participation in UN Peace Operations* (1994), 15.

45. Rakiyo Omaar and Alex de Waal, *Somalia Operation Restore Hope: A Preliminary Assessment* (London: African Rights, 1993), 20.

46. Michael Kelly (Lieutenant Colonel), discussion with Nick Reaburn, January 2001, p. 10.

47. Kelly, "Legal Regimes and Law Enforcement," 196.

48. David Hurley (Colonel), discussion with the author, January 25, 1995; McNamara, discussion with the author, as stated previously in note 18; Brian Millan (Lieutenant Colonel, Queenscliff Military Training College), discussion with the author, January 23, 1995.

49. The phrase is the author's but is derived from views expressed by Hurley, discussion with the author.

50. Mick Moon (Colonel), discussion with Nick Reaburn, February 2001, p. 10.

51. Robert Breen, *A Little Bit of Hope: Australian Force—Somalia* (St Leonards: Allen & Unwin, 1998), 339.

52. Commonwealth of Australia, Joint Standing Committee (April 8, 1994), 546; *The Washington Post*, November 21, 1993; Ioan Lewis, *The Times*, December 4, 1992.

53. Thomas J. Callahan, "Some Observations on Somalia's Past and Future" *CSIS Africa Notes*, March 1994, p 6; Walter S. Clarke, "Testing the World's Resolve in Somalia," *Parameters* 23, no. 4: 49.

54. Confidential source, State Department Bureau of Intelligence, January 25, 1994.

55. Peter Kieseker, quoted in Breen, *A Little Bit of Hope*, (note 44) 347–348.

56. Commonwealth of Australia, Joint Standing Committee (April 8, 1994), 546; Commonwealth of Australia, *Australian Participation in UN Peace Operations* (1993), 3.

57. Peter Kieseker, "Relationships Between Non-Government Organisations," 68.

58. Ibid., 68; Ian Wishart, quoted in World Vision Australia's submission to Commonwealth of Australia, *Australian Participation in UN Peace Operations* (1993), 15.

59. Murray Domney (International Policy Division, Department of Defence, Australia), discussion with the author, January 27, 1995; Kieseker, "Relationships Between Non-Government Organisations," 711–773.

60. Commonwealth of Australia, Joint Standing Committee (April 8, 1994), 481.

61. Ioan Lewis, "White-Washing the UN's Failures in Somalia," *Somali New Update (SNU)* [electronic mail], August 27, 1994.

62. Kelly, discussion with Reaburn, 23.

63. John L. Hirsch and Robert B. Oakley, *Somalia and Operation Restore Hope: Reflections on Peacemaking and Peacekeeping* (Washington, D.C.: United States of Peace, 1995), (note 7) 155–156.

64. Hurley, discussion with the author; Kelly, discussion with Reaburn, 34; Martin Stanton, *Somalia on $5 a Day: A Soldier's Story* (New York: Ballantine, 2001), 113.

65. Stanton, *Somalia on $5 a Day*, 113–114.

66. Moon, discussion with Reaburn, 7–8.

Chapter 5

1. Robert G. Patman, "The UN Operation in Somalia," in *A Crisis of Expectations: UN Peacekeeping in the 1990s*, eds. Ramesh Thakur and Carlyle A. Thayer (Boulder: Westview Press, 1995); Peter Woodward, *US Foreign Policy and the Horn of Africa* (Aldershot, UK: Ashgate, 2006), 71.

2. George Ward, "Peacekeeping: an Essential Tool," *New Zealand International Review* 19, no. 3 (1994): 23–25.

3. William Shawcross, *Deliver Us from Evil: Warlords and Peacekeepers in a World of Endless Conflict* (London: Bloomsbury, 2000), 102.

4. Joseph Frankel, *International Relations in a Changing World*, 4th ed. (New York: Oxford University Press, 1988), 99.

5. Bill Clinton, *My Life* (London: Arrrow Books, 2005), 552.

6. Richard A. Clarke, *Against All Enemies: Inside America's War on Terror* (New York: Free Press, 2004), 86.

7. Clinton, *My Life*, 552.

8. Warren Christopher, Secretary of State, "Building Peace in the Middle East," Columbia University, September 20, 1993, http://dosfan.lib.uic.edu/ERC/briefing/dossec/1993/9309/930920dossec.html.

9. Anthony Lake, Assistant to the President for National Security Affairs, "From Containment to Enlargement," Johns Hopkins University, School of Advanced International Studies, Washington, D.C., September 21, 1993, www.mtholyoke.edu/acad/intrel/lakedoc.html.

10. Bill Clinton (Address, UN General Assembly, New York, NY, September 27, 1993).

11. Madeleine Albright (Address, National Defense University, Washington, DC), quoted in Boutros-Boutros Ghali, *Unvanquished* (London: I.B. Tauris, 1999), 115.

12. Harry Johnston and Ted Dagne, "Congress and the Somalia Crisis," in *Learning from Somalia: The Lessons of Armed Humanitarian Intervention*, eds. Walter Clarke and Jeffrey Herbst (Boulder: Westview Press, 1997), 197.

13. Andrew J. Bacevich, *American Empire: The Realities and Consequences of US Diplomacy* (Cambridge, MA: Harvard University Press, 2002), 146.

14. Ibid.

15. *Department of Defense Appropriations Act of 1994*, 103rd Cong., 1st sess., *Congressional Record* 139 (October 14, 1993): S13434–S13481.

16. Ibid., S13436.

17. Harry Johnston and Ted Dagne, "Congress and the Somalia Crisis," in eds. Walter Clarke and Jeffrey Herbst *Learning from Somalia: The Lessons of Armed Humanitarian Intervention* (Boulder: Westview Press, 1997), 201–202.

18. *Department of Defense Appropriations Act of 1994*, S13448.

19. Ibid., S13454.

20. Ibid., S13467.

21. Ibid., S13474.

22. *50th Anniversary of the United Nations*, 104th Cong., 1st sess., *Congressional Record* 141 (June 26, 1995), S9025.

23. *Department of Defense Appropriations Act of 1994*, S13438.

24. Ibid., S13451.

25. Ibid., S13455.

26. Ibid., S13469.

27. Warren Christopher, quoted in *Washington Post*, October 17, 1993.

28. David Halberstam, *War in a Time of Peace: Bush, Clinton and the Generals* (New York: Touchstone, 2001), 263–264.

29. Shawcross, *Deliver Us from Evil*, 102.

30. Sarah B. Sewall, "US Policy and Practice Regarding Multilateral Peace Operations" (Working Paper 01-3, Carr Centre for Human Rights Policy, Harvard Kennedy School, Cambridge, MA, 2001), www.hks.harvard.edu/cchrp/Web%20 Working%20Papers/PKO.pdf.

31. Clinton, *My Life*, 552.

32. Steven Kull, "Misreading the Public Mood," *Bulletin of the Atomic Scientist*, March 1, 1995, 55–59.

33. Steven Kull and C. Ramsey, "The Myth of the Reactive Public-American Public Attitudes on Military Fatalities in the Post-Cold War Period," in *Public Opinion and the International Use of Force*, eds. P. Everts and P. Isernia (London: Routledge, 2001), 205.

34. Bill Clinton, quoted in Clarke, *Against All Enemies*, 87.

35. Clarke, *Against All Enemies*, 87.

36. *Department of Defense Appropriations Act of 1994*, S13436.

37. Bacevich, *American Empire*, 146.

38. David A. Welch, "The Impact of the 'Vietnam Syndrome' on US Foreign Policy in a Post-Cold War World," in *Globalization and Conflict: National Security in a "New" Strategic Era*, ed. Robert G. Patman (New York: Routledge, 2006), 98.

39. Walter Clarke, "Failed Visions and Uncertain Mandates in Somalia," in *Learning from Somalia*, eds. Clarke and Herbst, 3.

40. Thomas G. Weiss, "Overcoming the Somalia Syndrome: 'Operation Restore Hope,'" (Paper, Experts Meeting on State Sovereignty, Human Rights and Humanitarian Action, Montreal, Quebec, March 1–2, 1995), www.dd-rd.ca/site/ publications/index.php?id=1280&subsection=catalogue.

41. Anthony Lake, quoted in James K. Oliver, "US Foreign Policy after 9/11: Context and Prospect," in *The War on Terror in Comparative in Perspective: US Security and Foreign Policy after 9/11*, eds. Mark J. Miller and Boyka Stefanova (New York: Palgrave Macmillan, 2007), 20.

42. Bacevich, *American Empire*, 90.

43. Oliver "US Foreign Policy after 9/11," 24.

44. Madeleine Albright, "Myths of Peace-Keeping," *Dispatch*, June 1993, 464–467.

45. Madeleine Albright, "Building a Consensus on International Peace-Keeping," *Dispatch*, November 1993: 790–791.

46. Clinton, *My Life*, 554.

47. Clarke, *Against All Enemies*, 87.

48. Stephen Shalom, "Gravy Train: Feeding the Pentagon by Feeding Somalia," *ZMag*, February 1993, www.argumentations.com/Argumentations/StoryDetail_2907.aspx.

49. Bacevich, *American Empire*, 148–149.

50. Richard Holbrooke cited in Halberstam, *War in a Time of Peace*, 265

51. John Garofano, "The Intervention Debate: Toward a Posture of Principled Judgment" (Monograph, U.S. Army War College, Strategic Studies Institute Carlisle, PA, January 2002), 27, www.strategicstudiesinstitute.army.mil/pdffiles/pub293.pdf.

52. Peter J. Katzenstein, "Introduction: Alternative Perspectives on National Security," in *The Culture of National Security: Norms and Identity in World Politics,* ed. Peter J. Katzenstein (New York: Columbia University Press, 1996), 2.

53. *SIPRI Yearbook 2002: Armaments, Disarmament and International Security* (Oxford: Oxford University Press, 2002), http://editors.sipri.se/pubs/yb02/app01a.html.

54. Mary Kaldor, *New and Old Wars: Organised Violence in a Global Era* (Oxford: Polity Press, 1999), 115.

55. Shawcross, *Deliver Us from Evil*, 103.

56. *New York Times*, October 13, 1993.

57. Halberstam, *War in a Time of Peace*, 278–279.

58. Ibid., 275–277.

59. Alan Kuperman, *The Limits of Humanitarian Intervention: Genocide in Rwanda* (Washington, D.C.: The Brookings Institution, 2001), 35.

60. Darren C. Brunk, "Curing the Somalia Syndrome: Analogy, Foreign Policy Decision Making, and the Rwandan Genocide," *Foreign Policy Analysis* 4, no. 3 (2008): 301–302.

61. Arthur Jay Klinghoffer, *The International Dimension of Genocide in Rwanda* (London: Macmillan Press, 1998).

62. Philip Gourevitch, *We Wish To Inform You That Tomorrow We Will Be Killed With Our Families* (New York: Farrar Strauss and Giroux, 1998), 170

63. Former Acting Secretary of State Lawrence S. Eagleburger reiterated this point in "'The CNN Effect:' How 24-Hour News Coverage Affects Government Decisions and Public Opinion," *A Brookings/Harvard Forum*, January 23, 2002, www.brookings.edu/events/2002/0123media_journalism.aspx.

64. Bacevich, *American Empire*, 163.

65. Fraser Cameron, *US Foreign Policy After the Cold War: Global Hegemon or Reluctant Sheriff?* (London and New York: Routledge, 2002), 25.

66. Richard Holbrooke, quoted in Bacevich, *American Empire*, 163.

67. Shawcross, *Deliver Us from Evil*, 133–168.

68. Bacevich, *American Empire*, 164–165.

69. Lee Ann Matzinger, "The American Connection: United States Foreign Policy and Terrorism in Somalia" (Master's Thesis, Alliant International University, San Diego, 2002), 99.

70. Warren Christopher, Secretary of State, cited in "Somalia's First Lesson for Military Is Caution," *New York Times*, March 5, 1995.

71. Daniel Simpson, the U.S. Special Envoy to Somalia, cited in Donatella Lorch, "Last US Marines Quit Somalia as Escorts for the UN," *New York Times*, March 3, 1995

72. Gregory A. Pirio, *The African Jihad: Bin Laden's Quest for the Horn of Africa* (Trenton, NJ: The Red Sea Press, 2007), 61.

73. Ibid., 61–62.

74. Ibid., 81–82.

75. Ibid., 82.

76. David Shinn, "Ethiopia Coping with Islamic Fundamentalism before and after Sept. 11," CSIS Africa Notes, February 2000, www.csis.org/media/csis/pubs/anotes_0202.pdf.

77. Pirio, *The African Jihad*, 65.

78. Bruce Lawrence, ed., *Messages to the World: The Statements of Osama Bin Laden* (New York: Verso, 2005), 16.

79. Ibid.

80. Ibid., 9.

81. Ibid., 17.

82. Ibid., 39.

83. Ibid., 48.

84. Osama bin Laden, quoted in Lawrence Wright, *The Looming Tower: Al Qaeda and the Road to 9/11* (New York: Alfred A. Knopf, 2006), 189.

85. Al Qaeda document quoted in Pirio, *The African Jihad*, 60.

86. Michael Scheuer, *Through Our Enemies' Eyes: Osama in Laden, Radical Islam, and the Future of America*, rev. ed. (Washington, D.C.: Potomac Books, 2006), 151–154, 209–210.

87. Clarke, *Against All Enemies*, 92.

88. Ibid., 130.

89. Wright, *The Looming Tower*, 6.

Chapter 6

1. U.S. Senate Committee on Intelligence and U.S. House of Representatives Permanent Select Committee on Intelligence, *Joint Inquiry Briefing by Staff on U.S. Government Counterterrorism Organizations (Before September 11, 2001) and on the Evolution of the Terrorist Threat and U.S. Response: 1986–2001*, 107th Cong., 1st sess., June 11, 2002, http://intelligence.senate.gov/clark.pdf, 5.

2. Andrew J. Bacevich, *American Empire: The Realities & Consequences of US Diplomacy* (Cambridge, MA: Harvard University Press, 2002), 163.

3. Derek Chollet and James Goldgeier, *America between the Wars: 11/9 to 9/11—the Misunderstood Decade between the End of the Cold War and the Start of the War on Terror* (New York, Council on Foreign Relations, 2008), 138.

4. John Dumbrell, "America in the 1990s: Searching for Purpose," in *US Foreign Policy*, eds. Michael Cox and Doug Stokes (Oxford: Oxford University Press, 2008), 94.

5. Bill Clinton, "A Foreign Policy for the Global Age" (Lecture, University of Nebraska, Kearney, NE, December 8, 2000).

6. Richard A. Clarke, *Against All Enemies: Inside America's War on Terror* (New York: Free Press, 2004), 201.

7. Chollet and Goldgeier, *America between the Wars*, 147–148.

8. Bill Clinton, quoted in Bacevich, *American Empire*, 39.

9. Bill Clinton, quoted in Chollet and Goldgeier, *America between the Wars*, 247.

10. Bill Clinton, *My Life* (London: Arrow Books, 2005), 719.

11. Bill Clinton, quoted in Clarke, *Against All Enemies*, 129.

12. Full text of request reproduced at www.fas.org/irp/news/1996/WH_fact_sheet_10_96.html.

13. George Tenet, quoted in the *Washington Post*, September 9, 1998.

14. Clarke, *Against All Enemies*, 149–150.

15. Richard Miniter, *Losing Bin Laden: How Bill Clinton's Failures Unleashed Global Terror* (Washington, D.C.: Regnery, 2003), 110.

16. Ibid., 166; Clarke, *Against All Enemies*, 170-171

17. U.S. Senate Committee on Intelligence, *Joint Inquiry Briefing by Staff*, 8–9.

18. Osama bin Laden, quoted in Richard Miniter, *Losing Bin Laden*, 161.

19. Osama bin Laden's *World Islamic Front* declaration of February 23, 1998 reproduced in *Messages to the World: The Statements of Osama Bin Laden*, ed. Bruce Lawrence (New York: Verso, 2005), 61.

20. Osama bin Laden, quoted in "Context of 'May 26, 1998: Bin Laden Promises to Bring Jihad to US,'"*History Commons*, www.cooperativeresearch.org/context.jsp?item=a052698home.

21. Clarke, *Against All Enemies*, 153.

22. Michael Scheuer, *Through Our Enemies' Eyes: Osama in Laden, Radical Islam, and the Future of America*, rev. ed. (Washington, D.C.: Potomac Books, 2006), 210.

23. Ibid.

24. Chollet and Goldgeier, *America between the Wars*, 267.

25. Bill Clinton quoted in *New York Times*, July 29, 1996.

26. *New York Times*, March 20, 1998.

27. Chollet and Goldgeier, *America Between the Wars*, 123.

28. Bacevich, *American Empire*, 150.

29. Chollet and Goldgeier, *America between the Wars*, 188.

30. Office of the Secretary of Defense, *Defense Planning Guidance for the 1994–1999 Fiscal Years*, 102nd Cong., 2nd sess. (Washington, D.C., 1992); *New York Times*, March 8, 1992.

31. Frances Fitzgerald, "George Bush and the World," *The New York Review of Books*, September 2002.

32. Chollet and Goldgeier, *America between the Wars*, 199.

33. Ibid., 133.

34. John English, "The Ottawa Process: Paths Followed, Paths Ahead," *Australian Journal of International Affairs* 52, no. 2 (1998): 121–132.

35. Chollet and Goldgeier, *America between the Wars*, 274.

36. Fraser Cameron, *US Foreign Policy after the Cold War: Global Hegemon or Reluctant Sheriff?* (New York: Routledge, 2002), 164.

37. John Lewis Gaddis, "Setting Right a Dangerous World," in *Major Problems in American History since 1945*, ed. Robert Griffith and Paula Baker (Boston: Houghton-Mifflin, 2007), 532.

38. Osama bin Laden, discussion with CNN's Peter Arnett, March 1997, reproduced in *Messages to the World*, ed. Lawrence, 46.

39. Peter Woodward, *US Foreign Policy and the Horn of Africa* (Aldershot, UK: Ashgate, 2006), 73.

40. Gregory A. Pirio, *The African Jihad: Bin Laden's Quest for the Horn of Africa* (Trenton, NJ: The Red Sea Press, 2007), 68.

41. Yusef Khazim, "Islamists Regroup Their Forces after Ethiopian Preemptive Strikes,'" *Al-Wasat Magazine*, May 1999, 30–33, quoted in Scheuer, *Through Our Enemies' Eyes*, 191.

42. Lawrence Wright, *The Looming Tower: Al-Qaeda and the Road to 9/11* (New York: Alfred A. Knopf, 2006), 5.

43. bin Laden, discussion with Arnett, 54.

44. Scheuer, *Through Our Enemies' Eyes*, 190.

45. *U.S. v. Usama bin Laden, et al.*, S (7) 98, Cr. 1023 (2001), 1665.

46. Ibid., 2813.

47. Scheuer, *Through Our Enemies' Eyes*, 190.

48. Pirio, *The African Jihad*, 67.

49. Scheuer, *Through Our Enemies' Eyes*, 191.

50. Osama bin Laden, quoted in *Through Our Enemies' Eyes*, 211.

51. *U.S. v. Usama bin Laden, et al.*, 31, 1649, 5455, 7487; Woodward, *US Foreign Policy*, 140.

52. *U.S. v. Usama bin Laden, et al.*, 31, 1649, 5455, 7487.

53. Scheuer, *Through Our Enemies' Eyes*, 211.

54. Richard Miniter, *Losing Bin Laden*, 174.

55. Bill Clinton, "The Presidential Address" (Address, NewsHour with Jim Lehrer Transcript, August 20, 1998), www.pbs.org/newshour/bb/military/july-dec98/clinton2_8-20.html.

56. Ibid.

57. Ibid.

58. U.S. Senate Committee on Intelligence, *Joint Inquiry Briefing by Staff*, 9.

59. Sandy Berger, quoted in Chollet and Goldgeier, *America between the Wars*, 267.

60. Madeleine Albright quoted in Miniter, *Losing Bin Laden*, 225.

61. Clarke, *Against All Enemies*, 199–201.

62. Miniter, *Losing Bin Laden*, 169.

63. Clarke, *Against All Enemies*, 220.

64. Ibid., 221-22; Miniter, *Losing Bin Laden*, 203–206.

65. U.S. Senate Committee on Intelligence, *Joint Inquiry Briefing by Staff*, 9.

66. George Tenet, quoted in Chollet and Goldgeier, *America between the Wars*, 267.

67. U.S. Commission on National Security, *New World Coming: American Security in the 21st Century*. Washington, D.C.: Government Printing Office, 1999.

68. Clarke, *Against All Enemies*, 218.

69. Bill Clinton, "The 2000 State of the Union" (Address, NewsHour with Jim Lehrer Transcript, January 27, 2000), www.pbs.org/newshour/bb/white_house/jan-june00/sotu00.html.

70. U.S. Senate Committee on Intelligence, *Joint Inquiry Briefing by Staff*, 7.

71. Ibid., 50.

72. Miniter, *Losing Bin Laden*, 218.

73. Ibid., 215–217.

74. Ibid., 222.

75. Clarke, *Against All Enemies*, 223.

76. Michael Sheehan, quoted in Miniter, *Losing Bin Laden*, 227.

77. U.S. Senate Committee on Intelligence, *Joint Inquiry Briefing by Staff*, 56–57.

78. Ibid., 90.

79. Clarke, *Against All Enemies*, 216

80. Bacevich, *American Empire*, 151.

81. Ibid.

82. bin Laden, quoted in *Messages to the World*, ed. Lawrence, 60.

83. Ibid.

84. Clarke, *Against All Enemies*, 224.

85. Osama bin Laden, discussion with the Karachi-based Pakistani newspaper, *Ummat*, September 28, 2001, www.public-action.com/911/oblintrv.html.

86. "bin Laden's 'Letter to America,'" *The Observer*, November 24, 2002, www.guardian.co.uk/world/2002/nov/24/theobserver/print.

87. bin Laden, discussion with Arnett, 54.

88. Chollet and Goldgeier, *America between the Wars*, 224.

89. Osama bin Laden, quoted in Scheuer, *Through Our Enemies' Eyes*, 48.

90. Chollet and Goldgeier, *America between the Wars*, 240.

91. Ibid., 241–242.

92. Chollet and Goldgeier, *America between the Wars*, 315

93. Clinton, *My Life*, 812.

Chapter 7

1. Derek Chollet and James Goldgeier, *America between the Wars: From 11/9 to 9/11—the Misunderstood Decade between the End of the Cold War and the Start of the War on Terror* (New York: Council of Foreign Relations, 2008), 295.

2. Paul Rogers, "Global Terrorism," in *US Foreign Policy*, eds. Michael Cox and Douglas Stokes (Oxford: Oxford University Press, 2008), 362; Andrew J. Bacevich, *American Empire: The Realities & Consequences of US Diplomacy* (Cambridge, MA: Harvard University Press, 2002), 198–204.

3. George W. Bush, "National Press Conference, The East Room," White House, March 6, 2003, www.whitehouse.gov/news/releases/2003/200030306-8.html#.

4. Bill Clinton, discussion with Joe Klein, White House, Office of the Press Secretary, August 15, 2000.

5. Caroline Kennedy-Pipe, "American Foreign Policy after 9/11," in *US Foreign Policy*, eds. Cox and Stokes, 403–404.

6. Chollet and Goldgeier, *America between the Wars*, 308-9.

7. Condoleezza Rice, "Promoting the National Interest," *Foreign Affairs*, no. 1 (2000): 47–48.

8. Chollet and Goldgeier, *America between the Wars*, 296.

9. George W. Bush, quoted in "The Second Gore-Bush Presidential Debate, October 11, 2000," *Commission of Presidential Debates, Debate Transcript*, www.debates.org/pages/trans2000b.html.

10. George W. Bush, quoted in Bacevich, *American Empire*, 203.

11. Charles Krauthammer, "The New Unilateralism," *Washington Post*, June 8, 2001.

12. Rice, "Promoting the National Interest," 48–49.

13. Ivo H. Daalder and James M. Lindsay, *America Unbound: The Bush Revolution in Foreign Policy* (Washington, D.C.: Brookings Institution Press, 2003), 46–48.

14. Rice, "Promoting the National Interest"; George W. Bush, "A Distinctly American Internationalism" (Speech, Simi Valley, CA, November 19, 1999), http://georgebush.com/speeches/foreignpolicy.asp.

15. Richard A. Clarke, *Against All Enemies: Inside America's War on Terror* (New York: Free Press, 2004), 196.

16. Mohammad Yaghi, "The Palestinian-Israeli Conflict: A Case Study of US Foreign Policy after 9/11" in *The War on Terror in Comparative Perspective: US Security and Foreign Policy after 9/11*, eds, Mark J. Miller and Boyka Stefanova (New York: Palgrave Macmillan, 2007), 172-173

17. George Tenet, *At the Center of the Storm: My Years at the CIA* (New York: HarperCollins, 2007), 139.

18. Bill Clinton, quoted in Chollet and Goldgeier, *America between the Wars*, 306.

19. Clarke, *Against All Enemies*, 225–226.

20. Bob Woodward, *Bush at War* (New York: Simon & Schuster, 2002), 34.

21. Clarke, *Against All Enemies*, 231; Rebecca Leung, "Clarke's Take on Terror," *CBS News, 60 Minutes*, March 21, 2004, www.cbsnews.com/stories/2004/03/19/60minutes/main607356.shtml.

22. Clarke, *Against All Enemies*, 230.

23. Ibid., 231.

24. Ibid.; Leung, "Clarke's Take on Terror."

25. Michael Scheuer, *Through Our Enemies' Eyes: Osama bin Laden, Radical Islam, and the Future of America*, rev. ed. (Washington, D.C.: Potomac Books, 2006), 232; Jason Leopold, "Bush Ignored 9/11 Warnings," *Truthout Report*, January 31, 2006, www.truthout.org/article/jason-leopold-bush-ignored-911-warnings.

26. Clarke, *Against All Enemies*, 231–232.

27. Woodward, *Bush at War*, 35; Clarke, *Against All Enemies*, 234–235.

28. Osama bin Laden, quoted in Scheuer, *Through Our Enemies' Eyes*, 215.

29. *New York Times*, April 6, 2000; Scheuer, *Through Our Enemies' Eyes*, 243.

30. Scheuer, *Through Our Enemies' Eyes*, 243.

31. Peter Bergen, "The Bin Laden Trial: What Did We Learn?" *Studies in Conflict and Terrorism* 24, no. 6 (2001): 429–434.

32. Osama bin Laden (Statement to Delegates to the International Conference of Deobandis, Taro Jaba near Peshawar, Pakistan, April 9–11, 2001), quoted in *Messages to the World: The Statements of Osama Bin Laden*, ed. Bruce Lawrence (New York: Verso, 2005), 95–99.

33. Lee Ann Matzinger, "The American Connection: United States Foreign Policy and Terrorism in Somalia" (Master's Thesis, Alliant International University, San Diego, 2002), 106; Robert G. Patman, "Somalia," in *Political Parties of the World*, ed. Bogdan Szajkowski (London: John Harper Publishing, 2005), 539.

34. Andre Le Sage, "Somalia and the War on Terrorism: Political Islamic Movements & U.S. Counter-Terrorism Efforts" (PhD Thesis, Cambridge University, Cambridge, 2004), 61.

35. Gregory A. Pirio, *The African Jihad: Bin Laden's Quest for the Horn of Africa* (Trenton, NJ: The Red Sea Press, 2007), 85–86.

36. Ibid., 89–90.

37. Ibid., 70.

38. George W. Bush, quoted in Woodward, *Bush At War*, 39.

39. U.S. Senate Committee on Intelligence and U.S. House of Representatives Permanent Select Committee on Intelligence, *Joint Inquiry Briefing by Staff on U.S. Government Counterterrorism Organizations (Before September 11, 2001) and on the Evolution of the Terrorist Threat and U.S. Response: 1986–2001*, 107th Cong., 1st sess., June 11, 2002, http://intelligence.senate.gov/clark.pdf, 10.

40. Leopold, "Bush Ignored 9/11 Warnings."

41. Clarke, *Against All Enemies*, 230; Chollet and Goldgeier, *America between the Wars*, 326.

42. Clarke, quoted in Leung, "Clarke's Take on Terror."

43. Chollet and Goldgeier, *America between the Wars*, 311.

44. Clarke, *Against All Enemies*, 235.

45. Woodward, *Bush at War*, 4.

46. Leung, "Clarke's Take on Terror."

47. U.S. Senate Committee on Intelligence, *Joint Inquiry Briefing by Staff*, 62.

48. Clarke, quoted in Leung, "Clarke's Take on Terror."

49. U.S. Senate Committee on Intelligence, *Joint Inquiry Briefing by Staff*, 63.

50. Clarke, *Against All Enemies*, 236.

51. U.S. Senate Committee on Intelligence, *Joint Inquiry Briefing by Staff*, 63.

52. Stephen Hadley, quoted in Clarke, quoted in Leung, "Clarke's Take on Terror."

53. Leopold, "Bush Ignored 9/11 Warnings."

54. Woodward, *Bush at War*, 35.

55. Ibid., 36.

56. Ibid.

57. Leopold, "Bush Ignored 9/11 Warnings."

58. U.S. Senate Committee on Intelligence, *Joint Inquiry Briefing by Staff*, 63.

59. Leopold, "Bush Ignored 9/11 Warnings."

60. Rice, "Promoting the National Interest," 47–48.

61. Clarke, *Against All Enemies*, 5.

62. George Tenet quoted in Woodward, *Bush at War*, 4.

63. George W. Bush (Address to a Joint Session of Congress and the American People, September 20, 2001), www.whitehouse.gov/news/releases/2001/09/20010920-8.html.

64. The criteria used here for deriving a causal association were adapted from Austin Bradford Hill, "The Environment and Disease: Association or Cause?" *Proceedings of the Royal Society of Medicine*, 8, no. 5 (1965): 295–300.

65. Robert H. Dorff, "Failed States after 9/11: What Did We Know and What Have We Learned?" *International Studies Perspectives* 6, no. 1 (2005): 22–24.

66. Chollet and Goldgeier, *America between the Wars*, 310.

67. Clarke, *Against All Enemies*, 222–224.

68. *Messages to the World*, ed. Lawrence, 16.

69. Ibid., 9.

70. Craig Unger, *House of Bush House of Saud: The Hidden Relationship Between the World's Two Most Powerful Dynasties* (London: Gibson Square Books, 2004), 19–36.

Chapter 8

1. Christopher Andrew, Richard J. Aldrich and Wesley K. Wark, "Preface: Intelligence, history and policy" in *Secret Intelligence: A Reader*, eds. Christopher Andrew, Richard J. Aldrich and Wesley K. Wark (New York: Routledge, 2009), xv.

2. Michael Evans, "Mastering Krulak's Children: Land Warfare Challenges in the Early 21st Century", Massey University, Chief of Army's Conference on *Enduring Conflict: Challenge and Responses,* Palmerston North, September 2, 2009.

3. Edward J. Perkins, former US Ambassador to the UN, "Fact Sheet: Somalia—Operation Restore Hope," Department of State *Dispatch*, 3, December 21, 1992, 898.

4. Hew Strachan, "Strategy in the 21st Century: Rethinking Clausewitz," University of Otago, August 27, 2009.

5. Osama bin Laden, quoted in *Messages to the World: The Statements of Osama bin Laden*, ed. Bruce Lawrence (New York: Verso, 2005), 96.

6. Steve Smith, "The Concept of Security in a Globalizing World," in *Globalization and Conflict: National Security in a 'New' Strategic Era*, ed. Robert G. Patman (New York: Routledge, 2006), 35.

7. Andrew J. Bacevich, *American Empire: The Realities & Consequences of US Diplomacy* (Cambridge, MA: Harvard University Press, 2002), 135.

8. General Jack Keane, former Vice Chief, US Army, *Lehrer News Hour*, April 16, 2008 cited by Michael Evans in "Mastering Krulak's Children . . ."

9. Ibid., 134.

10. U.S. Senate Committee on Intelligence and U.S. House of Representatives Permanent Select Committee on Intelligence, *Joint Inquiry Briefing by Staff on U.S. Government Counterterrorism Organizations (Before September 11, 2001) and on the Evolution of the Terrorist Threat and U.S. Response: 1986–2001*, 107th Cong., 1st sess., June 11, 2002, http://intelligence.senate.gov/clark.pdf, 43.

11. Andrew J. Bacevich, *American Empire: The Realities and Consequences of US Diplomacy* (Cambridge, MA: Harvard University Press, 2002, 137

12. Eliot A. Cohen, "Defending America in the Twenty-first Century," *Foreign Affairs* 79, no. 6 (2000): 40–42.

Index

About the Author

ROBERT G. PATMAN is Professor of International Relations in the Department of Politics at the University of Otago, New Zealand, and director of its multidisciplinary Master of International Studies program. His research interests center on international relations, U.S. foreign policy, post–Cold War security, and the relationship between order and justice in a globalizing world. He is the author or editor of seven books and is coeditor of the forthcoming book on *The Bush Leadership, the Power of Ideas and the War on Terror.* He is coeditor of the Praeger Security International (PSI) series on the Ethics of American Foreign Policy and a Fulbright Senior Scholar and a Senior Fellow at the Centre of Strategic Studies, Wellington. He also provides regular contributions to the national and international media on global issues and events. Professor Patman's Web site is www.robertpatman.co.nz.